Evolutionary Human Education

Philosophy, Psychology and Human Being

Dr. Edward Schellhammer

Original edition in German 2014

English translated edition 2021

© **Copyright. Dr. Edward Schellhammer. All rights reserved.**

ISBN: 9798536330906

Imprint: Independently published

www.schellhammerinstitute.com

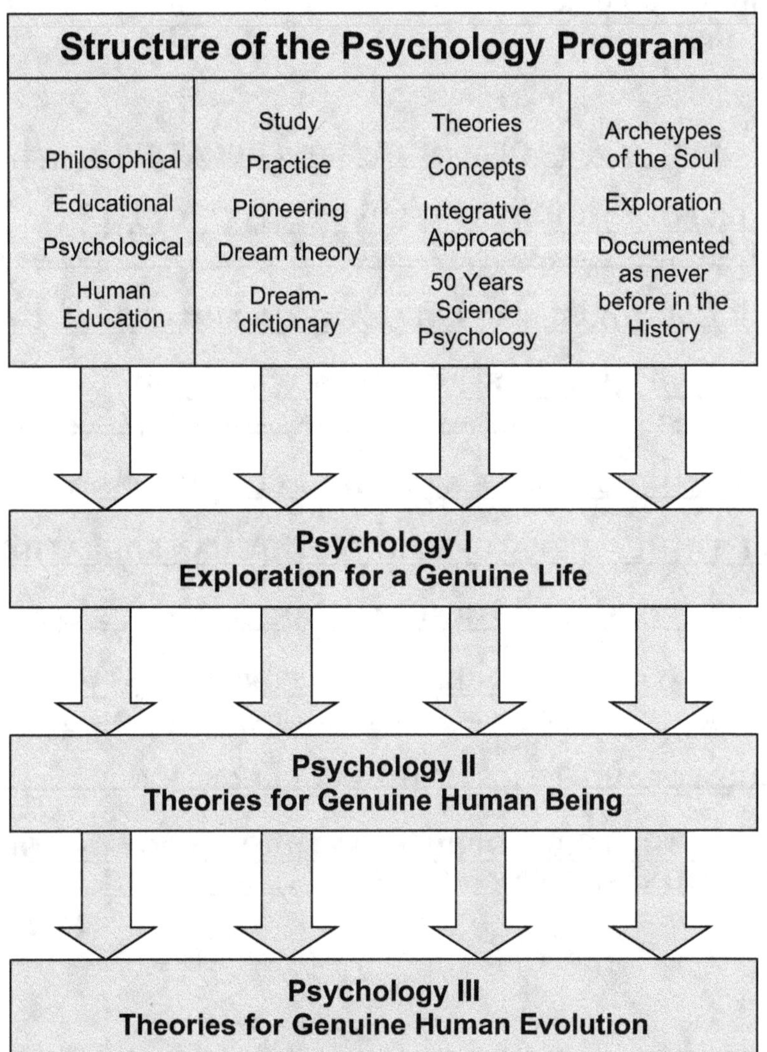

Structure of the Psychology Program

Philosophical
Educational
Psychological
Human
Education

Study
Practice
Pioneering
Dream theory
Dream-
dictionary

Theories
Concepts
Integrative
Approach
50 Years
Science
Psychology

Archetypes
of the Soul
Exploration
Documented
as never
before in the
History

Psychology I
Exploration for a Genuine Life

Psychology II
Theories for Genuine Human Being

Psychology III
Theories for Genuine Human Evolution

Table of Contents

INTRODUCTION: UTOPIA OF HUMAN EDUCATION 6

THE DISPUTE ABOUT THE "PERSONALITY" AND ITS "EDUCATION" 19

STRUGGLE FOR HUMAN EDUCATION IN PHILOSOPHY 41

HUMAN EDUCATION OR PSYCHOANALYSIS AND PSYCHOTHERAPY? 54

IMPASSE OF PEDAGOGY AND ADULT EDUCATION 69

HOLISTIC HUMAN KNOWLEDGE FOR HUMAN EDUCATION 88

DUE TURN IN SCIENCE OF HUMAN EDUCATION 114

PARADIGM OF HUMAN EDUCATION FOR THE 21ST CENTURY 135

MARKS FOR DIDACTICS OF HUMAN EDUCATION 156

DRIVING THE PHILOSOPHICAL ANTHROPOLOGY OUT OF EDUCATIONAL SCIENCES 198

List of illustrations

Illustration 1: Models of Psyche and Personality (1)

Illustration 2: Models of Psyche and Personality (2)

Illustration 3: The Psychic Organism

Illustration 4: Evolutionary Human Being

Illustration 5: System Model of Andragogical Reference

Illustration 6: The Cornerstones of Andragogy

Illustration 7: Education in Networking

Illustration 8: Formation of the Psychic Organism

Illustration 9: Learning through Realistic Motivation

Illustration 10: The Network of Success

Illustration 11: The Human in Interaction

Introduction: Utopia of Human Education

"Personality development", "self-realization" and "emancipation" are today buzzwords that in the field of pluralist democracy, school and practical psychology have become to the signboard at almost all educational intentions today. Under these labels, many personality ideals are offered for sale as commodities in psychotherapy and in the psycho-esoteric market. Pedagogy and adult education also use such words to describe their educational idea. A kind of recreational education has emerged that has "squeezed out" all of words that the language has to offer in this context. Many words can be listed, for example: Holisticness, happiness, higher consciousness, conflict-free personality, self-fulfillment, transcendental and cosmic experience, harmony, inner peace, success, ecstatic feelings, oneness with the higher self and vitality.

These are ideals about life. These are also ideal human images. The fact is that such words have become empty formulas and nice talk. They are trite as marketing labels. For long different suppliers have recognized that the merchandise "personality education" must be sold with advertising psychology. There are no limits to the play with words, sounds, colors, shapes, and associations. The longing for redemption of humans from the prison of their unconsciousness, out of their inner loneliness and their need for security and genuine love is in part shamelessly being exploited.

Some sellers outbid each other with superlatives and "peak experiences". It has arisen in psychology and in psychological adult education a real market power struggle, who is now the new resp. the "great power" in the "modern" and "postmodern" flow. The free space of pluralistic society allows such a diversity.

But the new danger nobody will take responsibility for: The stimulus satiation of ideals, values and ways of salvation makes it for the individual almost impossible to recognize and to live bindingly for oneself what really is coping with the personal inner life. How is this supposed to be recognized from the vast variety of concepts and methods? The core question affects everyone: How do they justify their personality ideals and their practices?

The sects also operate with a diverse vocabulary, especially crowning the summit of superlatives with words such as "redemption", "God's chosen" and "apocalypse". Everywhere, they claim that the "devil" is doing his work and the "evil" dominates. "Highest illuminates" represent God on earth today. From the concrete doing and the teachings of this "salvation bringers" one can identify their pathological ideas and ways of life. The media regularly pillory some of them, which tends to encourage the throng here and there. Meaningful and dangerous is the ideological dogmatic the claim of force and power of the sects and as well as the connected psychically strayed personal situations of their guidances.

All want to build the "theocracy on earth", the "kingdom of God", the "cosmic and divine regime" and the "paradise". And some want to "clean up" with the "perfidy of godless people". None of them have a constructive relation to his psychic inner life.

The history of religions is full of claims to power and seductions of humans. Again, and again, new movements have emerged that secretly or publicly taught and practiced their ideas of human being and God. The history of esotericism, the Gnostic movements, the Templar order of the Rosicrucians and the Freemasons as well as all their many splinter groups show us the almost infinite abundance of possibilities for human education and self-realization.

The common basic question is this: How do they justify their ideals about the human and their practices for human education?

Indeed, today there are, probably like never, vital reasons for human education to new ideals and to renewed values. The civilization in industrialized countries has reached an extremely high technical level of development. But the psychic-spiritual evolution of the individual human is lagged significantly. The destructions of environment have reached huge dimensions. Nobody will want to deny that. The armories are gigantic, and the armies worldwide well prepared for the "last great war". Violence, social conflicts, and crime have reached a degree that can barely to be managed.

The accident statistics reflect a kind of "war" of its own. Addictions of all kinds, in particular drugs, alcohol and medication addiction do harm devastating suffering. Mental disorders and psychosomatic sufferings increase significantly, even in school age. Millions suffer from meaninglessness, loneliness, and hopelessness.

Self-lie and life-lie dominate everywhere. One does not have to paint the "apocalypse" on the wall. Nobody must talk about a dramaturgy of the future in people's ears with eloquence. More than half of the humanity today has too little of all that is necessary for life. In thirty years, this will lead to hardly controllable explosions. The children, young people, and adults in their mid-life today will experience that future. The search for new personality ideals and new concepts of the human education is very understandable and necessary.

Here, too, the same basic question arises: How can new educational ideals and educational practices be justified?

The search for knowledge about the human, for ideals of human being and for the "good life" is the history of a tradition that has developed again and again new teachings since the beginnings of Western philosophy in the Greek ancient world. The pedagogy has the mandate from the state to educate the humans so that the democracy and the diversity of the social systems remain viable. Many variants of theory forming, and practical education have been developed for the education of children and people.

For about two hundred years, the pedagogy and the psychology have the humans systematically explored. This resulted in human images, goals and methods.

Probably all directions and positions agree on one thing: The human with his psychic forces, unformed or wrongly formed, unconscious and chaotic in his inner life, in aberration due to the lack of love, thinking little and dominated by his drives, is the causer of the today's social problems, locally, nationally, internationally, and globally.

But is there even a demand for new personality ideals and ways to achieve them? If there are ideal human images and methods that comprehensively and holistically integrate all psychic life in the human, who would be specially interested in? Who wants real comprehensive self-knowledge? Who wants to develop all his psychic forces and to form a balanced functioning unit? Who wants to let grow the force of love in oneself and live it in a binding way?

The psychoanalysis teaches since the beginnings that the human struggles with a rigid persistence against any amplification of consciousness about himself and about life. All ideas and ways can be presented to humans; many are always ready to live them. But they never want the truth about themselves and about the human being. This triggers enormous resistances. The human prefers to accept any form of suffering, destruction, and war. The arrogance of the "I" towards its own inner reality and towards the psychic life of humans in general is marked by enormous defense. The love for the psychic life has in the humans rarely depth and stableness.

Personality ideals, human images and especially the practical human education must start at the reality of psychic life. The big problem here is that the various positions in pedagogy, psychology and andragogy cannot agree on an overarching conception of psychic life and the educational ideals that are rooted in it. Freeing oneself from fixations to the doctrines and position battles, the reported scientific knowledges of pedagogy and andragogy resp. psychology can be merged to a new entity of the inner psychic life. This creates a basic reality on which the human education can be andragogically justified put for discussion. This means that the decisive elements are available that a holistic personality education must contain.

It is possible to integrate the knowledge of depth psychology of all directions, behavioral psychology, cognitive psychology, transpersonal resp. spiritual psychology and humanistic psychology into an entity. All key models of learning psychology from the most different directions of research and scientific theoretical positions may be combined in a dynamic systemic model. Building on this, a human image can be created philosophically and education theoretically, which is the base for realistic and practicable ideals, for the design of a new versatile human being and thus in general for the human education in the future.

However, we cannot completely clarify the question of holism of human education. It is our point of view that no paranormal abilities are necessary for comprehensive self-formation in the sense of the individuation.

That is why we exclude several special phenomena from our term "holism"; such as: Telekinesis, levitations, telepathy, clairvoyance, contacts to the afterworld, body leaving, spiritual healing, ecstasy, magic powers, stigmatization, and wonder signs resp. wonder skills of all kinds (see Murphy 1994; Keller 1979). Astrology and numerology do not free extra-psychic forces, which form or determine the human to a certain extent beyond his psychic organism. Returns in past lives may open transcendental prospects, but for the personal development and individuation they are irrelevant.

We opinion that the human potentials do not lie in such paranormal possibilities, but in the very ordinary structure of psychic dispositions (forces) and its development resp. education within the frame of an integrative balanced process. We do not know a single argument that justifies the thesis that psychic-spiritual development in its highest level must produce paranormal abilities. With this, however, we do not exclude that in the future the anthropology of andragogy can and should include cosmic dimensions (cf. Resch 1973; Capra 1991) in the empirical-analytical and humanistic elaboration of a new human image.

Well-founded knowledges of human education, versatile, balanced and newly compiled into a complex entity, provide the starting point for substantial effects of action-oriented educational goals, such as:

Reduction of psychic and psychosomatic sufferings, drastic reduction of accident rates, massive decrease of environmental damage, decisive diminution of violence and crime, efficient ways of solving social conflicts and the making wars impossible. The back bonding to the scientifically proven facts of comprehensive psychic life, the learning and the forming are the only communicatively manageable alternatives to sects, to psycho-religious movements, to ideological and dogmatic systems and to an educational science that is not amazingly effective in social sub-areas.

New future-oriented models as the basis for ideals and forms of life are in demand and vital if the humans do not want to indulge in the idleness principle of the social forces. Political power and rule cannot pave new ways.

No "savior" can lead the situation to the good for the humans. Everyone must "redeem" himself. This is only possible through a comprehensive, holistic personality education.

Here, the pedagogy and the andragogy bear the great responsibility for the future. Educators and andragogues should settle to a round table, develop solidarity and together establish the enormous value of their knowledge and their acting instruments for the benefit of the humanity. They owe this to the humans. Because they have taken their knowledges from the humans. What should the knowledge of pedagogy and andragogy serve for, if not for children, the young people and the adults?

We have attempted to connect central aspects of the basic knowledge of educational science (pedagogy / andragogy), psychology of all directions and philosophy resp. philosophical anthropology into a new whole. Of course, we had to limit ourselves to the essential and were not able to work on every single scientific finding. That is the task of pedagogy and andragogy in the future.

But this is certain: The inner reality of the human can effectively be compound to a holistic psychic system. This results in the "psychic organism" with its various subsystems. There is no "black hole", no psychic space without base and no part entity without meaningful connection with the other units. It may seem strange to the scientist that we are also talking about "love" and "spirit" and still claim that these realities can be scientifically included as fundamental psychic forces in the human. But philosophy without love and spirit is not real philosophy and pedagogy resp. andragogy without love and spirit are not able to guide the human to himself.

We have taken a decisive step further based on a long tradition of philosophy. We wanted to know, whether it is possible to unfold this psychic system from an unshaped resp. malformed state to a new state of wholeness and all sides balanced integratedness of all individual forces. Against all claims of psychology resp. psychoanalysis and psychotherapy, we can say with certainty today:

It is possible to form the human in his psychic forces till he has reached the highest possible psychic-spiritual level of all-round balanced entity and wholeness. We term this process as "individuation", where we must add immediately that our model is developed significant differently than the well-known one from the history of psychology (C.G. Jung, Jungian school). This psychic-spiritual evolutionary process can be identified and evaluated scientifically just as the psychic organism, especially also justified resp. discussed educational theoretically and structured didactically for education processes.

From these basis we can formulate first general personality ideals: Comprehensive systematic self-knowledge of all psychic forces, differentiated self and life consciousness, free from defenses and projections, flexible open integration of all life realities, formed strong will and pronounced self-control, completely liberated and integrated unconscious life, differentiated perception and thinking, clearly identified and realized basic needs, versatile balanced and used emotional life, viable and operational capacity to love, flexible and vital psychodynamics, cooperative communication with the spirit (i.e. the force that creates the dreams and can be used intelligently in the imagination), and the set-up of a new entity and wholeness of the entire psychic life centered in this spiritual force. These ideals are realistic. They can be built up in sub-steps in the process of individuation.

This is the psychic-spiritual evolution of the human. In the individuation the human lives these personality ideals, step by step, always more comprehensively, more differenciatedly and more consciously. Because the acting is expression of the formed psychic forces, separated from external determinants.

The working methods result from the knowledge of different effects of psychic forces. The basic forms of work are: Acquiring didactically structured knowledge and experiencing it in exercises; mental training for relaxation, revitalization, and psycho hygiene; dream interpretation and symbol work; imagination, resp. contemplation, analytical rational and meditative life handling, and life processing; self-critical systematic reflections on the consciousness contents; as well as psycho-energetic exercises and rituals.

This kind of human education is life formation and lifelong education. It mediates an inner anchoring in the psychic subsystems that are increasingly developing themselves on all sides in a constructive and progressive way. Instead of ideologies or dogmas, instead of empty words or emotional choppiness, instead of fighting about normative decisions, the contents, objectives, and ways arise from the reality of the psychic organism itself. The human builds up new life values from his inner spirit, from the force of love and from the experience of this inner growth process. What is being built new inside can be controlled by the "I" and implemented in the life. This is the evolutionary path to a new human being in the future.

Never a sect, a psycho-religious movement, a life philosophy, a psychological direction, an ideological doctrine, a political program, a fundamentalist thinking, or a religion replace what the human can find and develop in himself.

Each idea system that offers the humans ideals and paths outside the psychic organism and outside the individuation process cheats the human about what he is inner psychic and must become from his inner being: A living image of the supreme archetype, the "circle-cross-mandala". This archetype is on the other hand also the image of God. This is not an attempt to recoup by the backdoor what enlightenedly resp. "emancipatoryly" and scientifically by many is considered "to be completed".

The "individuated human" is the living and realistic ideal. The life in the individuation process is an evolutionary solution path out of the worldwide problems of humanity. In the psychic-spiritual development "happiness", "joie de vivre", "peace" and "self-realization" become concrete goals of personality development. Such values become a living reality in the life of the individual through the process of individuation. Individuation is the holistic comprehensive educational concept of andragogy.

We define the andragogy as the science of adult education in its real core with "science and practice of human education resp. personality development and individuation". The andragogy defines itself in the alignment with the psychic organism and its development processes. The acts of the human in the life systems of industrial society and the resultant educational needs are the second orientation. These realities set the criteria for the epistemological basis of the descriptive and normative statement systems as well as for the research concepts and methodologies.

The science of andragogy must have the autonomy to be able to focus the "thing" itself as the object of its interest in knowledge and act. It needs a certain freedom in relation to political ideological time appearances, trends of the leisure industry and the economic further education demands. Only in this way it is possible to process scientifically the reality of the human psychic life and the related educational interests. Thus, the andragogy serves in the core the humans and the pluralistic democratic society. Individuation as an education process creates certainly psychic "healthy" humans with comprehensive life competences, with life forms rooted in love and spirit, a psycho-social peaceful life and a human-centered environmental design.

Without many healthy core cells (individuals, families, life communities) a state decomposes. Many politicians no longer have this in mind. They are already overloaded with damage repairs.

Solution paths are here: As science and research, the andragogy can base objectively, theoretically, and normatively the psychic-spiritual education of adults in the industrial society. It must have the courage, building on this, to discuss openly the educational concept for humans. It is essential that the scientist, researcher, professor, teacher, advisor and "andragogue" first research himself and lives what he proposes to the humans as educational goals and paths in the sense of individuation. In "Bildungsforschung und Bildungspraxis" (in Switzerland), we read: "Should the education research in their basic functions be realized, it needs to relate to the current situation" (1988, 30). We consider the state of universal human education in terms of personality formation and individuation with all the painful and conflictive consequences as a fundamental aspect of this "current situation." Let us take a quick look at this "current situation".

Wemmer / Korczak inform in their data report (1993; see also: Statistisches Jahrbuch für die Bundesrepublik Deutschland und für das Ausland, CD, 1996) on the situation in Germany in an annual overview:

Around 10.000 suicides, at least 200.000 child abuse, 500.000-800.000 medication addicts, approx. 2 million alcoholics with 30.000-40.000 deaths (as immediate consequences), 140.000 early deaths due to excessive smoking, traffic accidents with over 430.000 injuries and 7.500 deaths, 4-7% of children with psychic disorders, plus drug addicts and drug deaths, plus sexual abuse, plus serious physical injuries, plus violent crimes of all kinds, plus work and household accidents, etc. The authors also paint a dramatic picture of the environmental conditions. The authors call for "prevention as a task of the adult education" (289).

Lorenz (1993) sketches the "eight deadly sins of the civilized mankind": Overpopulation, devastation of natural habitat, technological race, loss of all strong emotions, genetic decay (advanced infantilization), breaking of tradition, increasing indoctrinability of mankind, armament with nuclear weapons. Jungk (1993, 91) supplements these deadly sins with the "megatrends" (176): Economic crisis, democracy deficit, cultural crisis, crisis of the family and loss of identity of the individual. The unemployment is a long-running topic in books and the press. The associated psychic and psychosomatic sufferings, the family burdens and the subsequent social conflicts take on enormous (highly explosive) dimensions. The "new poverty" in Europe is one of the greatest humiliations of "capitalist" achievements. Despite the scarcity on the one hand, Schulze (1992, 38) paints a picture of the society where "experience orientation as basic motivation" dominates the lifestyle of millions.

The "mass culture" (Eco 1992, 42-49) is characterized by: Low average of taste, homogenization of individuality, people without consciousness about themselves and the world, a market with deception through suggestion for the purpose of artificially fueled consumption, passivity in thinking, decision-making, judging and acting. "We amuse ourselves to death" writes Postman (1994, 8, 193): "In the brave new world the humans are controlled by inflicting pleasure on them"; and: "Censorship (is) no longer necessary, amusement takes on this task". According to Bourdieu (1994, 576), this is the new ethical task of the avant-garde: "Duty to pleasure".

The "postmodernism" is arriving. Vester (1993, 15, 31, 34, 38) outlines its characteristics, i.e.: Blending and mixing (pastiche-like and collage-like is lived); lacerated boundaries between culture, commerce, consumption, and production; the effect of the rhetoric is important, not the correct ascertainment; "the antihero is the ironic rascal"; the "postmodernism is the celebration of forgery". Beck (1986, 73, 105) marks clearly this "current situation": "The risk society is a disaster society"; "The phase of latency of the risk threat is coming to an end". What does the adult education do for (or against) this?

There are problematic solution paths: Anyone who promises the humans the "quick happiness", the "easy success" and the "short path" to life fulfillment and "enlightenment" lies and deceives them. Of course, most people want to be betrayed, to live life lies, and only use "drugs" for self-anesthesia. Anyone who offers "salvation" and "healing" with magical-technical short-cut, is a "drug dealer". The shameless misuse of terms such as "truth" and "holism" on the market for human education promotes alternative solutions. One can understand that many would rather have such "drugs". For most people, the psychic-spiritual life is worth less than the paper on which these realities are revealed to them. That is the reason why the terrible horror breaks out somewhere in the world every few decades. This is where the roots of hatred, greed, envy, lies, intrigue, exploitation, violence, and war lie. Who does not want this have to know: Self-knowledge resp. self-formation is hard work that has to be done thoroughly and systematically if it will become sustainable in life, and bear "rich fruits"? However, this is not the trend of postmodernism.

True psychic-spiritual human education as a business has little chance in the highly industrialized market economy. Because personality development cannot be turned immediately and directly into tangible capital. There is hardly any social recognition for this. However, if fewer and fewer humans take their psychic life seriously and educate it, then the day will come when no one can love himself and others anymore.

Anyone who does not want to be able or does not have the courage to represent, educate and protect the values of psychic-spiritual life and live it in solidarity has not be surprised when opposing forces increasingly determine how one should live.

But should one leave the world and leadership in social life to those who trample the psychic-spiritual life, who only express mockery and scorn or indifference about it? That leads to the failure of the collective psychic-spiritual evolution of the human. So, who should stand up for the values of the psychic life if not those who have the chance to discover these realities within themselves? Isn't it the central requirement of life to look for oneself and to form one's entire psychic-spiritual life? And isn't it the primary task of a science of andragogy to research and offer knowledge and ways for this?

Looking at how most people live, and interpreting the cultivated habitat as an expression of the formed psychic life of humans, then one has not to ask for psychotherapy: Human education is necessary, in all psychic forces, thoroughly and systematically, didactically built-on and educational theoretically founded, historically linked back to the tradition of philosophy and pedagogy, future-oriented and integrated into the holistic psychic-spiritual development process called "individuation". We are trying to contribute to this with this study.

To the science of adult education some critical aspects are also to discuss: As a "value-free" science it runs the risk to include little of the real everyday life of "ordinary" people in the industrial society. Some researchers seem to have little knowledge of the harsh, often amoral reality of the capitalism. Some have little idea of psychological mechanisms in the psyche of the "hardliners" of today Marxism-Leninism. Others do not give the impression of being able to see psychologically sufficiently through the phenomena of religions in their concrete form and in their dogmatism.

Some theories hardly give a deep psychological clear sight into the human dramas as it happens with several million people every day. There are projects that are well founded in terms of the science theory, but they hardly go beyond the "village spirit" of their scientific institute. They do not include the life of powerless and mentally weak people. They do not grasp the concrete world, despite the "lifeworld reference".

Certain concepts modify their (German) educational theory little and discuss their life ideals hardly in context with other variants. Some educational "paradigms" cannot include that personal management (we are thinking of billions of people) is not yet possible today with modern (European) educational principles.

If the science of adult education is to be an acting science, it will still have to learn a lot in this regard. The crucial problem for the science of adult education lies deep and includes the responsibility: "... human acting is guided by purposes and determinations, oriented on intentions and beliefs. Each educational acting is therefore connected with certain interests and does not allow any retreat to the position of neutral intermediary." (Lenz 1986, 158). A new paradigm is called for (Grof 1993, 27, 42).

Our paradigm of personality development is:

■ Personality development is the basic key qualification for professional and personal life.

■ In the future, personal development will be the essential basic education for every demanding professional further education.

■ Personality development creates the competences for constructive positive relationships (friendship, marriage, family, work, cultural life).

■ Personality development reduces many risks in the personal life and in the social networking of one's own life.

■ Personality development can be used anywhere, takes versatile effects, and dynamically stabilizes the self-identity.

■ Personality development means life knowledge and everyday acting that is thoroughly thought out and processed on all sides.

■ Personality development qualifies to leisure design, to optimal handling with the lifetime and the own possibilities.

■ Personality development creates inner security and confidence in one's own forces, especially in times of great stress.

■ Personality development leads to an all-round balanced psychic organism in steadily progressive development.

■ Personality development is essential in all life phases for real enrichment and substantial fulfillment.

■ Personality development integrates a high ethical responsibility for oneself, for others, for the job, for the society and for the habitat.

■ Personality development is an investment for the future, especially because the social developments present great challenges.

■ Personality development is the categorical prerequisite for every responsibility in education, consulting, care, leadership, and management.

■ Personality development reaches the human in his deepest psychic-spiritual being, also in the most decisive meaning questions.

■ Personality development and individuation form a type of human who will be in demand in all systems of the society in the future.

The pedagogues and the andragogues have considering the immense psychic-spiritual formation deficits and their social consequences ("risk society") a significant responsibility. It is precisely in this that a common solidarity must be developed beyond the theoretical positions. If pedagogues and andragogues authority and leadership in the human education, with personality ideals from the psychic organism cannot integrate and promote showing solidarity then they have not resolved their own father conflict. Strong personalities with courage and pioneering spirit are required, free from neurosis, compensation, drive repression and envy. These are above all those humans who are open to the unconscious, dreams, spirit, love, wisdom, and those who practice themselves practical individuation.

The personality development and individuation that we develop as an educational concept in this study are of vital importance for the individual, for economy and for social life:

"The time urges" warns Weizsäcker (1987). "It's ready" writes Ditfurth (1988). "The deadly progress" by Drewermann (1991) is a mirror about the destruction of the earth. "Our Common Future" is a terrifying analysis of "The World Commission on Environment and Development" (1987). "Global 2000" is a report of megatrends that could hardly be imagined. "The nuclear threat is growing more than ever" analyzes us Senator Tom Harkin (1990). We also wrote about the "Lage der Welt", based additionally on many dreams on this subject: The "Point of no return is very close" (1988).

Numerous other experts could be consulted to confirm: Human education with new personality ideals, with love and spirit from the individuation, is the most important task in the future. It seems almost without a chance to us, yet: The utopia of a human-centered society in the future can become a reality with suitable leaders in human education (pedagogy and andragogy). The economy policies and especially the professional further education can only create the welfare of citizens, build up stable peace and social justice, and promote happiness and love with a comprehensive psychic-spiritual human education. Many humans want family security, a peaceful world, freedom, self-respect, happiness (contentment) and wisdom (Inglehart 1989, 156). An *"European Conference of Pedagogues and Andragogues"* on human education is urgently needed.

That is the freedom of human: To live and to become what the human is in himself as psychic-spiritual reality, or to deny it. By turning to the developed education ideals, the human decides about his future and ultimately about the future of humanity. If the politicians cannot come up with a new educational policy, then they too - and thus the state - must bear the consequences. Nobody can make this decision for another. Nobody can go for any other the path of the individuation. The young people today cannot simply inherit from their fathers and mothers. They must find new goal orientations and thus new forms of life. The orientation is a human-centered society. We have developed orientations and goals from the current state of knowledge about the psychic-spiritual human. In this we see a realistic chance for a hopeful future and for the love to the human being from the inner spirit.

This is our utopian vision of human education.

Dr. Eduard Schellhammer

The Dispute about the "Personality" and its "Education"

"Personality development" has been the buzzword in the field of psychological and psycho-esoteric practice scene of popular education since the 1970s. But the topic is ancient. The great philosophers have spoken of "human education and development" since ancient times. The topic has reappeared again and again through the centuries under different words.

"Personality development" served as a concept vehicle and still serves for ideologies, religions, philosophies, esoteric orders, and secret societies, for political interests, for psychologies, psychotherapy, and the psycho-esoteric market. "Self- realization" is the message of humanistic psychology. But what does this term mean in the sense of a psychological-spiritual formation of the personality?

Basically, the following first general definition can be established: The adult human - that is: The personality or: The person - is in the focus of the personality development as affected person and as a self-educating individual. The adult is also the one who educates other (adult) people. We can also say: The adult educates himself (self-formation-self-education). We have so two components: First, the human as "personality" (individual person) and, secondly, the term "education".

"Educating" means commonly: Acquiring knowledge, shaping, compounding, realizing, designing, developing, expanding awareness, understanding, reflecting, adapting etc. "Education" has undoubtedly to do with learning processes (Wehnes 1991, 256). Learning processes are on the one hand contemplating-heuristic (i.e., understanding through empathy, inner viewing, and interpreting) and on the other hand technical-practical (i.e., acquire, practice, inform, process, copy). Education tends obviously to change behavior and psychic forces resp. dispositions (Ortner 1991, 304).

The term "education" cannot be defined alone by the characteristics of learning, socialization, enculturation (cultural appropriation), individualization and professional qualification. In the use of the term, education has always been understood in connection with certain educational intentions (educational goals).

The meaning of this term has in the context of educational (human-forming) targets got always new accents since the ancient Greeks to the present day. The views in the pedagogy are spread across the whole spectrum from the complete rejection of the education term to the "postmodern" educational theory (Wehnes 1991; Brezinka 1978; Klafki 1971 and 1985; Röhrs 1967; Ballauf 1986; Mollenhauer 1987; Roth 1991, Becker 1992; Lenz 1987).

In the Greek cultural sphere, education was intricately linked to values such as: The happiness, the good, the beautiful and the virtue. With the beginning of metaphysics, currently, the educational ideal was: "To realize the highest being with its origin". In the Roman Empire one taught the ethical and cultural maximum development of all forces. In the patristics, human education was linked with Christian theological education ideals. The Scholasticism produced different directions of thoughts. Essential educational ideals can be placed in the context of knowledge, belief and free will. In the mysticism (13th / 14th century) the actualization in "God's own likeness" was considered as educational idea (Jakob Böhme, Meister Eckhart, Paracelsus). During the Renaissance (1350-1510) the ideal of the "pure human education" was as the highest self-development (again) in view. The Enlightenment sat cross-accents: "The emancipated human" was considered the highest educational goal. The Humanism generally spoke of "self-realization" and "self-creation". Education is an indisputable condition of human being. However, the content and the methods must always be redefined.

"Education" has been redefined, repeatedly, depending on the cultural environment of the time. The Humanism is generally regarded as the model that has human education as its content. The human with his inherent forces is the center of educational goals in all humanistic conceptions. The "freedom of the individual" in the neo-humanism ended with the void of life of general education. The decline of humanistic educational ideals in the 19th century led to the "self-realization of empirical human" (positivism, materialism, Marxism) and since the middle of the 20th century to decisive technocratic reorientations in the context of technology, work, leisure, and society.

Old humanistic ideals and concerns have been rediscovered and modernized in the last few decades.

The target formulation of this "educational work" sees itself as "holistic" in the sense of the psychic-spiritual entity of the human. In the center of interpretation and models are since about 1970 "self-actualization", "freedom", "maturity", "responsibility", "solidarity", "self-realization", "self-determination" and "self-fulfillment" (Brezinka 1978, 48). At the same time, it implicit the "good and happy life". Concerns of the four major schools of ancient Greece are retaken in variations. "Education" is defined as concept for the lifelong learning in the context of age and living environment par excellence (Roth 1991, 480). Education creates the necessary basic prerequisites for coping with life situations (Pfniss 1988, 14, 18, 36).

The concept of education is changing through all times. Where today some separate between general human education and professional resp. economic related education, say others, that this separation is "artificial" (Steinringer 1994, 29). Education is to be determined in a complex network: Human, world, personal development, coping with the existence with individual, social, sociological, intellectual, societal, and professional components (Albers 1987, 38). The following components of the term "education" are generally recognized:

1) Education takes place in the acquisition and examination of what concerns the human collectively; 2) Education implies formation for all; 3) General education includes versatility; 4) Education is embedded in culture, and therefore in space and time; 5) Education is design and realization of the individual life history; and 6) Education depends on personal contribution (Wittenbruch 1994, 36). Today, the term "education" in pedagogy and andragogy is increasingly discussed in the context of "value education" (Brezinka 1994, 47-60). As a result of the current cultural crisis and the "risk society" (Beck 1986) character formation, love to values resp. generally value-oriented education are demanded again. "Good life values" are endangered by indolence, indifference, overstimulation, prosperity, emphasis on reason, experience-orientation, and egotism (Beck 1986, Hufer 1993, Brezinka 1994).

With a few key words - we are aware of the incompletion and incompleteness of this foray - this first overview of the history of education illustrates in particular: The definitions of the term "education" are in the history of human development manifold and contradictory.

Some emphasize metaphysical aspects. Christian theologians place their ideas of God at the center of education. Others understand education as character formation or conscience formation. Still others see the "moral human" as the goal of education. In many cases, education is simply about acquiring knowledge for the capacity for life in the industrial society (work, leisure, family, state).

"Education" is a basic term in education. Its use today is downright inflationary and alienated from the human - with all his psychic forces and spiritual values: educational policy, educational opportunities, educational deficits, educational economics, educational planning, etc. Some therefore reject this term. They also circumvent it, especially since the new "educational science" (approx. 1965), because it cannot be operationalized. Should the term "education" be abolished because it was defined in a wide variety of factual and historical contexts? The term "psychology", for example, is no less meaningful. But hence no psychologist wants to abolish it.

For a clear application of the term "education" there is a lack of coherent definition and delimitation criteria (e.g., compared to the term "learning"). As starting point for the development of a new conception of human education, we want to limit the "human education". First, we exclude all forms of training (of learning processes) of professional, continuing, and further education. We also exclude what has to do with the learning of skills for the daily life, including music, art, and leisure opportunities. The so-called "general education" is also excluded. Of course, we are not saying that everything we exclude here has nothing to do with "education". We only determine the "space" in which we want to think and analyze in our study.

For our term use, we isolate "education": The human as psychic-spiritual entity is what has to be "educated" through an evolutionary process. In this sense we speak of "human education". In a topical view, the human is situationally integrated into certain social locations and must cope with concrete incoming tasks (Kaiser 1985, 42, 135). General elements of knowledge, situation-related aspects of ability and inner-psychic dispositions interlock in our "human education". Our understanding of education is characterized by learning, development (growth) and education in the entirety of the person (Dominicé / Finger 1991, 21-22).

This brings us to the term "personality". The definition of the term is no less problematic. The field of personality psychology is marked by diversity, interpretation richness and heterogeneity. Personality theory is like a Babylonian confusion. We find about a hundred theories of the personality: A world ranging between Skinner (or Pavlov) and Plato; between learning machine and spirit being.

The total personality research is still today in an awkward position, as stated Roth in 1969: "To give a preliminary definition of the term "personality" turns out to be unworkable. In the literature can be found as many proposals as there are writers working on the area. It is also not known a criterion that would allow to decide which of these definitions would be preferable to others." (Roth 1969,10). Bischof (1983, 13-16) gives a detailed report to the personality theory. He cites various scientists of which especially Adelson in 1969 has clearly stated the situation: "The field of personality today is characterized by abundance, prolixity and lack of unity ... of considerable overlaps of social and personality theory ... it depends purely by lust and humor on how we classify the many studies ... personality theory is a rampant confusion ...". That has not changed in 1993 either: "At the present time there is no recognized definition of 'personality'." (Pervin 1993, 17).

It seems not yet been possible to classify the definitions about "personality" coherently. Theories determine the research methods and research methods limit the theories. The whole is also be interpreted on the background of life realities of research and science. Financiers determine research projects. Publishers decide on the publication of certain research results. Scientists underlie the coercion of fitting to be able to build their careers and to obtain research funds. To these critical aspects, we can add another problem: The theories of Freud, Jung, Adler, Szondi, Frankl, Rogers, Maslow, and many others became the legitimacy of professional institutions (psychoanalysis, psychotherapy, pedagogy). Are those institutions once established and economically functional, then the responsibles can no longer integrate their teaching and practice in an overarching theory system. The capital interest is in front of the scientific knowledge interest. A thorough innovation of theory and practice would eventually question the legitimacy of the institution based on its teachings.

In the past, the topic of "personality" was about will, reason, drives, feelings, conscience, strivings, character and the "individual peculiarities of the overall structure of the person". In the history, the human education revolved around aspects such as: Character, conscience, virtue, disposition, religiosity, mind, heart, will, reason, understanding, spirituality, motivation, and spirit. Thus, today the personality psychology is concerned empirical-analytically, with its sub-areas: General psychology, developmental psychology, motivational psychology, differential psychology, and social psychology. Aspects of psychoanalysis can also be assigned here.

The personality psychology also has a philosophical direction: Transpersonal psychology, psychosynthesis, existentialist psychology, "logo" psychology, psychological anthropology, metaphysics, all psychology concepts with "mind" and unity "body-soul-spirit", parts of analytical psychology (especially the collective unconscious with the theory of archetypes) and humanistic psychology. Philosophical anthropology resp. philosophy is an essential integration science of the adult education (Reifenrath (1983, 50).

For some, the structure of the individual psychic forces is in the foreground. Empirical experiencing is the central characteristic. Others emphasize ideal, spiritual, and metaphysical considerations. The positions seem to be incompatible. They also reflect history and zeitgeist (Pervin 1993, 28). Brezinka sums up the problem: "... as early as 1937 there exist at least 50 meanings of the word 'personality'; on 70 pages of an educational report from 1960 there have over 80 terms with the word part 'educate'" (Brezinka 1978.89).

In general we can say that the focus of the human education since the antiquity has been the human: With all his psychic and psycho-transcendental forces, with his inner spirit, with his psychic-spiritual development (as possibility and necessity), with his psychic-social life field, with his life happiness (love, hope, happiness, joy and meaningfulness) and life suffering (crises, conflicts, difficulties and sorrow experiences), with his acting as well as with his questions about himself, about the "right" life and about the meaning of life par excellence. However, the positions are characterized, they all try to reach the human and his being from their theories and teachings.

The teachings answer in different ways the fundamental questions about human and his being: Who is the human? What can the human become? What can the human find in himself? What is the "good life"? What is the meaning of life? How should the human live? How should he shape his cultural and social life? What is wisdom? What is love and happiness? How do one achieve inner peace? What is hope? What is psychic-spiritual evolution? Where does the inner unfolding lead? What are "transcendent experiences"? What is "supreme enlightenment"? How should the human treat the challenges of life? Should or must the adult be trained and guided? How should the human be guided and educated? What does self-knowledge and individuation effect in personal and social life?

Let us record in key words some fundamental aspects about the human in the context of the "human education", regardless of the difficulty of synthesizing existing personality theories.

Many psychic forces are part of the human: The "I" and the consciousness, the will and the self-control, the defense and the integration, the feelings and the meaning-value experience, the basic needs and the driving forces (e.g. sexuality), the personal unconscious, the rational functions (perception, thinking, intelligence), the transcendental abilities of the inner spirit (e.g. in dreams and imagination), the psychic energy and of course all aspects of personality that manifest themselves in direct behavior (such as: Lifestyle, skills, roles, love, temperament, psycho-physical reactions).

We call the overall of these forces "psychic organism". Because we assume that all these psychic forces are interdependent and work together as a complex structure. This psychic organism is at the center of the actual human education. The psyche as organism is thus the field of educational work. This is where the "education" of individual psychic forces begins. We define "personality" as "the individually formed psychic organism" that can be further shaped, developed, changed, and differentiated.

With the term "personality education" we emphasize the individual formation of the psychic organism. "Personality" accentuates the individual formed and moldable. When we talk about "human education", we broaden our horizons with philosophical-anthropological dimensions.

"Human" means the psychic-spiritual reality that is present in all humans.

The inner psychic evolution also belongs to the human life, that means: The psychic-spiritual development of the entire "psychic organism". That implies spirituality and "higher consciousness" about oneself and life. This development we name "individuation process". Individuation is also the process of inner regeneration, complete rebirth, catharsis of the lived life back to the prenatal period, psychic-spiritual transformations up to the completely integrated holistic person and - since Plato - development of the human up to the "highest sages".

The question on the human, contains substantially the possibilities and ways of psychic-spiritual development (referred as "individuation"). Individuation - and of course as a steady condition (base) self-knowledge - is the central subject matter of personality formation.

Our thesis is: *Individuation is the basic topic of human education.*

We can characterize the psychic-spiritual evolution under some polarities:

● Rejection of the psychic life	● Integration of the psychic life
● Dogmatic-ideological bindings	● Binding to the individuation
● Unconsciousness of the inner life	● Awareness of the inner life
● Disorder in the psychic forces	● Order in the psychic forces
● Destructiveness of psychic forces	● Constructiveness of psychic forces
● Expansion in quantity	● expansion in quality
● Mindlessness in life	● Live in connection with the spirit
● Power to exploit / dominate	● Power to balanced leadership
● Avoidance of life (necrophily)	● Devotion to life (biophilia)
● Regressive binding (inside / outside)	● Progressive development / differentiation

This spectrum of polarities reflects two images of human images: At the beginning there is the "archaic human" and at the end of the process there is the "evolutionary human".

The humanity is still at the beginning of this evolutionary process. Most people do not even know that there is a psychic-spiritual development and what it should be used for. Culture, Civilization, and technical progress are not yet the evolution of the whole human. Everywhere there is a lack of deeper knowledges and insights over the evolution of the human being as an inner-psychic process.

Before one can talk about topics like "emancipation" and "self-realization", one must know exactly what the "psychic organism" consists of and how the process of individuation resp. inner evolution takes place. If the andragogue and the pedagogue do not really know this comprehensively, they always define education and educational targets only partially according to their point of view and theoretical position. With this, however, parts are explained as the whole, where there is no question of wholeness. This leads to complete misorientation. In this way the science and the practice of human education moves away from the reality of the genuine human being. That must lead to "educational disasters".

The basic questions of existence arise from the point of view of evolution: Where do humans come from? Does the human exist as a "soul" even before the conception? Where does the human go after his death? What does the human live for? What is "psyche" resp. "soul"? What is earthly life for? What do "inner experience" and "consciousness" mean? What is "spirit"? We set the thesis here: Through the process of this evolution (called "individuation") the human finds all the answers in himself. The dreams and imaginative meditations inform about this. *The inner lively process itself is the answer to such questions.*

The human is also a cultural and social being. He shapes his ecological and cultural environment. He shapes himself relationships, social systems, and work. This designed world has an impact on the individual life. The shaped habitat essentially determines psychic life and development possibilities of everyone. It also gives orientation about the need for education and reflects moral and spiritual values as well as human images that act implicitly or explicitly as a yardstick. The shaped habitat is thus in the focus of human education. Because the human also recognizes himself in what he lives and creates, just as he is limited and shaped by these objectivations. He can form himself by recognizing himself as an image in this created world. This interplay of forces between human and habitat is the frame for personality development.

We consider the term "habitat" to be relatively unspecific here. We think the habitat such as: Relationships and encounters, work and working space, politics, business, school and education, religions resp. churches, ethics, norms, zeitgeist, undeveloped environment (nature / wildlife), built environment, culture and entertainment, goods, capital, and food.

Every human is looking for happiness and joy, for hope and love. On the other hand, there are crises, conflicts, difficulties, and suffering of all kinds. These are not mental illnesses, but conditions that are always part of the human life. The main ones to be mentioned here are stress, marital crises, midlife crises, depressions, fears, restlessness, nervousness, despair, loneliness, sexual difficulties, tics, insecurity, feelings of inferiority, neurotic conflicts, inner emptiness, mysterious dream life, compulsions, unhealthy habits, hopelessness, aggression, grief, concentration weakness, learning inhibitions, suppression, communication difficulties, contact problems, boredom, lack of drive, divorce and much more.

In industrialized states the human today is in an overly complex habitat with personal challenges that never were given in such a manner in humanity history in quality and quantity: Leisure and experience culture. The "free time" is a particularly topical time issue, closely intertwined with the question of personality development. Today "leisure is everyday life and an illusion at the same time. Many people need the colorful illumining to be able to endure everyday reality" (Opaschowski 1994, 6). The daily leisure time is in 2001 about 6 hours per day, 6 weeks per year and 15 years per lifetime; the tendency is growing up to doubling in 2010 (Nahrstedt 1990, 48). Opaschowski characterizes leisure time with the following elements: Personal time, educational time, social time, nice thing (and full of problems / conflicts that nobody wants to see), purely private matter (which is never true), full decision-making freedom (with massive foreign influence), have fun, relax, can be spontaneous, free of obligations, not strenuous as opposed to work (Opaschowski in: Roth 1991). Leisure time also means "being driven", "demonstration to the outside", "displacement to the inside", "boredom", "stress and inability to be alone" and generally a "highly conflictual area" (Opaschowski 1994, 13-17, 212-243) Furthermore, the leisure time scientist means, that most people miss their options in their free time, although never have been open so many options. In addition, everyone is controlled more from the outside than most people assume. Opaschowski assumes that personality formation should be a part of leisure education: Discovery of own interests and opportunities, for the activation of self-activity to cope with information flood, to find the correct use of consumption opportunities, to contact ability, to life joy and sense orientation (Opaschowski in: Roth, 1991, 933-944). The core of this leisure science revolves around the goal "to get more enjoyment and satisfaction". (Nahrstedt / Popp and Wegener-Spöhrig and Opaschowski, 1994, 425-444). Their education term is constituted by general educational concerns such as "leisure mature", "leisure capable" and "leisure competent"; "leisure pedagogy must seek its perspective in the actual core questions of the development of the human, the world and the cosmos" (Nahrstedt 1994, 433; and 1990, 176).

In this perspective, the chances of leisure for human education are enormously rich. The human - and according to sociological studies especially singles (also known as "the cuddly children of the consumer society") - needs more than good eating and drinking, bathtub, television, radio, car, nice neighbors, a nice apartment, hobbies and garden to be happy. In our opinion, he can only find his happiness through individuation. The fact that the human wants experiences (television is at the forefront of leisure activities) does not mean that he will find them. The question remains open, "whether it will be possible to produce this experience" and it is not certain whether the experience consumer really experiences this happiness with suggestion (Schulze 1992, 431, 542-543). For example, the television may "transform our culture into a huge arena for show business" and may man and woman greedily experience images in rapid change and dynamic variety out of boredom and let the shows become the content of their religion (Postman 1994, 102, 115, 153), there is no real happiness and no real inner joie de vivre, especially not life fulfillment. What Bourdieu claims may apply in part: Adult education, meditation, yoga, parapsychology, esotericism, body expression and psychotherapy are "barely veiled expression forms of a dream to escape the society" (Bourdieu 1994, 582). Today, the science of the adult education can offer to this social situation an education that cannot be interpreted or abused as an escape from society. Another positive aspect that should be emphasized is that many people are searching.

Sociologists and pedagogues paint a picture of the situation of the human in Europe that contains two main characteristics: Risks and loss of value (Beck 1986, Brezinka 1994; to name just two authors). The humans are strongly guided by the outside world, released from previous compulsions (including mythologies) and tied to the "here and now experience culture" through offers and purchasing power. This leads to a strong simplification of the reality and to a personality education excluding values. The strong experience orientation (Schulze, 1992; Opaschowski; in: Klein 1993) causes instability in norms and disorientation. The "value insecure society" is in a "culture and value crisis". The value-based education is again required (Brezinka 1994), a development of personality with partial elements such as "critical self-concept, concrete acting abilities, social responsibility, yes to the own live" (Wollenweber, 1994, 3-26) and "moral sensitivity, reflexivity, rational argument ability" (Hufer, 1993, 314-316). The adult education must be tied back to values.

Every human is also in external developments during his life course. In this, he is often confronted with unexpected difficult situations that can be significant challenges. The personality education includes the diversity of the individual psychic life situations and their possibilities for positive coping with. Human education as professionalized practice acquires here an important necessary task. It provides practical life education, life counseling, life support (again also for self-education) and thus personality development.

The objectives of human development can be developed in retrospect at the designed position analysis created in a first delineation. Differentiation and in-depth justification will be rolled out in the individual chapters.

The basic goals of human education are:

1. To know all own psychic forces and understand its symbolic language; to include their effects in acting and to understand their historicity (past and present).

2. Order, correction, and catharsis of all psychic forces; restructuring of the entire potential into a wholeness; integration and differentiation in the consciousness.

3. Growth and development of all psychic forces combined with the necessary inner-psychic transformations and the specific psychic-spiritual evolution steps (individuation).

4. To understand, integrate, appropriately manage, and resolve crises, conflicts, disturbances, difficulties, and sufferings; to learn all the necessary instruments and competences.

5. To find answers to the basic questions of human being and life from self-knowledge and individuation; development of a differentiated human image and life understanding as well as of values such as love, meaning, freedom, happiness, spirit, and wisdom.

6. Shaping of the personal, social, and cultural life from inner anchorage in the individuation; taking responsibility and living collective solidarity so that this human being finds expression in the life and these objectivations reactivate a supporting effect on the human and the social life.

Much and significant things can be presented for the topicality and legitimacy of personality education. But does the human in our time want to develop his "personality" with such goals?

Most people think: "The psyche is not important ... I know myself enough ... I am sufficiently developed ... I can cope with all life problems myself ... The unconscious does not exist ... Dreams are unimportant ... Meditation is nothing for men ... Social problems have nothing to do with me ... Personality development does not make my life any better ... I know what love and wisdom are ..." The depth psychology has proven many times that self-knowledge is an exceedingly difficult undertaking. Because the human tends to self-deception, has by nature enormous resistance to his unconscious life, and through censorship mechanisms his consciousness is considerably one-sided and particular in the self-image and in the "world-you" image. Those who do not want to see their resistance and censorship mechanisms do not see them either. What is so kept away from consciousness does not exist. A discussion about repression and defended realities is almost impossible.

Every year the Europeans hear: "No more Auschwitz and never more war in Europe". But what many millions have done against the dignity of the human is not simply an outward image of what characterizes the society today (as it was then): The feelings are not taken seriously; the basic psychic-spiritual needs are suppressed; the love is mocked; the spirit (experienced in dreams, imaginations and contemplations) is dismissed as a ridiculous pipe dream; the unconscious is ignored; the wisdoms are coldly and arrogantly left to those who "want higher up"; and the truthfulness is stupidity to the naive. From the "simple citizen" to the scholars (especially in pedagogy and andragogy and in the peripheral areas of human education) there are far too many people who talk about the psychic life without even only once have looked in the own mirror. All of them, one with scientific acumen and the other with clumsy words, sometimes friendly-politely and sometimes quite cynically, talk about the human and his education without knowing what humility is. Don't they all contribute to making war and an "Auschwitz" possible again?

Many believe that they must cope with their difficulties, conflicts and disturbances on their own and that they simply have to deal with them "somehow". Some think that the basic questions of life are a matter for churches or philosophers. Or they seek their answers in communities that transfer their teachings and ways to happiness and wisdom without self-knowledge and individuation.

The unconscious living human creates himself as an "archaic person" an archaic world. The world's population today must master enormous problems. The question is rightly asked whether these can still be resolved politically in Europe and worldwide. But these problems start with the individual: The human causes most social and ecological problems through the lack of personality development - that is, through the lack of self-knowledge, through the lack of psychic-spiritual growth and through incorrect behavior.

Social problems include ennvironmental pollution, some illnesses, accidents of all kinds, misuse of raw materials, noise, aggressions, violence, wars, crime, unemployment, fanaticism, racism, corruption, drug abuse, alcoholism, malnutrition and much more. From these few examples alone, it can be concluded: There is a lack of systematic popular education - in the sense of human education - for shared responsibility and a corresponding way of life, which would mean that the humans cause fewer and fewer such problems and at the same time adequately could cope with the existing problems.

The human is every day exposed to countless influences: Mass media, the built environment, other people, work, leisure activities and much more. The individual can no longer consciously regulate his feelings that are triggered by the multitude of influences. He is no longer able to reflect about everything and to form a judgment about everything. Motives of behavior and experience cannot be sufficiently reflected. The experience of meaning and values is reduced to meaninglessness and worthlessness. What creates displeasure or pleasure is suppressed or acted out inappropriately. Life-hindering ideals and totalitarian values are formed without that the human can recognize them as such. Here are some of the causes of unhappiness, suffering, harm, and disturbances.

Many institutions offer happiness, wisdom, love, and experiences of God without dreams, without imaginative meditation, without processing the personal unconscious, without comprehensive self-knowledge and without the process of individuation.

But this leads away from the human and away from real essential and constructive answers about human life. It is missing an integrative concept of human education and a professionalized practice that systematically mediates ways and methods for personality development that really lead to the whole human - the "whole psychic organism".

Holistic personality development is a catchphrase on the psycho-esoteric market today, a promise that hardly any of the offerors can honor. So "emancipation", "self-realization" and "freedom" remain melodious words. They will never become a fully viable reality in the habitat. If scientists and professional actors in personality education do not find consensus about the psychic life of the "personality" and cannot justify the education of the human in it, then they will all still for long argue about theories, dogmas, ideologies and paradigm to "personality" and "education".

There are some major facts about life:

Human education is a serious and great challenge. The psychic-spiritual development in the sense of individuation is the highest value of human life. "Self-knowledge" means "working on oneself". This can be exhausting. Love and truthfulness in life are difficult and often painful learning processes. Consciousness amplification about oneself and one's psychic life requires constant effort. In-depth personality development requires humility and ability of insight. Intangible psychic values are not in great demand in society today. Anyone looking for real wisdom can no longer participate in many areas of social life. Solidarity and loyalty to the cause of human education are essential. Because their value is enormous and therefore needs to be protected. But who still takes it seriously today? For almost everything, people go on streets and protest or appeal; but never for self-knowledge and individuation and never for their holistic psychic-spiritual well-being.

Religious movements and esoteric groups, with many illusions and empty promises, often with pathological aspects, have discredited the practical personality development. Base reflexes of antipathy by emancipatory thinking and acting humans are understandable.

But they must be overcome. Inertia and convenience are natural forces of the human. Working less and less, more and more comfort and more and more consumption, all embedded in illusionary ideas of life, conveyed daily from the advertising, make a society on long-term to the roots "cancer sick". After all, who wants to develop systematically self-knowledge and inner development over years? Pleasure-stimulating offers have stronger impulses. In addition, money and power are still exclusive goals in life for many people. Where this leads collectively when these people do not develop any psychic-spiritual development, the whole world population finds out today.

The psychotherapy has increasingly created an awareness in the recent years, that the human and the life estimate falsely in the most normal base characteristics: Who has crises and disturbances is "sick" and requires psychotherapy. For many people this leads to a fundamental defense: "I'm not mentally ill." New attitudes about human life are to be conveyed: There is no life without conflicts, problems, crises, disturbances, difficulties, and suffering.

The advertising in the esoteric and psychological market has devalued all valuable terms about the human and the life into empty shells. More recent developments, understanding itself as psychology and psychotherapy, are virtuoso word constructions. But its anchoring shows mockery of the seriously searching person. Many promises massively exaggerated goals that can never be achieved with the given work units and the work concept behind them. Quality in personality development can therefore no longer be brought closer to target groups with words of objectivity.

The core problem is, in a nutshell: The greatest "guilt" that the human has in himself is that he owes to himself his own personality development, i.e., his self-knowledge and individuation. We can also talk of "heritage guilt", in the sense that almost everyone takes over from his parents and from society these "debt". It is almost as if there is some secret and authoritative conspiracy going on in individual and collective life:

"Human never find yourself. Never investigate your unconscious life. Never seek to fathom the depths of your soul. Educate yourself externally, but at all costs, however you can, prevent the discovery of your inner spirit."

The "fall of the human adverse God" (Eissler 19 75, 64) consists in the fact that the "I" refuses to integrate its own psychic reality into the consciousness and to live responsibly for it. If a person does not do this, then ultimately his instinct for destruction (death instinct) always wins. Freud analyzed this clearly already estimated hundred years years ago.

The andragogy must integrate difficult opposing forces: Hardly anyone wants to look really in the depths, to process of his own lived life in the unconscious and to create consciously his individuation centered in the inner spirit through dreams and meditation for years. The personality education is certainly a difficult task. On the other hand, the risks of a lack of human education in the sense of our concept are considerable. The "business" is difficult, as some looks as if he is speaking true, but is in fact a liar. "The misconception that only what can be rationally understood or even what can be scientifically proven is part of mankind's permanent knowledge, has a pernicious effect" (Lorenz 1993, 70).

The psyche has a decisive influence everywhere the individual and collective life: Unformed psychic forces, not integrated into the consciousness or not adequately formed for the demands of life, have consequences for all humans. To this end, we are presenting a "brainstorming", compiled from five issues from a Swiss newspaper.

The stressful effects of inappropriately shaped psychic forces are key words for the "lack-, experience- and risk-society":

Murder	Obesity	Dogmatism
Robbery	Ignorance	Neurosis
Vandalism	Housing shortage	Idle work
Assault	Ozone hole	Poison in the ground
Violence	Poison in drinking water	Lack of drinking water
Drug addiction	Floods	Sleep disorders
Alcoholism	Oil spill	Desertification
Medication - abuse	Radicalism	Overexploitation
Suicide	Terrorism	Species extinction
Attempted suicide	Cancer	Slander
Traffic accidents	Overpopulation	Exploitation
Disability	Atomic bombs	Circulatory disorder
Leisure accidents	Injustice	Armament
Workplace accidents	Tropical forest deforestation	Armies
Household accidents	Poisons in the air	Residential silos
Dispute	Denunciation	Animal cruelty
Divorce	Excessive television	Death penalty
Separation	Nature mutilation	Greed for consumption
Scam	Industrial filth	Useless driving
Sadism	Civil war	Feces in the sea
Neglect	Wars	Gas bombs
Unemployment	Abuse of power	Chemistry abuse
Bad work	Drown	Lack of education
Aggressivity	Traffic chaos	Building up of ground
Oppression	Economic crimes	Self-harm
Depression	Climate catastrophe	AIDS spread
Anxiety	Coercion	Political intrigues
Insomnia	Forest decline	Polluted beaches
Nervousness	Bribery	Deprivation of liberty
Tensions	Stutter	Allergies
Migraine	Drug trafficking	Mountain landscape disfigurement
Vegetative disorders	Heart pounding	Arm trade
Tobacco abuse	Difficulty falling asleep	Chronic ailments
Sexual perversion	Masochism	Heart diseases
Child abuse	Shoplifting	Culture damages
Lying	Forced internment	Psychopathy
Intrigue	Hunger	Ostracism
Arrogance	Doings	Population explosion

Harass	Secret service	Monoculture
Betrayal	"New Poverty"	Humiliation
Too much eating	School failure	Mental illness
Wrong nutrition	Blackmail	Illiteracy
Poor personal care	Mafia "culture"	Isolation
Anorexia	Fundamentalism	Sports accidents
Fanaticism	Nuclear waste	Ideologization

From the time of conception, the human is formed by his environment. All psychic forces, all aspects of personality and lifestyle are formed from the beginning of the life. In this respect, the human is a "learning product". Still, the human is not a machine. The individual dispositions determine the forming process. The human has individual possibilities to expand and correct these shaping processes through personality development. On the other hand, the human also influences his environment from early childhood. He shapes his life systems in the way that his psychic forces are formed. In this sense, psychic life is at work everywhere in people's life. Shaping life is an expression of the human education. The individual free life design and self-actualization are simultaneously restricted resp. determined by the world that he creates for himself together with his collective. He is already born into this created world. The humanistic ideals of human education face a harsh front of reality.

If a person wants to face himself and his life – and not to flee, if he does not want to remain in the unconscious and thus in the "archaic" stage of development, he must develop himself psychic-spiritually throughout his life. To this, he needs knowledge about himself and human life. He needs instruments to form and to develop himself to master life challenges. The human needs leadership in personality development and individuation. Love, wisdom, inner happiness, and inner peace are life qualities that can and must be learned and developed systematically. The human needs support in times of excessive demands. He needs advice in difficult situations. Training is also important about what he could (can) not learn neither at home nor at school nor in his personal environment or must re-learn. Much can be listed about it; here are just a few key words on the methods: Psycho-hygiene, dream interpretation, autogenic relaxation, mental training, meditation methods, instruments (checklists) for self-reflection, instructions on crisis and conflict management, etc. There are few humans today who recognize this need and create their own personality development themselves.

The human education has far-reaching social implications. Personality development is an individual and collective necessity. The topicality is clear.

The legitimacy is beyond doubt. Personality formation is to pick up newly as a scientific topic and to master comprehensively. The scientific and social responsibility of a new theory and practice of human education is enormous.

We have hereby outlined the area of "human education". We orient us now on the term "pedagogy" and expand our term definition: "Human education" in the broadest sense of the word is "andragogy". Andragogy means: "Human formation". One can also translate as "human leadership". (Note: Human; ago: lead / form; cf. Pedagogy: Child [boy] lead / from (Böhm, 1988, 23). Andragogy is often used synonymously with the general concept "adult education", but thus has not won recognition (except in Holland) (Klafki 1971, III, 237; Pöggeler 1974, 20-36; Reifenrath 1983, 1-3). It seems to us that the term "andragogy" has been used more frequently in German-speaking countries in recent years.

According to our term analyzes and definitions, we can formulate as a basis and orientation frame for our study: *Andragogy is the science of human education. Personality development and individuation are practical andragogy.*

The fundamental legitimacy of andragogy has its roots directly in the human. In concrete terms: The legitimacy is not based primarily on technocratic-economic needs, not primarily on socio-critical arguments, not first on political need analysis, not primarily on holistic-ecological concerns and not on a "modern life understanding" (e.g., the "leisure human"; the "experience culture"). If the andragogy would justify on these subject interests, its legitimacy would merely be "imported" (Siebert, in: Roth, 1991, 635-638).

On the other hand, we are not saying that there are no weighty arguments here. Much more it comes to justify the andragogy as a science on its own with own an essential question. The topic here revolves around the so-called "pedagogical resp. andragogical reference". The andragogue forms as professional and as himself formed in individuation another human or a group in an organized evolutionary process from a certain initial state in direction of certain personality ideals (resp. objectives). The learner ("student") practices the methods of education independently with increasing ability in the sense of self-education (self-formation).

As the next step, we want to first discuss those areas that deal with human education in a practical and scientific manner. These are mainly three departments: 1) The philosophy and philosophical anthropology; 2) The psychoanalysis, psychotherapy, and psycho-counseling; and 3) The pedagogy (educational science) and adult education.

The field is wide, manageable to a certain limit and the sources can hardly be counted. There are plenty of institutions, many individual professionals, many doctrines and a varied professional experience with certainly over 300 methods of human development, including esoteric practice. We focus on three aspects: 1) Subject matter of the department in the historical horizon; 2) Basic problems of the department and its areas; and 3) Conceptual and theoretical problems. Our recognition interest is limited the outlining and highlighting of some central characteristics. The guiding questions revolve around key words such as: Diversity of knowledge, terms, science claim, working methods, positions, evaluation, practical applications of the science, personality development of the professionals, social relevance.

Some comments on these key words offer the approach to the definition and foundation of the human education as a science and practice. Building on this, we want to present a new concept: The andragogy for the 21st century.

Andragogical visions in 12 theses: "Andragogical training analysis" for educators, pedagogues, andragogues, social pedagogues, education experts, education researchers, teachers, and education administrators?

1. The (ped-) agogical actor has an unconscious, i.e., a "reservoir" full of life experiences since the prenatal period, images of people and life, images with meaning and value, images of norms, commandments and sanctions, images with a complex character or "critical" load etc. This inventory is mostly unconscious, often emotionally highly charged, full of contrasts, partly constructive and partly destructive resp. suitable and unsuitable for the life fulfillment. Many (ped-) agogical actions are controlled by it. *The pedagogue can only "educate" as far as he recognizes, and can shape, form, change, consider this reality in himself and in the educandus.*

2. The pedagogue on the one hand - and the educandus on the other hand - has a variety of defense mechanisms and projection tendencies that always influence the (ped-) agogical interactions. Many educational interactions fail because the analytical-methodical principle "resistance comes before content" is not recognized and consequently methodologically (educationally) not properly observed. *The pedagogue "educates" as he recognizes the defense mechanisms and the projection dynamics in himself and in the educandus and can deal with.*

3. The pedagogue and the educandus have a variety of basic psychic needs, for example: Autonomy, self-identity, love, security, truthfulness, authenticity, trust, happiness, psycho-social security, integrity, development of all psychic forces resp. potentials, etc. *The pedagogue can*

only "educate" to authentic development as far as he recognizes these needs in himself and in the educandus and can thus prepare the way to fulfillment.

4. The pedagogue and the educandus each have a variety of feelings with quite different characteristics, for example: Intensity, duration, mode of action, expression, causes, meaning and value. Some feelings are quickly overlaid by other feelings, transform in other feelings through repression or are the expression of a biographical chain reaction. *The pedagogue educates in the emotional area in the way he recognizes, considers, and can cope with his own emotional world and that of the educandus.*

5. The pedagogue and the educandus have dreams every night. Dreams contain messages about the human and his life, about all aspects of human being. Dreams inform, warn, advise, guide, educate, prepare changes and solutions. Dreams are about the whole psychic-spiritual and real being of the human. Dreams are created by an inner spiritual force with andragogical intent. Only this force - and never a theory - can lead a human completely to himself. *The pedagogue achieves the human being "educationally" as far as he takes seriously his own dreams and those of the educandus, understands them and takes them into account as a crucial life function.*

6. The love is a complex psychic emotional efficiency, for example: Developing life holistically, building joy of life, taking seriously, and developing all psychic forces, integrating the entire psychic life, shaping the habitat from within, realizing the psychic-spiritual evolution "with spirit". The love can forgive, reconcile, understand, exercise patience, live kindness, let someone have his way, renounce, and transform what is suffering. What is the human being without love? *The pedagogue can only "educate" with love and to love as far as he forms and lives his own force of love with self-analysis and self-development.*

7. The life of the humans is largely characterized by life lies and partial schizophrenia - that is: The humans ignore their inner being and split it off, although it is sufficiently shown that what is repressed always "strikes back". Everywhere we encounter lying, twisting, distorting, intriguing, covering, acting and being dishonest towards oneself. Masks and facades as well as narcissism and egocentrism characterize the self-being. *The pedagogue "educates" to authenticity, how he recognizes the types of distortion of human being with self-analysis and self-development, becomes free from and can deal with it constructively.*

8. The human life is full of difficulties, crises, problems, and conflicts. This is a completely normal part of the life. Even so, most people deceive themselves and others in this regard; they suppress their own "conflictual

being". One must learn life techniques, coping methods and strategies for solving this. And that also means holistic self-education. *The pedagogue can only "educate" to cope with the conflictual human being as far as he can competently manage his own conflictual human being with self-analysis and self-development.*

9. Christian, esoteric-spiritual and psycho-ideological education do not practice the all-round balanced formation of the comprehensive psychic human being. They exclude the unconscious, defense mechanisms, function of libido in projections, the dream life and individuation with its archetypal procedures to a large extent or entirely. Their education is based on myths, on spiritual constructions or on technological reduction. *The pedagogue only has educational competence for the all-round balanced human education as far as he can practice and exemplify a comprehensive, internally rooted, evolutionary image of human through his own life.*

10. The primarily human consequences of previous concepts of formation and education are due to a lack of life competences and self-management as well as a result of stressful biography or social stress: Depression, migraines, social phobia and chronic fears, spinal problems, suicidal thoughts, sheep disorders, chronic pain, impotence, obesity, constipation, postural deformity, victims of violence in the family and acts of violence in marriage and family, accidents of all kinds with many deads and insureds, children with asthma, adolescents with hearing damage, language disorders, addicts (nicotine, alcohol, drugs of all kinds, medication, games, consumption, chocolate, pornography, food, television, mobile phone, etc.) and psychic or psychosomatic sufferings as a result of an unsuitably educated psychic-spiritual human being. - *At least 50% of these sufferings can be reduced with a balanced formation and education! However, this requires that those who are educationally (agogically) active in research, teaching and practice teach, "educate", and realize a well-balanced human being.*

11. Individuation is constitutive for formation and education in the third millennium; at its core, it includes: Self-analysis, processing the unconscious (biography), integrating and shaping all aspects of the person and the inner-psychic opposite sex, shaping the self-identity (as a man or woman), integrating sexuality with love and understanding, living out of the force of love, getting rid of neurosis and egocentrism, learning social competences and coping methods to the conflicting human being, living culture and environmental shaping with this inner education, inserting in the andragogical force of the spirit (which creates dreams and properly designed meditations), all-round balanced education of all psychic forces for the purpose of the completion of the archetypal procedures to the evolutionary human being, and on the goal level: Realization of the

highest mandala of human being. *If the pedagogue wants to promote such processes in the educandus, he must live himself in this educational process of individuation. Individuation greatly facilitates the agogic work and significantly increases the efficiency of agogic interaction.*

12. Traditional concepts of pedagogy and andragogy lead to believe: The unconscious is insignificant; defense and projection mechanisms are unimportant; basic psychic needs are to be observed only to a limited extent; feelings are to be repressed; dreams are just "brain-physiological waste"; love is a private matter; individuation is educationally and andragogically irrelevant; narcissism, egocentrism and the conflictual human being have little to do with pedagogy, social pedagogy and andragogy. - What kind of educational conception and educational practice is this that almost ignores the entire inner-psychic reality and thus the individuation? What are the collective long-term consequences if formation, education, and further training do not integrate the above-mentioned human areas as an integral part of their human image and in the center of their practice? Therefore: If pedagogy (social pedagogy and andragogy) wants to form the humans to their authentic human being in teaching, research, and practice - and this also for the good of society as well as the natural and animal world, it needs a new visionary andragogical human image for the third millennium. And this implicitly includes: *The individuation is the indispensable "andragogical teaching analysis" for all (ped- / social ped-) agogical professions in teaching, research, and practice as well as in education administration.*

These 12 theses are to be justified step by step in the following chapters.

Struggle for Human Education in Philosophy

Philosophers say: "Philosophy is love for wisdom and truth" and "Philosophy is the queen of sciences". The philosopher is the wise. He stands "above the life", as in static distance and (in awareness) at looking over space-time. He thinks comprehensively, farsightedly, and down to the deepest depths of being, things and life. "Serving the humans" should be the philosopher's task. But philosophy is what a philosopher writes and teaches: Many idea systems, ideologies, terms, constructions, and abstractions of abstractions. This shows the history of philosophy. Philosophy is epistemology, art of life, and the "religion of the educated" (Brezinka 1978, 190).

Isn't the human the most central object of philosophy? Philosophy has to do with ethical living, morality, religious, human images (philosophical anthropology), with culture, but also with logic, epistemology, science theory, metaphysics (ontology) and aesthetics. Our interest is: What do philosophers say about the human? Many designs have been made to this.

We want to briefly touch those elements from a hardly manageable number of philosophers and literature that address topics about the human and his education (upbringing). Some philosophers have thus touched only marginally, others have realized within their life engagement (Höffe 1985, Störig 1965; Baldwin 1960; Hügli / Lübcke 1991, Kerényi 1971, Rocek / Treasure 1972).

It is a tradition that popular education was understood as a part of philosophy and mystery schools as early as ancient Greece. "Recognize yourself" is the name of the Delphic temple saying, a paradigm for life help. Socrates (470-399) taught human images and the general questions about life: What is virtue? What is the conscience? He encouraged self-reflection and self-knowledge. Plato (428-348) founded his "Academy" in 385, which lasted around 900 years. He had a clear concept of the psychic-spiritual development of the human, which leads to the highest level of enlightenment and wisdom, to the highest perfection. Life issues take significant space: Moral goals of the human, virtue, truth, harmony, the good life, education, personality development, maturation and much more.

The life goals Plato has rooted in the "imaginative". The body, as a mortal shell of the human, is the source of lust and aspiration (power). Rational forces are recognition, learning, "I", and reason. The soul itself is immortal. In the soul is the deity, the transcendency and the good. The aim of life is the harmonization of these three force areas, which leads to the "art of living" as ethical behavior. This human education implies the all-round balanced order of all forces. So, also justice, honor, courage, prudence and wisdom develop. The harmony of the soul is the ideal for the formation of states. The ideal state is of the same order structure.

Aristotle (384-322) also taught human education, first at Plato's Academy, later in his own "school", the "Lykeion". Here, too, we find the moral improvement of human behavior, a doctrine of virtues and ideas about felicity for people and politics. Felicity results from the morally valuable action that is directed by the reason. Finding the "right center", i.e., living balanced inside and outside without extremes, is the principle of action. The education takes place through experience to the insight, through practice and doing. Repressed emotions are the source of suffering and therefore special attention should be paid to. They can be reduced through music, theater visits and art.

Epicurus (341-271) founded another school called "Epicurus Garden". He taught the humans the liberation from superstition, gave instructions for a happy and good life. His teaching is individualistic and atheistic. The pleasure-displeasure-mechanism is the source of all behavior. The human can and should guide these forces with his mind. The goal is a positive balance of pleasure and displeasure. That means soul peace, being free from desires, humility, being free from irrational fears and superfluous wishes. He understood his ethics in this interest.

The STOA (since 300 BC.) is considered the fourth classical school of Greek antiquity. Zeno of Kition (340-262), is the founder of the stoic school. Practical life-help for people was the formative commitment consisting of instructions and teachings to the "right life". The focus is on acting according to the principle of reason. The human finds felicity in: Passion lessness, calmness of the mind, inner independence, and asceticism. The reason is above the feelings.

The philosophical schools of antiquity taught and practiced all methods of the psychic trainings such as meditation, concentration exercises, rules to the way of life (discipline, loyalty, obedience, self-control) and methods of soul guidance.

In the Roman Empire we also find the popular education as philosophy, poetry, and rhetoric, for example in Cicero, Virgil, Horace, and Ovid. At the same time, the teachings of early Christian Gnosis (as mysticism and as knowledge) is to mention (Manichaeans). From the early days to Middle Ages, church teachers and philosophers made significant contributions to popular education. We mention here three outstanding figures who have dealt extensively with self-knowledge, human education, and human guidance:

Augustine (354-430) places self-knowledge at the beginning and at the center of all life. Its content is not just psychological self-examination. The path of knowledge leads from oneself through analysis of the own lived life, quasi after or behind the sensual and rational knowledge to God. To recognize oneself means to know God at the same time. Human depravity and desire for self-enjoyment are essentially based on the lack of love ability, which in turn is an expression of a lack of knowledge, thinking, insight, awareness, and truth. Only the love capable human can find true happiness.

Thomas Aquinas (1224-1274) taught the pre-existing soul. It is the real human. The human is body, life, meaning and spirit (reason) in one. Intellect, reason, and belief in God are the three cornerstones of human education. The virtue teaching includes, e.g., Wisdom, courage, prudence, justice, faith, love, and hope. Moral behavior consists of the one hand of these virtues and the use of reason. On the other hand, the highest morality is dependent on grace. The greatest felicity lies in the knowledge of God. The mystical union with God becomes the highest value of the being at the end of his life. The final fulfillment of the human resp. this felicity is transferred to the hereafter.

Meister Eckhart (1260-1327) sees the salvation for the human essentially in knowledge. Knowledge is based above all on intuition, the inner vision, and the inner sources. Faith, love, and hope are central virtues. What God is can ultimately only be manifested through the human. Inner experience ultimately leads to God.

Bonaventure and Bernhard of Clairvaux are other mystics from that period who taught and practiced themselves the inner vision of the divine truths as the last and highest goal of the human.

Only a few centuries later the time begins when great thinkers liberate the question of the human from theological-metaphysical systems. The courage to investigate the question for the human with the reason breaks the fetters of dogmatism and opens the way to emancipation. But isn't this emancipation an ideology and an illusion again? Let us briefly touch on the history of philosophical thought about the human:

Descartes (1596-1650) wants to put ethics on scientific bases and hopes from this a re-education of the human: From the fool to the clever, from the coward to the brave, from the emotional labile to the affect controlled. The mastery of the outer nature should lead to the mastery of the inner nature.

Human education is embedded in the relationship with God. Because ultimately only the relationship with God makes happy.

Leibnitz (1646-1716) made the individual to the focal point of thinking. Meditations are self-reflections of the thinking human. Only symbolic knowledge can make possible the knowledge of God. Reason makes possible belief and does not stand in opposition to it. We find here for the first time (?) the concept of the unconscious.

Kant (1724-1804) outlines a new human image in which he justified the capability of reason. He prompts the humans to create a law of virtue free of force through the ethical natural state. The human is rooted evil and must overcome this condition by using the reason. The greatest of all questions "What is the human?" is placed above the three basic questions of philosophy, which are: What can I know? What should I do? What can I hope for? There is also a practical aspect to be found: In the "big world" the human has to behave "sophisticated" and to do this he needs knowledge of human nature. Reason and free will regulate the happiness.

Hegel (1770-1831) advocates that the motives of moral acting must be strengthened. Politically oriented, religious popular education creates a free people. The alienation of the human in the structure of society is to be brought to new life by regaining the context in moral acting.

In his external nature, the human is an archaic deficient being. The distinction to animal nature is to be sought within. The human being is characterized by its possibilities and limits of changeability in space and time. Philosophy should not recognize God, but the human: His person, his moral point of view, his place in the family and his role as citizen.

Numerous philosophers and poets since the Enlightenment and then in modern times can also be understood as popular educators. Many names should be mentioned. We can only highlight a few key words from the last 200 years:

Schopenhauer (1788-1860) viewed the human in an instinctual manner, in which the "will" obtains the decisive function. The intuition leads to the inner experience of this driving force, which in its natural state is geared to economic and sexual exploitation. The felicity comes from giving up all aspiration. The human is "the animal that can beat".

Kierkegaard (1813-1855) claims to be a human is a free decision, everyone can also refuse. Whoever puts the sensual enjoyment above the ethical principle makes himself unfree. This also removes the ground for self-liberation, self-determination and "being able to be oneself".

Marx (1818-1883) was a time-critical committed intellectual. Realization of philosophy meant to him the design of the societal reality, according to the laws of reason. His criticism of philosophy is an expression of his engagement: Changing the world, not just interpreting it. The ideal of human emancipation is understood socially. The human is a creature of nature, which realizes himself by working. Alienation of work and working conditions must be reflected in an action-oriented manner. The human affects the nature, changes it; and this in turn changes the human.

Nietzsche (1844-1900) analyzes the necessity and ways of reshaping the illusory world and illusions of the human. He sets clear contrasting accents: God is an illusion of the week, a myth, and a symbol for values without perspective. The human is challenged to live his own will, to give meaning to himself and to life itself. The evil is the best human force. The human is "the sick animal".

Scheler (1874-1928) looked at the "position of the human in the cosmos" (1966). The foundation of human life are irrational feelings and impulses. Body and soul are one. There are not just physiological differences between humans and animals that make the human humanly. It is the spirit that makes the human to what distinguishes him from the animal. Spirit is super-spatial and timeless. Spirit is intelligence and choice ability. Spirit enables the view of ideas, the abstraction of objectivity. The human can detach himself from the environmental relation (in contrast to the animal) and thus to recognize the things (life) in their "intrinsic nature" through the liberation from instinctual pressure. Spirit enables "pure knowledge". In this respect, spirit is an ascetic principle. The experience of God and "God- realization" are embedded in this knowledge. Becoming human and becoming God are reciprocal, mutually dependent processes.

Marcuse (1898-1979) understood revolution as a liberation of human instinct nature. He sketches the "one-dimensional human" (1968). His philosophical treatises are social and cultural-critical studies. The practice is at the beginning of theory; translated: The life of the human comes before the personality theory. The real interest of the individual is real freedom. This cannot be found in hedonism. The reality of happiness is the freedom as lived self-determination.

Gehlen (1904-1976) creates a human image under the heading "deficient being" (1971). The human is helpless; he not only lives; he must lead his life.

From this he justifies institutions which must provide in education and formation processes. The human is a product of tradition and zeitgeist. To that extent he is a cultural being. A pluralistic ethics as social regulation instance allows a reorientation adverse biological, psychological, and social forces (1969).

Horkheimer (1895-1973) sees the human in the tension field between those who enjoy (have) property and those who resign and suffer as a result. Philosophical-psychological occupations about the "authoritarian personality", about "authority and family" and about society characterize a human image in the view of "critical theory". His philosophy is "philosophy of life".

Adorno (1903-1969) sees in the clarification of the unconscious an act of enlightenment. The lack of consequences of thinking has driven the human into a "delusional overconfidence". The "education to maturity" (1973) is the focus of practical commitment.

These are a few small excerpts that highlight aspects of human education. These philosophers traced - along with many other philosophical topics - the basic questions of the human and the "good life". For some, the guiding principle of ancient Greece was elementary: "Self-knowledge is the beginning of wisdom" and the basis for a happy and good life. Again, and again, the Socratic "Daimonion" - the divine element of the spirit in the human as the top goal of ethical-personal maturity - stood in the center of philosophical efforts. Forming innate morality and practicing dialogue with God within, is the core issue of human formation of all metaphysically oriented philosophers to positions in the new philosophical anthropology (Rothacker 1966; Landmann 1969). Other philosophers are more oriented towards empiricism (English empiricism) and distance themselves from a Platonic-Aristotelian metaphysics. The focus is on the right of sensual experience. Space-time categories take precedence. We have increasingly found social conditions as a frame for human being and the opportunities for self-development since the middle of the 19th century.

Again, and again, in human images of great philosophers appears the "spirit" as the main characteristic of being human. But what is "spirit"? Many accents are set, such as intelligence (thinking) and reason, creative force of the cosmos, power of God, creative force in the human, the connecting in the unity body-soul and in the unity body-soul-God, the unity creating force in the human, a normative principle (because cosmic and / or divine order) and the force in the human that frees him from the space-time dimension. This spirit, however understood, places the human in a creation plan where he can no longer be interpreted as a random product of evolution (Monod 1971). Such interpretations receive an additional horizon, for example if it is taught that the human is bound by memory and his unconscious to what he has lived, created, thought, and experienced. Or from another perspective: The human unfolds himself in the interplay of culture (which he creates) and intra-psychic reality. The social conditions and the formed psychic forces are the determinants of every possibility of development. The history and the life determine what a person is and can become.

The question is obvious: Is there a definitive human image at all? Is it still possible to create a "wholeness" out of the psychic, educational and philosophical fragmentations? Is the question "What is the human and his humankind?" (Pestalozzi) maybe even a pure language game? Is it possible to detach knowledge processes at all from the individual psychic forces and their reciprocal functioning, which in turn are embedded in historicity? Various philosophers answer these questions differently, some inner-orientated, others external-orientated. Truth is to be found inside or truth is to be found by thinking performance; or: The social reality is the truth. This makes it difficult to define "knowledge". The matter becomes even more problematic when it is asked whether philosophy should be purposeless or action oriented. Technocratic understanding stands next to "pure science". Who can really take responsibility for his own definition, not just with committed words on paper?

With Scheler (1928), Portmann (1956), Plessner (1965) and Gehlen (1969) at the latest, philosophical anthropology is an independent philosophy that deals with the "being of the human". Recently there has also been the saying of "psychological anthropology" (Gadamer / Vogler 1973, vol. 5). Philosophical topics are as far threaten here, this "philosophical anthropology ", and as far as the subject of discussion are knowledges of psychology and psychoanalysis, we relate it to psychology. Finding knowledge about the human and his possibilities, in the context of historicity, is the task of philosophical anthropology. Empirical research stands next to meaning interpretation. The increasing novel ideologization by methodological reduction with simultaneous abstraction of the sense questions is rejected. Anyone who asks about himself is always looking for the meaning and interprets himself and his life. Life is always to be understood hermeneutically (Habermas et al. 1973). Purpose freedom and action relevance identify the positions. There is a tendency for all thought systems of this new science from the recorded facts in an educational postulate: The human needs education and capable of education, since birth, and throughout his life.

We would like to distinguish this understanding of education from that humanism, which is characterized by hedonism or eudemonism, sometimes mixed with a little "spirit" and "transcendence". The human basic needs as the starting point and goal of the being are a reduction of the human image to present and moment. The "intelligence of the spirit" is missing, and it is not considered that the life of the human always includes crises, conflicts, disturbances, and difficulties.

Life always includes life suffering. From the point of view of wisdom, one even has to say: There is no comprehensive psychic-spiritual evolution without inner suffering. There is no thought system with which one can get rid of suffering. In our opinion, this problem is an important basic topic of philosophical anthropology.

A manageable, lifelike philosophical human image should make it possible to understand behavior and condition of the human, his thinking, and his way of life in a larger context. It should also be able to capture difficult life questions. Let us make clear a few basic questions:

Why does the human suppress his psychic life every day? Why does the human live physically and psychically unhealthy and self-harming, even though he is aware of it? Why does the human repeatedly undergo formalized ecclesiastical, political, and social rituals? Why does the human intentionally inflict psychical and physical harm on other humans, including torture and killing? Why does the human wage war? Why does the human live sexual perversions that no longer have anything to do with love and natural drives? Why does the human always look for God and contact with a hereafter, where God and hereafter have never been "proven"? Which forces bring a human to take his own life? Why is the human looking for the game? Why do the humans intentionally ignore the most self-evident laws that they give themselves? How do mental disorders such as anxiety, compulsions, depression, neglect and "inner voices" arise? Where do the dreams and images in imagination come from? In other words: How can the intelligent information of inner images be explained? Why do the human need "home"? Why has the psychic-spiritual evolution been "forgotten", resp. rather for most people without meaning?

Many thinkers have been investigating the basic questions of the human, certainly before ancient Greece. We left out some. The following should also be mentioned: Plotinus, Anselm, Bacon, Hobbes, Pascal, Spinoza, Hume, Fichte, Husserl, Steiner, Heidegger, Plessner, James, Portmann, Sartre, Popper and Habermas; and this list, too, is only a selection from the series of philosophers.

On the fringes of philosophy, some esoteric movements and secret orders have dealt with the human education. To mention here are mainly Freemasons, Rosicrucians, Gnostics, Anthroposophists and mystical schools of all kinds. They operated all (and operate) in their own system self-awareness, personality development, as well as philosophical and / or religious education of the human (Doucet 1980, Miers 1980).

The secret doctrines and secret orders have a tradition that goes back to the time of ancient Greece. It is not possible to give a summary here. Just a few notes may illustrate that there have been other organizations and still are that practice much "popular education", be it in terms of the general life philosophy, be it in the sense of popular esoteric and personality training (character education, self-knowledgeable, awareness formation, spiritual growth, transformation to inner unity, etc.). Gnostic-theosophical orders, grail communities and kabbalistic schools of all kinds have educated with teachings, cult and rites millions of humans since Plotinus (204-270). There are to be mention the Freemasons with all their various groups, the Rosicrucians, the Illuminati, the gnostic-Neoplatonist hermetism, the pansophic currents, the Jewish mysticism, the alchemy, the templar orders and many other occult societies with mixtures of Christian doctrines, Buddhism, and magic practices. The "mystery human" as an object of knowledge and a needing education is always the focus of teachings and practices. All want ultimately always self-development and self- actualization of the human. How the personal and the collective unconscious had already been the subject of practice, for example, shows the alchemy, with precursors dating back to Pythagoras (Jung 1972; Frick 1978, I, II, II; Lennhoff / Posner 1980).

They all have influenced the policy, human education, and social living since ancient times at least as strongly as the classical school philosophy. They taught (and teach) about life and death, about sexuality, about magical forces, about the spiritual, about self-knowledge and experience of God, about virtues and moral values, about good and bad, about the stages of spiritual development and much more.

From this brief overview with just a few key words from the field of human education in philosophy, we can highlight some characteristics:

Many philosophers of the occident since ancient times have practiced useful life philosophy. Some more inquiry-studying in the own educational institutions or - later - in universities and others especially through practical popular education (lectures, essays, consultations, political activities). Today, philosophy seems to be experiencing its great identity crisis. The absolute truth is at an impasse and the metaphysical master thinker have become unpopular. It is unclear what today can be counted to philosophy. The theoretical concepts are different in content and scope. There is an increasing tendency today to relate the aspects of the human to philosophical anthropology. But the reality shows that this is practically impossible to achieve. Characterized by a plurality of heterogeneous language constructs and life meanings, a plurality of incompatible concepts, like the Babylonian confusion (Hugli / Lübcke, 1991, 7).

The science has always given reason to heated arguments, polemics, and mutual condemnations. Certain directions as positivism, hermeneutics, existentialism, hedonism, metaphysics are used as insulting terms. In the philosophical anthropology today, it is undertaken an attempt to integrate different approaches to a wholeness. But it is also evident: The authors define content and method not according to generally accepted criteria. This is the freedom of philosophy. So, we find the old directions again in philosophical anthropology.

The working methods in philosophy are different. It is always thinking processes and doctrinal conversations that should lead to "valid knowledges". Social scientific methods are used today to supply "material" to the philosophical reflection resp. thinking processing.

As indicated, there are many different directions of thinking. It is not clear who can be considered a "classic of philosophy" and who cannot. There is a certain tendency, that a professor, who writes books and articles, even to highlight as a philosophical reference for a factual issue. The size of the print run and topicality in the press also seem to be a factor in identifying a new position. In many cases, philosophers have triggered "movements" which were then "dead" again after 50 years. Certain philosophers clearly declare that they do not regard or consider this or that philosopher as philosophers at all.

We have no knowledge of a success judgment as to what the human education of philosophy achieves. The world shows which new concepts are creating changes in science and practice. No philosophy has changed the world so much in such a short time as Marxism. And many theories have only led to combat on paper. In the richness of ideas there is always a delicacy for new thought constructions. In practice, philosophy is a teaching and fighting arena. There are losers and winners here, many speakers, but no evaluation of the educational performance in the world of life.

There is no clear idea how philosophy should affect the human and life. Some positions see their task in the direct change of the human and society. Others, however, are above worldly engagements. With rare exceptions, psychoanalysis has still not succeeded in moving the philosophers to seek the "truth of the human" and that of God and spirit in the depths of the unconscious - and for example in dreams. It can be interpreted that the actual inner reality of the human in philosophy has not enough attention received by far.

The professionalization tends to academic career. Most of the philosopher is a professor, teacher, or freelance writer. Some were active in journalism, with literary works, with historical research or in government functions. In the past, rich people afforded their "house philosophers". This is no longer common today. "Philosophical consultant" does not exist as a profession. The philosophy as science today has little practice. It is a "free art" at universities and some of their products also reflect the unconscious life of their authors. The philosophy has its claim to human education and human guidance in this century - perhaps ever since the independence of pedagogy - not honored, with some exceptions.

We can also examine the philosopher - and the gnostic and the "enlightened one" - in what he does depth psychologically. Many philosophers and "sage" still owe the self-reflection.

The questions of cognition interest are, among other things: How does the philosopher place the "libidinousity" of the human, if he cannot live his own sexuality? Where does he seek clarity in assessing the "evil" if he is burdened in his superego since early childhood and does not know his own destructive psychic forces? Which human image characterizes his studies when it comes to the habilitation or the recognition of his achievements among colleagues? What position relevant to practice does the philosopher take when the "eye of the educational department" looks carefully towards the teaching institution? How does the philosopher see the difference between man and woman when he lives his own relationship in a strained relation? Where does he look for God if he believes he is rationally liberated from his own religious upbringing? How does the philosopher react if he has bad dreams about what he thinks, teaches, and lives? How does the philosopher solve his own "guilt"-problem if his "I" with all imaginable constructions wards off continuously, what should be assimilated in the consciousness about himself as human, as psychic-spiritual being? How does the philosopher live his own personality development and individuation?

There is a lack of professional image building, which involves the psychic-spiritual development, along the scientific expertise, by the philosopher scholars. From the point of view of individuation one can assume that a philosopher who has not completed his own psychic-spiritual evolution to the goal is only a "half philosopher"; and that the philosopher who does not know the unconscious, love and dream language, has essentially rather little to say to personality development - and in general for human education.

The social significance of philosophy is, indirectly, enormous. It shapes the understanding of sciences. Again, and again, it has produced ideologies and dogmatic teaching systems that have made "history". Looking back into the history of the occident, the combination of ideology and dogmatism with the power of state had often devastating consequences. Whenever philosophy was ideological and dogmatic, it has served as a vehicle for warfare and oppression. Conversely, philosophy has led to liberation and breakthrough to new forms of life and government. If love, wisdom, and inner experience of a deeper meaning in life (with or without God) are the core interests of philosophy, then occidental philosophy has failed. For the most part, it has not reached or educated the human in this matter. It served only itself and the careers of its representatives as well as church and politics.

For the foundation of human education as a science and practice, some conclusions result:

The andragogy will be able to find a lot in its search for valuable knowledge about the human and life in the history of philosophy. A psychological and socially critical processing of knowledge can certainly expand usefully the human image in andragogy and pedagogy. But it is an exceedingly difficult undertaking and resembles the work in a diamond mine: A small uncut diamond in the rough to ten tons of stone and earth. The absorption in the literature of the entire esoteric can especially provide proposals. The material available to us on this is no longer usable from the point of view of scientific nature and state of knowledge of psychology. Some issues of human education raise questions to philosophical anthropology.

Feedback of philosophy to practice resp. a manner of action-oriented knowledge acquisition can always be an asset. The conversation about epistemology also leads to the unconscious and to the dreams. Who has not completed systematic and in-depth self-knowledge, steps aside his unconscious life inventory, has not developed love force and does not understand the intelligent spirit that creates the dreams, is maybe a "Chair-philosopher", but he knows little about the human, and life? Some philosophers still have their own enlightenment ahead of themselves if they want to be interlocutors of (new) andragogy. This is also an orientation for the own philosophical reflections of andragogy.

The andragogy as science and practice of human education treats the basic themes of the human with social scientific methods, with hermeneutic, with interpretation of symbols, and with depth-psychic methods (introspection, imagination, projection). Despite the necessity of a positivistic (mechanical-materialistic) cornerstone, we consider its absolutization to be an illusion and therefore ideological and subjectivistic. The "other reality" in the human cannot be put away.

The philosopher must process his own history and that of philosophy generally in the sense of catharsis. This personality development leads to inner freedom and to a reconsideration of the meaning of life. Those who have done this no longer need to cling to positivist ideals. Inwardly free, he can "philosophically" turn to the reality of the human. Then a completely different kind of knowledge begins. The andragogy develops an integrative understanding of its practical activities, which also includes philosophical and thus ethical education.

For our interest, it is sufficient for the time to mark those areas that can be considered as philosophy of life. We use this term synonymously with "practical philosophy" and mean "the philosophy that reflects the human and his life in such a way that the human can benefit from it". Philosophy of life is part of andragogical practice. These are those parts that philosophically and ethically the human and his being examine from the perspective of "good life", transcendence, para psychological reality in the human, spirit (the "higher self") and psychic-spiritual evolution. The relationship of inner spirit (in dreams and in the imagination) to the "I" of the person is the source of moral duty. We consider this back bonding to be essential for a human-centered theory and practice. This also includes elements of gnostic and mysticism, albeit to be understood today in new practices, symbols, and terms. Nothing is as important in these areas as clear terms that have a clear place in the psychic organism.

One might be inclined to divide classical philosophy into andragogy and philosophy. But there are some problems. Because philosophy also includes logic, epistemology, ontology, aesthetics, ethics, mystics, gnosis, philosophy of language and state, theory of science, metaphysics, philosophical and psychological anthropology, and much more individual topics. It may affect a lot of philosophical conversation if one wanted to clearly define what belongs to andragogy and what is "pure philosophy". Nevertheless, the andragogy as an independent science can eliminate those areas that are relevant for the theoretical (anthropological) foundation of human education. "Human education" as theory and practice imply philosophical questions and reflections.

Human Education or Psychoanalysis and Psychotherapy?

The field of psychotherapy, psychoanalysis and psychic counseling is wide. The main points to be mentioned are psychoanalysis, neo-psychoanalysis, analytical psychology, individual psychological psychotherapy, fate analysis, existence analysis, bioenergetic psychotherapy, logotherapy, transpersonal psychotherapy, cognitive psychotherapy, hypnosis and suggestion therapy, humanistic psychotherapy, behavior therapy, gestalt psychotherapy, anthroposophical psychotherapy, psychagogical therapy and clinical psychotherapy. Aside there are other processes: Dance therapy, wholeness therapy, music therapy, teleoanalyse, imaginations therapy, positive psychotherapy, psychodrama, transaction analysis, integrative body psychotherapy, NLP therapy, psycho-organic analysis, respiratory therapy, and flowers therapy as well as some more word combinations. To present all these here would go beyond the scope and our objectives (cf. Pervin 1993; Schlegel 1973, I-IV; Bischof 1983; Pongratz 1973; Hilgard / Bower 1970).

We cannot roll up these directions individually below. It must suffice here to outline the development history and the situation of psychotherapy, psychoanalysis, and psycho-counseling (a term that we introduce here for the sake of simplicity; synonymously with "psychic counseling") to be able to clarify essential basic problems for andragogy.

The history of psychoanalysis, psychotherapy and psycho-counseling starts in the 19th century with the research on the unconscious. In the 20th century the application follows scientific methods in the context of independent departments of psychology that gradually come to development and adopt clear contours. Wundt (1832-1920) founded the first psychological laboratory in Leipzig. Till then, philosophy and pedagogy had dealt in thinking with the "soul life". Psychology was part of philosophy.

The practice of psychoanalysis and psychotherapy has its precursors already in the antiquity. On the one hand, there are the philosophical schools. On the other hand, it must also be mentioned the temple system: Healing through dream incubation, by magical rites and natural healing practices (Kerényi 1971).

The temperament teaching, for example, goes back over Knigge (1752-1796) to the antiquity. It understood itself essentially as human education. No doubt the Christian church practice since its existence has developed its own practice of life counseling, consultation, self-knowledge and psychocatharsis. Witch expulsions were methods that Charcot tried to re-develop with hypnosis. The confession can be understood as a practice of psychocatharsis. In addition to the classical pedagogy the church practice counts as a forerunner of today's psychotherapy and psychic counseling. We find further forerunners in the Gnosticism, in mysticism and in secret orders such as Rosicrucians and Freemasons.

The systematic exploration of the unconscious began in Charcot's circle (1825-1895), with a history of development going back to Mesmer (1794-1815). Ellenberger (1973, I, II) documents extensively that Janet (1859-1947) extensively researched on neuroses, the unconscious, psychic energy, psychological analysis, complexes ("idées fixes") and its pathological expressions (e.g. hysteria). Janet claimed in 1913 at the international congress of medicine in London methods of psychotherapy, rapport, resistance resolution and catharsis healing of neuroses as his discoveries. He strongly criticized Freud's interpretation of dreams. Theories and therapy forms of all major researchers in the field of the institutions Salpetriere and Nancy were based on clinical pictures of psychiatry. To this circle also Dessoir can be counted, who wrote the famous book "about the double-I". In it he presented the concept of superconscious and subconscious and explained that dreams give access to the subconscious. The history of systematic exploration of the unconscious began with this. On the first "International Congress on experimental and therapeutic hypnotism" under the honorary chairmanship of Charcot (8.-12.8.1889) were also names like Freud, Janet, Forel and James (see in: Ellenberger, 1973; Helmchen / Linden / Rüger 1982).

Freud (1856-1939) has taken some ideas with him from his stay with Charcot in Paris. He also rejected some things (e.g., hypnosis) and probably found confirmation in others. Freud's theoretical works can be grouped into four main parts: Personality model ("I", id, super-ego, resistance), method the psychoanalysis, neuroses teaching, and (later) cultural and religion analysis.

The repression of sexuality and its destructive effect (on psyche, body, culture, and politics) is expected as a central social critical education request being applied also to the "healthy" human. Religion as a "childhood neurosis" was a topic that did not primarily address to the psychiatry but aimed at the whole Christianity and Judaism. Freud then tried to protect his teaching on psychoanalysis for the future with a secret society (in the sense of a lodge). His drive-oriented conception met with fierce opposition and at the same time international interest.

Adler (1870-1937), member of the Psychological Society by Freud has vehemently been rejected of Freud with his theories about the psyche. His studies revolve around themes that can be indicated with a few key words: Power and inferiority, striving for compensation and superiority, social factors and thinking as significant factors in the noseology of neuroses. In 1911 Adler said goodbye to this group. He founded his own society.

Jung (1875-1961) had also raised serious concerns about the sexuality theory. Freud and Jung broke off their relationship in 1913. Jung developed his own work: The collective unconscious with the theory of archetypes, individuation process, complexes and psychic energy, the theory of types with the aspects of anima-animus, mask-persona, introversion-extraversion and the psychic functions, later then religious-psychological topics. Jung has more and more removed himself from his psychiatric research. His main works have hardly anything to do with psychiatry, psychopathology, and psychotherapy. The "numinous", i.e., the mysterious depths of human soul with its symbolic expressions have a humanistic, gnostic, and metaphysical dimension. For Jung, this dimension was essential for understanding the human.

Reich (1897-1957), after clashes with the Freud-school and exclusion from the International Psychoanalytic Association from Vienna emigrated to United States, dealt with own concepts of psychotherapy: Character plating, social causes of neurosis, Orgon (psychic energy / bioenergy), character analysis, emotions and psychic reactions, technique of psychoanalysis, etc. His extensive pioneering work has created a new line of development in psychoanalysis with Lowen.

During this period, the development of psychoanalysis is to settle the Gestalt psychology of the Berlin School: Wertheimer (1880-1943), Koffka (1886-1941), Köhler (1887-1967) and Lewin (1890-1947). Gestalt psychology teaches that the psychic is originally always present as "Gestalt" and not as "elements". Wholenesses are organized according to certain laws. They are dynamic and not mechanical. This basic concept of psychic space or field can be transferred as a formal model of thinking, needs, learning, development, memory, and behavior.

With the political development in Germany from 1932 onwards, psychoanalysis in Europe experienced a break. Many analysts have emigrated. The beginning of Neo-Freudianism begins in the USA and after the Second World War in Germany. It is hardly possible to classify the development in homogeneous groups. The contributions of many psychoanalysts are orientated on entirely different issues and interests. Social psychological considerations, society critical approaches and philosophical foundations of a new psychoanalysis are only a few keywords. Individual contributions to the so-called "Neo-Psychoanalysis" - now away from the classic pathology cases such as hysteria and schizophrenia towards narcissism and everyday life - provided above all Horney, Sullivan, Kohut, Sandler and Schultz-Hencke. Let us accentuate a few examples:

Ms. Horney (1885-1952) desexualized Freud's theory and recognized that many neurosis forms neither have their causes in childhood nor in impulse disorders, but simply in life problems and life conflicts such as illness, fatalities, unemployment, money problems, and workplace problems. Sullivan (1892-1948) developed an interpersonal theory of personality with the "self-system", analyzed the fear as core emotional factor of neurosis and designed a dynamic development psychology as an alternative to Freud's concept of phases (anal-oral-phallic). His commitment to a "better society" reflected his hopes for the positive opportunities of the human. Erikson (1902-1994) advanced the understanding with his model on the psycho-social development stages. His personality theory is based on eight phases of "I"-development that extend into old age. Fromm (1900-1980) expanded the theoretical foundations of psychoanalysis with studies to love, good and evil, narcissism, the freedom of the human and to a "new society". In contrast to Freud, his human image is rather optimistic.

In Switzerland, Boss (1903-1990) developed the Daseinanalysis. The experience-based approach in space and time plays a central role in it. Being developing and world exploration receive central psychic importance. The path to one's own self-being, to psychic-spiritual wholeness is the course of psychoanalysis. The love plays in the application of psychoanalytical technic a main function. Boss rejects the concept of unconscious categorically. He puts the psychotherapy on a new basis: Philosophical understanding gets a more human-fair meaning than instinct-oriented scientifical approaches. He was awarded the "Great Psychotherapists" prize by the American Psychological Association, with which his approach - based on the philosopher Heidegger - has found international recognition. Szondi (1893-1986) expanded the "I"-analysis and the drive analysis with his "fate analysis". He analyzed with a meticulous system, the relations between genetics (pedigree) and the psychic reality. He has developed a categorization of aspirations and needs, that should serve as explication of psychopathological appearances. He created the concept of "familial unconscious", which contains the entity of the ancestral claims. This gives his psychoanalytic practice completely new work forms.

Psychoanalysis in the USA has lost the "culture of psychoanalysis in Europe". It developed a "well reserved psychoanalytical professional status" (Russell Jacoby 1990). Medically oriented psychoanalysts still claim that they are the only ones who have the right to call themselves psychoanalysts and to practice psychoanalysis. The history of psychotherapy from about 1920 runs this claim away. However, it was argued - and is still debated - about the so-called "layman analysis" of non-medical psychoanalysts. Outside of the orthodox psychoanalysts are the "wild psychoanalyst" and "layman analysts," then as today.

Mitscherlich, Adorno, Sartre, Jaspers and Holzkamp - to note just a few names - opened extended discussions in the 1960s and 1970s on the question of the human resp. psychology and neurosis teaching of psychoanalysis and psychotherapy. Socio-critical considerations close again the bow to Freud's commitment to culture and society economy.

Parallel to the neo-psychoanalysis - and to the other psychology concepts - a new movement had been developed in the USA, later in Europe, far from the depth psychology: The humanism in psychology. Rogers (1902-1987) started with the idea that in every human are "immeasurable sources" which help to transform his life and to become himself. In the center of his personality theory is the concept of the "self". The attitudes and feelings that the human has of himself, is opposite to the ideal self. Self-actualization and self-development are in the focus of his interest. To this, he has developed a special form of therapy, known today as "client-centered conversation psychotherapy". The self-realization takes up a lot of space at Rogers. However, this concept may be given little theoretical value, as well as his conception to the personality (the "self"). Fear, resistance analysis, sexuality (drive dynamics), guilt and depression are little in his interest area. Roger's engagement shifts to the so-called "encounter groups". Openness, honesty, sympathy, and the updating of the "here-now" are characteristic for his method. The philosophical orientation lies in humanism, partly certainly also in the religious.

Maslow (1908-1970) is the main exponent of this humanistic psychology. He sees this path as a real alternative to the orthodoxy of Freudianism. The transcendent and the transpersonal acquire an elementary meaning in the understanding of the human and his suffering. The focus is on a new way of life, not just healing a suffering. However, he does not have the (psychiatric) sick human in his line of sight, but the "normal healthy", disabled in his realization as a human. Links to James (1842-1910) and Dewey (1859-1952) can be seen here. He believes in love, in the good in the human and in the possibilities of a new world, shaped by this psycho-transcendental humanism. The satisfaction of basic needs is a prerequisite for this. His model of the self-realized human is shaped by this hope and love. The Gestalt therapy of Perls (1893-1970) can be classified into these psychological development line, at which psychoanalytic elements and ideas of existentialism are shaping too. The gain of sensory perception and body feelings are training elements in the psychotherapy that direction.

Frankl (1905-1997) belongs to the second Vienna generation. His comprehensive work is lauded as "overcoming the psychoanalytic nihilism", as "re-creation of God in the soul", as "... fulfilled of glowing humanism". His meaning-oriented "logotherapy" is considered the "Third Viennese School" along with Adler and Freud. Frankl has written over 25 books that have been translated into 14 languages and have gained wide recognition, especially in America. However, there is no place for them in textbooks on personality theory. The meaning question of life and generally metaphysical questions about the human and life are frame and centering forces in his psychoanalysis and neurosis teaching. The religious in the human and the meaning question of being have already found their foundations in James, for example in his study of human nature (The variety of religious experiences, 1901/1902); an approach that did not arouse interest by Freud at the time. Earl Dürckheim (1896) also belongs to this series. His intellectual asset is based on the Gestalt psychology, the work Jung's and especially Meister Eckhart. He described the religious bottomlessness as the main cause of "not sound being". We find central connections to humanistic psychology in Frankl and Earl Dürckheim. Their roots are to settle by James (1842-1910), who in contrast to behaviorism hold the introspection as an essential path to the analysis of consciousness. Today's "transpersonal psychology" developed from this field (Assagioli, Grof, Tart, etc.).

Today's relaxation techniques, hypnosis and imagination have their origin in psychiatry, also as early as the 19th century, partly from the same field around Charcot, Bernheim and Liébault. Schultz (J.H.), Langen and others, as well as Chertok in France have following this tradition developed methods of suggestion, hypnosis, and relaxation - as parts of psychoanalytic practice - not only concerning the psychiatry. In America, too, hypnosis is being taken up again as psychotherapy (cf. Erickson M.H). Mental training, imagination and autogenic training have found their way into general education across Europe.

Is this direction "neo-psychoanalysis" or a completely new development in the theory and practice of psychoanalysis? Janet said in 1919: "The decline of hypnosis in the history of psychotherapy is a momentary accident ... hypnotic suggestion will come back." (Chertok 1973).

In fact, today this tradition has found a revival in medical practice and above all in the sector of practical life support, psycho-esotericism, and naturopathic practice. "Neuro-linguistic programming" (NLP) makes use of this (Grinder /

Bandler 1991; Bandler / MacDonald 1991).

In parallel with the development of psychoanalysis, neo-psychoanalysis and humanistic psychology, behaviorism increasingly formed a challenge for psychoanalysis: Watson (1878-1958), Hull (1884-1952), Skinner (1904-1990) and Eysenck (1916) dealt with psychic forces and their learning processes as well as with a general personality theory. To do this, they created a variety of scientific methods. The factor analytical (nomothetic) personality theory and the laws of learning are the main results. They laid the foundations and carried out pioneering scientific work in the fields of experimental psychology, learning psychology, social psychology, and perceptual psychology. From this, behavior therapy emerged as an original new concept, independent and far from psychoanalytic theories and techniques. In the essence, the behavior therapy focuses on clearly operationalized therapy goals in behavior, thinking and feelings. The re-learning happens in many variants, for example: Re-conditioning, model learning, self-assertion training, aversion therapy, systematic desensitization, etc. The application areas tap into the broad field of mental disorders and deviance, including addiction and delinquency.

The psychology of behaviorism, as it was understood by Watson, for example, should be a thing of the past: "Psychology is a completely objective, experimental branch of nature science that needs just as little introspection as chemistry and physics" (1913). However, with the behaviorism - which includes Pavlov (1849-1936) approaches and research methods have been developed that without doubt have to take a crucial place in the psychological research in the future - among many other concepts of gaining knowledge and theory forming.

The clinical psychology sees itself as a connection to Piaget's clinical method in developmental psychology and thus as an applied science (Baumann 1979). With its scientific claim it belongs to the rank of behaviorism.

The "clinical psychologist" works in socio-educational institutions, in homes for children and young people, in welfare offices, in clinics, in psychiatry and geriatrics, in addition also in the own practice. The clinical psychology deals with psychic and psychosocial reactions in terms of illness, difficulty, and disorder. Clinical work is prevention, therapy, consultation, analysis, social-pedagogical work, and diagnostics. The philosophical-anthropological orientation is centered humanistically: "Much like in psychotherapy the individual should be brought (with the clinical psychology) actually to the conflict-free development of his personality (Schraml / Baumann 1975, I, 716). The clinical psychologist can use the entire repertoire of methods of education, counseling, psychoanalysis, behavior therapy, milieu therapy, analytical group psychotherapy, child psychotherapy, marriage counseling, conversation psychotherapy, relaxation, and hypnosis as well as psychagogical methods. The clinical psychologist is not doctor, i.e., not either psychiatrist. Clinical psychology is the attempt of a technologically oriented professionalization of the psychologist beside the medical psychoanalysis (Petermann / Schmook 1977, I, II; Baumann / Berbalk / Seidenstücker 1978).

Psychotherapy and psychological counseling cannot be clearly delineated in terms of their practical activities. Therapy and counseling are communication processes. A group of counselors differentiates itself with its defined activity obverse the psychotherapy. They are marriage counselor, education counselor, youth counselor, sex counselor, life coach, advertising psychologists, psychagogue, coach, learning support consultant, career consultant, group dynamicist, sociopsychologist, business psychologist, etc. These professionals are specialists in a practical crises sub-area or in areas such as communication groupdynamics, school, media, environment, economy, health, police resp. legal system, politics, etc. Some overlaps with the clinical psychology can be identified (see: Lück, 1986, 29).

The starting point in the practical consulting activity is, for example, a conflict, problem, difficulty, a special challenge of the client. The activity is oriented towards: Situation analysis, elimination of information deficits, strengthening of self-confidence, clarification of values and goals, learning support, change of attitudes, reduction of constraints, activation of motivation, determination of decision criteria and above all also the promotion of self-management in the problem situation.

In general, the activity field of psychic counseling does not include individuation. They do not see themselves as human educators in the psychic-spiritual evolution. The psychological human education is limited by the focused subject matter (the "problem"). The complete renewal of the human from the "inner rebirth" to the new completely integrated wholeness (the so-called "Individuated human") is not their work goal. Most consultants have an academic qualification and orient themselves in their activities on their specific expertise.

The terms "psychoanalyst", "psychotherapist", "clinical psychologist" and "psychic advisor" conceal a variety of theories, methods and "object fields". The meanings can no longer be mutually delimited. The "gray area" is ambiguous and in practice so rich as the lives of their clients. In addition, any working person has his personal inclinations. Some persons move away from their "school" in their professional years and work as the life situation in the individual case urges.

What is declared as a so-called "teaching analysis" has a very divergent reality between the different schools. At least two third of a teaching analysis in our opinion could be done in groups without limitation of the educational performance. We know of no evaluated theory that this thesis contradicts. Not without reason Balint has discussed the conflicting position of psychoanalysis also from the perspective of the (transmitted) father-son problem (Balint 1981, 307-346).

The general market for "popular esoterism" (e.g., New Age movement, practical parapsychology, magic, spiritual healing, psycho-religious movements), including the esoteric-psychological life counseling, is considered an adjoining activity field of psycho-counseling. The market offer is wide. According to advertisements, a lot is offered: Therapy, respiratory therapy, applied neurosystemics, mental healing, body-oriented therapy, NLP-training, awareness through movement, organic spirituality, Gestalt work, psychodrama, theater education, training against eating disorders, astrology, chirology, personality development, autogenic training, yoga, graphology, encounter, guided affective imagery, esoteric wisdom, aura analysis, spirit healing, return, practical magic, contacts with the beyond, ufology, health with minerals, aromatherapy, Huna, mental alchemy, development of the personal potentials, mystical experiences, higher consciousness, ecstasy, clairvoyance, future looking, evolution of the psyche, tarot, oscillation, light experiences and much more (see magazines "ESOTERA" and "PSYCHOLOGIE HEUTE").

The responsibles are diverse and almost entirely commercial: Centers, house of rest, holiday education center, practice, seminar location, school, institute, forum, training center, academy, life school, fairy tale center, healing center, therapy house, teaching center, meditation center, etc. In addition to autodidactics and "self-made-men" (-women) there are also academically qualified specialists in this activity field who practice an integration of scientific practice and spirituality. Several suppliers also supply different training programs for psychotherapists, analysts, consultants, experts, or teachers.

We have thus roughly outlined the field of psychotherapy, psychoanalysis, and psycho-counseling. We are aware that the list of the (few) women and (many) men who have made valuable contributions - especially their own theories and concepts - should be supplemented by other names: Janov, Kelly, Cattell, Maeder, Loewenstein, Moreno, Grof, Allport, Berne, Jones,

Binswanger, and others should be mentioned.

The sketched overview is sufficient to assert some essential characteristics:

The terms that identify the schools illustrate some initial problems: How can be grouped the different directions resp. teaching systems? There are a variety of science areas. What is therapy? What is analysis? The practice is complex and variable. What is a theory of personality? For example, is individual psychology really depth psychology? Is a metaphysical approach in psychoanalysis still psychoanalytic theory and practice? Is analytical psychology more "analytical" than Freud's psychoanalysis? Isn't behavior therapy just as much an "analytical" (i.e., "decomposing") psychology as psychoanalysis? The humanistic psychology cannot be called "the third force" (beside psychoanalysis and behaviorism). For there are before, beside and after Rogers and Maslow some teaching systems or schools, that also can be identified as "significant forces" in the history of psychology of this century. The transpersonal psychology declared since about 1968 as the "fourth force", as a "higher psychology", just transpersonal and transhumanistic. Cosmic experiences, partly in the sense of mysticism, partly in the sense of the beyond reality should lead over the own learning history. Far Eastern elements about the paths of enlightenment are unmistakable in this psychology (Grof 1985; Tart 1978).

The various schools and teachings are largely incompatible in their conceptual systems and in their theories (concepts, models). Freud, Jung, Adler, and others developed quite different dream theories. There are positions that consider the dreams resp. the dream interpretation to be unimportant. The definitions about the unconscious differ considerably from one another.

In some schools the unconscious does not exist at all. The concepts of human development are quite different. There are drive-oriented models, socio-psychological models, and more spiritual transcendentally rooted models. Jung's model of the individuation process is unique in the entire field of psychology and psychotherapy. The images about the human and life of the individual teachings deviate substantially from each other.

Such contradictions can already be seen from the beginning of the development of psychoanalytic teachings in the period from around 1890 to 1920 (Ellenberger, 1973, 1, 14). The old "fightings" between the individual schools last still and have lost nothing of hardness of mutual disqualification. (See a regional example in this regard: Bischofberger A., Pfusch auf dem Psychomarkt, page 41 ff; and Gutberlet M., "Verhaltenstherapie gegen den Rest der Welt, pages 47-48; in the Zeitschrift der Schweizerischen

Gesellschaft für Psychotherapie "Brennpunkt", No.53, Nov.1992, vol. 14; and "Riss", Zeitschrift für Psychoanalyse. 7.Jg., No.21., 1992 "Laienanalyse als Symptom").

The scientific nature of psychoanalysis, and humanistic psychotherapy, is fundamentally questioned by some experts (of other positions). Analytical psychology and general concepts about the intellectual development of the human are also classified as "extra-scientific" by representatives of empirical science. The dispute over theory formation and research methods is repeatedly conducted new on an academic basis.

There are over a hundred individual therapy methods (Seifert / Waiblinger 1993; Linden / Hautzinger 1981). Many of them are incompatible with one another; some of them have changed little since decades and are even represented doctrinally. What some consider to be necessary, others ignore at all. Some take a technocratic position, while others covenant the spirituality. The build upon human education has necessarily practical consequences.

Concepts of short therapy promise to solve problems, where others say that many hours of depth psychic work are necessary. Parapsychological working methods (e.g., hypnosis, mental training, psycho-energetic work forms) held almost all as charlatanry, at least as irrelevant. It is unclear whether psychoanalysis is only a therapy method (with its own personality theory), or a personal deep psychic formation for self-recognition and development. The same question applies above all to humanistic psychotherapy. It is likely that the "healing factor" in the psychotherapy has extraordinarily little to do with the specific method and the corresponding theories, but rather basically happens because the client deals with himself at all and knows that he has to learn new things - that is, to form himself in order to change his position. But that is personality development.

The dependence on the founders (e.g., Freud, Adler, Jung, Rogers, Reich, and others) is often evident and formative in practice today. The developments must also be examined critically from a commercial point of view. A state-approved and to the medical resp. social-pedagogic system integrated professionalization means jobs and health insurance financing.

The discussions about individual success rates are conducted more in the background resp. on a scientific level. A look at the literature shows: The success controls are sometimes poor, and the ascertained successes are mostly unconvincing. They are mostly in no relation to the effort and the training qualifications. The discussion about methodological problems is as topical today as it was years ago. The difficulty arises from the different approaches to the human understanding. The "conflict-free development of personality", for example, must be described as unrealistic humanism, as a longing for the paradise and as illusion. A control of success would not be feasible at all. The general problem of success assessment is in the range of long-term control, of the wholeness and the hidden problem shifting. But external factors influence the course of success situation considerably: New external situations such as unemployment, financial changes, new relationships, changes in the workplace and / or in the family, the course of a career, a disease, or an accident and many more can revive the old problem structures in new forms. Another question is: How can be measured "empirically" (just three keywords) meaning experience, self-realization, happiness experience and inner contentment?

It is fundamentally questionable whether all sufferings that psychotherapists are trying to cure can even be referred to as "mental illnesses" and thus fall under health care legislation. The different concepts of neurosis, conflicts, crises, and disorders make this problem clear right from the start. While Freud, Adler and Jung first wanted to find explanations and healing methods for the mentally ill (in the sense of psychiatry of that time), today the focus is on the human with his real-life difficulties, life problems and dissatisfactions, especially in humanistic psychology and "psycho-transcendental therapy". From teaching concepts, and, also in practice one can see: What is actual self-knowledge, self-education and self-development is declared as "psychotherapy" resp. "psychoanalysis". In our opinion, psychoanalysis is elementary self-knowledge and personality development (cf. Hartmann 1973, 70). Where crises, conflicts, difficulties, and life sufferings (which are always part of life) are declared as therapy cases, non-suffering and the "conflict-free personality" become the criteria of health (of the emancipated person?). But in our opinion, this is a perversion of life.

The professionalization in the field of psychotherapy and psychoanalysis shows some considerable problems. This results from the different positions. The innovative ability of individual schools seems to be generally rather low. The insight in some documents of the post-graduate courses of studies illustrates among others: Different curricula, in part extremely high costs, different durations and "credit points", different demands on the own analysis and inner development of the candidate.

Based on literature and personal encounters, we have not been able to find a single representative of these directions who would have achieved psychic-spiritual development (individuation) to the goal. We assess the state of the personal development of the psychoanalyst resp. psychotherapist considering the requirements (long-time own analysis) and the authoritative set images by the majority as moderate to low. A certain "narcissistic conflictuality" seems despite training analysis often have not been able to clarify (Battegay 1979, 137).

Finally, the general question to be asked is what social significance has the individual schools over the centuries. It is still a fact that an estimated 80% of the European population does not take part in this service, marginal encounters are not considered.

Formerly the relevant circles designated the Lake Zurich as the "psychologist lake". That can still be said today (cf. Obermüller Klara: Marktplatz der Seele. Die Weltwoche. Zurich, August 17, 1995, no.33). But: How many Swiss can afford this help at their own expense over a longer period (e.g., one year)? In Spain, for example, the situation is even worse. Probably 90-95% of the population could not even finance themselves psychological help - psychoanalysis, psychotherapy - for a few months. The density of psychologists is accordingly. Lück (1986, 55) sees group work to provide financial relief while maintaining psychoanalytic and psychotherapeutic goals. Freud called for "psychotherapy for the masses" (Balint 1981, 320). It seems to us that the psychoanalysts missed this educational mandate.

The whole psychology - especially psychoanalysis and psychotherapy - is as science in constant development. To this day, the psychology has not yet succeeded in making the humans in the industrialized countries fully familiar with the psychic reality. The downright gigantic sect system in the US (Ruthven 1991) and increasingly in Europe clearly shows how vulnerable the human still is for ideologies, dogmas, and myths as well as for fundamentalist thinking.

One may wonder which ideas will soon be raised as "fifth force" or "sixth force". Conceptually, however, there is hardly any way left open: From "stimulus-reaction" to "unconscious", to "numinous of the collective unconscious" to "self-realization", "transcendence" and "cosmos", all dimensions are already leased. The "new cosmic world order" and the "universal life" are already making claims to power.

For the foundation of andragogy as a science and practice of human education result from this some conclusions:

The andragogy is neither psychiatry nor medical psychotherapy, nor psychoanalysis in the sense of orthodox doctrine, nor a teaching of psychotherapy. The andragogy is no cure for psychic or psychosomatic illnesses.

The criteria of psychotherapy to distinguish it from andragogy may apply (Becker 1982, 42):

1) Need to medical attendance.
2) Need for care.
3) Disability in independent living.
4) Reduction / restriction in general forms of life.
5) Inability to work or limited ability to work.
6) Topicality of self-harm.

The andragogy does not deal with diseases and disorders that have these components. These fall within the competence of medical and clinical psychotherapy. On the other hand, all forms of disturbances, crises, difficulties, and human (psychic-existential) sufferings that do not have these components fall within the competence of andragogy. General neurotic disorders are quite a work area of andragogy because, by definition, over ninety percent of the people are already "neurotic" to some degree. Many therapists and analysts work with clients that do not fall under this list of criteria. This client group can therefore be described as "healthy". Its "therapy" is therefore an andragogical practice, i.e., human education.

From our philosophical-anthropological point of view it can never be the goal of human education to want to completely abolish suffering through psychic practices and to declare the "happy life without suffering" the highest goal. We consider this to be an arrogance towards life, and a rather childish illusion. Suffering is always part of the human reality. Suffering is neither an "evil", nor a "wrong" nor a "cruelness" in itself (Assagioli, 1992, 142/260). Suffering is also part of the psychic-spiritual evolution. Because there is no development of love force without suffering and there is no decisive expansion of consciousness without suffering. We set that as a thesis.

The future andragogy in theory and practice is inconceivable without the integration of the theories of depth psychology. It is the task of andragogy to develop an integrative personality model that includes the elements of the different schools. Against all disputes among experts, this is entirely possible. Finally, the various teachings have scientifically founded forms of work, which are also considered part of andragogy. The working target and the individual conflict issues decisive to the application of a particular method.

The various professional groups cover a part of andragogical practice that attend humans advising, supporting, helping, comforting, teaching, and leading in moments of crises, failures, difficulties, and problems of life of all kinds. The psychocatharsis and formation of the individuation process, in turn, requires other methods. Segments of psychological, therapeutic, and analytical practice are an area of andragogy as we have defined this subject area. The andragogy must develop a concept of how clients are to be advised and supported on the one hand in crises, conflicts, difficulties and life sufferings and on the other hand in the area of individuation and self-knowledge.

In general, it should be emphasized that nothing other than self-knowledge (self-reflection), self-education and self-development (self-renewal) in many variants and theoretical concepts is hidden behind psychoanalysis, psychotherapy, and psycho-counseling. Core objectives of psychoanalysis, such as, e.g., "strong critical I", "free of unnecessary identifications", "free of automatic transference" and "free of thinking patterns" and similar more are certainly central goals of personal development in the sense of individuation (Balint 1981 317). This is nothing other than "ordinary" personality education resp. human education with life advice. The concept of classical psychoanalysis and psychotherapy, what school anyway, is unsuitable for general personal development and individuation. The specific counseling situation client-analyst resp. patient-therapist is justified only by the specific interest and need to be able to discuss and work on certain very personal things in an intimate setting. Regardless of the intimacy of certain life issues, there are also factual issues that do not belong in a group with participants from all kinds of social and professional groups. The predominantly larger part of analytical and therapeutic learning processes can, however, just as well - we claim, even better - be achieved in a group (teaching). One can also process objectively and meditatively on the unconscious and the dream work in a group without having to create a particularly therapeutic transference situation.

Extending analytical and therapeutic learning processes to a comprehensive personality education and systematizing the corresponding knowledge appropriation and experience through training to learning units, so one can create a didactically substantiated program of personality education. Content and process are not given by chance of the group dynamics (or single hour), but clearly structured as a systematic integral personality and life education. Daily homework, exercises and reading are part of the program. Because everyone knows: One cannot achieve high goals in the life without exertion. Personality education and individuation, possibly connected to life counselling means work, path and destination. This is our new educational understanding of andragogy.

Impasse of Pedagogy and Adult Education

Till the 18th century pedagogy was a branch of philosophy: Pedagogy was considered as practical philosophy. Then the time of real pedagogy began. In the following period, all the the great pedagogues have also dealt with popular education, i.e., with human education. Some of them refer to Plato or Aristotle. Probably the first theory of education can be found in Plato's "Politeia". Virtue, competent thinking and acting as well as liberation and inner freedom are counterpart of the professional abilities (for making money). Awareness formation is the core of Plato's human education. In the medieval concept of education, "education" is interpreted theologically and, according to Meister Eckhart (1260-1327), it is given the highest intellectual expression in the "unio mystica". The concept of education of the enlightenment is far from such depths. Reason, own strength, and right virtue are the contents of education, currently (Wehnes 1991).

Upbringing and human education have been central tasks through the whole history of Christianity. The philosophy of Middle Ages finds its essential active pedagogical expression in church practice. The Christian churches can therefore be described as the decisive educational institutions in the occident, at least till the 18th century. We want to briefly examine some aspects of human education from the history of education (Knoop / Schwab 1992; Horney et al. 1970; Böhm 1980; Scheuerl 1985).

Comenius (1592-1670) is considered the first great theoretician of a systematic and comprehensive pedagogy, including the education of adults and elderly. The human is capable of learning, in need of learning and deserve to be appropriately treated or educated as "God's creature and member of the universal human community".

Rousseau (1712-1778) interpreted the human in the tension field between society and individual possibilities: "Everything is good and degenerate in the hands of people." Freedom, equality, and emancipation were the goals of his idea of the "new human". His culture criticism revolves around the problem of "overestimation of the head", the alienation through rationalization and mechanization of life.

Humboldt (1767-1835) started a comprehensive education theory. In the disruption of his time, education is given outstanding importance to him. Education leads to self-confidence, an all-side harmoniously formed individuality and self-development. Education is separated into general human education and vocational training. The dominant principle is the "general human and all-round harmonic education".

Herbart (1776-1841) taught about morality as the highest good of human education. He is considered "the last philosopher among pedagogues and the last pedagogue among philosophers". Questions of public life are viewed from an educational perspective. His human education centers around the morality - as "the crowning glory of the character formation" - which ethics provides the goal and psychology the ways and methods to achieve it.

Fröbel (1782-1852) founded the "Allgemeine deutsche Erziehungsanstalt" and dealt with "human education" (1826). The human should experience himself connected with cosmos and God. The human is to return to himself to discover his "higher purpose in life". "Life union" with nature, with humanity and with God is the guiding principle of this understanding of human being.

Pestalozzi (1746-1827) is known worldwide for his teaching on "head, hand and heart formation". The "modern popular education" has received lasting suggestions from him to this day. He understood upbringing as "fulfilling of the own destiny" and integrated people, family, and fatherland into it. He was never just a child educator. He was also a theorist of popular education. One of his key words is: "The life educates". Purpose of general people education is the rise of formation of inner forces of human nature. Vocational training is therefore subordinated to human education.

Schleiermacher (1768-1834) founded pedagogy as action science (theory and practice) with historical and ethical responsibility. The model was the maturity of the individual in the state. Pedagogy and state have a common interest basis: The maintenance of the state. The human education is thus in a dialectical relation to the interests of society. Morality and drive nature, ideal and real as well as reason and individual nature are dialectically related to one another.

Dilthey (1833-1911) understood education as "molding of all psychic functions". He designed a teleology of soul life, a doctrine of psychic functions and methods of understanding (hermeneutics). He understands the soul life as a holistic structure, embedded in the historical cultural areas. Despite all historicity of human life, the soul life is given independently. This is where the educational idea and human education are based.

Natorp (1854-1924) dealt with "social folk culture and personality culture". He was close to the workers', family, and women's movement. Popular educational tasks took up significant space. As a neo-Kantian, he saw the goals of human education in the enforcement of the law of reason. Ethics and the doctrine of virtues are based on this. The human as part of the community is to be educated for rational activity and truth. Drive, also will, and reason, are classified in a context of meaning and value.

Kerschensteiner (1854-1932) made considerable contributions to the workers' school as well as to theory and practice of civic education. The human image is practically oriented: The basic axiom of his education is that "the character is forming itself through acting". He sees vocational training as the "gateway to human education".

Spranger (1882-1963) was particularly committed to the subject of education in the interplay between spirit-soul-culture and to popular education ("general education"). He also designed a culture pedagogy and a humanities psychology. He also developed the three-step model: Basic education - vocational training - general education. Not the free development of personality is the highest goal, but to take the "best values" from the social entity and to give back the best own values. He sees the adult in a constant process of transformation ("stages of life"), whereby permanent learning and constant growth must implicitly be regarded as natural.

Montessori (1870-1952) is known for her "pedagogy from the child". In her commitment she has sharp criticism to adults as causer of wars, famine, injustice, misery and as inventor of the atomic bomb. The adult is to change, has in his self- education to become more mobile and to develop new forms of the own life. Not only the child is dependent on the adult; the adult also stands dependence on the child.

Litt (1880-1962) designed his pedagogy based on philosophical considerations. He placed the human as an educational topic in the dimension of spirit and being. He understood the realization of meaning on the one hand in the context of metaphysical ideas and on the other hand in connection with work and profession. Here human education is taking place.

Flitner (1889-1990) was remarkably close to popular education ("Volkshochschulbewegung"). Lifestyle, culture traditions and upbringing forms stand before the theory. According to him, human education is always to be understood in the larger context of occidental intellectual and cultural history. Questions of meaning and values are just as much a part of the understanding of education as philosophical thinking. By highlighting the special responsibility of pedagogues and adult educators he wants to be understood the education and upbringings as an independent science, especially emphasizing the social and humanistic practical relevance. Adult education is life teaching. The human needs education till the end of his life.

A first turning point in the history of education since the 18th century can be seen at the beginning of the 20th century. Flitner (1889-1990), Nohl (1879-1960), Weniger (1894-1961), Roth (1906-1983) and others made significant contributions to human education in the first half of that century. Historical-hermeneutical reflections, thoughts on education philosophy and culture resp. value education were guidelines in the study of human education. The pedagogy and "education of the human" receive science character, first, hermeneutic, pragmatic, then gradually also empiric.

A profound analysis of education processes following the knowledges of depth psychology has not been made (with a few exceptions; for example, Aichhorn (1878-1949). "The structure of the person" of Lersch, "The layers of the personality" of Rothacker and the "Fundamentals of character study" Klages (1872-1956) are considered as personality theories of pedagogy. These teachings were revolutionary for the human education in pedagogy. Some basic terms and findings have today its place in the everyday language, such as "choleric, melancholic, sanguine, phlegmatic", the "life forms" of Spranger (religious, social, economic, esthetic, theoretical human, and the man of power) as well as the constitutional types of Kretschmer. The scientific personality psychology emerged from this characterology.

A second reorientation - to a certain extent the scientific revolution in education - begins around 1955-1960 (we are mainly talking about the German-speaking area). The pedagogy becomes systematic empirical science. Great pioneering work in the shaping of new scientific understanding have done Roth, Röhrs, Klafki, Brezinka, Mollenhauer and Blankertz. Gradually the teaching and curriculum research and the education reform was developed. In didactics, education is understood in two ways: On the one hand the material and on the other hand the human. Dealing with world, subject awareness and meaning understanding characterize this new education understanding of didactics. The adult education is declared to be "permanent education". The German Education Council (1970) called for state responsibility for adult education; without success, states Mattl (19 91, 529).

While in psychology and psychoanalysis enormous theoretical pioneering work has been done from the end of the 19th century, the pedagogy found till after mid-20th century no profound theoretical revolution separate from the "reform education" (ca. 1900 to 1914, 1920 to 1930). Gradually the pedagogy influenced its scientific identity from the humanities hermeneutics to the empirical science. We find great achievements in practical teacher training and elementary schools as well as in the establishment of adult education and educational advice. Pioneering work has also been done in the broad field of social education, i.e., in social pedagogy for children and young people as well as in social work. The social pedagogy posed the same challenges for pedagogues as for psychiatrists in institutional psychiatry at the turn of the century? (e.g., Montessori).

Another reform development in this century, in the period 1960-1980, expanded the interest in education with comprehensive school reform programs, curriculum theories and a new understanding of science. The search for a new understanding of education takes up a lot of space (Roth 1991). Humanistic concerns and commitments are at times significantly in discussion. Pedagogues argue for an ethically better individual and social life. Emancipation and freedom from ideology and dogmatism as well as technical-practical skills characterize the educational concept of this new era.

From about mid-1975 the whole area of pedagogy and adult education is deeply explored and broadly expanded. Scientific-theoretical confessions based on Habermas (knowledge interest), Albert (ethics and critical rationality) and Topitsch (freedom from ideology) are part of the introduction of many studies. The "Frankfurt School" (Adorno, Horkheimer, Habermas) and positivism (Popper) significantly influenced the search for identity in pedagogy and its new view of theory and practice for human education. The linguistic formulations move so far away from the everyday reality of what "personality formation" is that a new kind of alienation from the practice of education has arisen. Maybe it is only the theoretical distancing to understand the objective and operational knowledge interest.

The unconscious, the dream life and the drive conception of psychoanalysis have not yet found a comprehensive inclusion in the educational theory. Pedagogy professors and pedagogues of all types of schools have not yet been able to come up with an own "teaching analysis" (or shall we say: "education analysis") (Habermas 1973, 262 f., 290 note). Concepts of psychic-spiritual development, for example in the sense of Jung and Fromm, are still far off the education idea. Of religious "conscience formation", metaphysical "meaning questions" and Christian "virtues" some pedagogues of the younger generation had experienced enough. Curriculum research and school reform programs are in the focus of "modern pedagogues", with a few exceptions, of course (Oser 1976; Brezinka 1978). A turn in the direction of "values education" resp. the conscience formation can be seen again today (Oser / Althof 1994; Oser / Althof / Garz 1986).

At the beginning of the century, year 1900, human education saw itself as popular education. The older terms "popular upbringing and popular education" come from the pedagogy. They cover the entire spectrum of adult education. In the 19th century, popular education was pursued by the labor movement, the churches, and the bourgeoisie (so-called "bourgeois-liberal popular education"). In the 1920s the term "free popular education" was introduced in Germany.

The term adult education was only introduced after 1945. In the 20th century the popular education developed in political, religious, Christian charitable and educational organizations as well as in university institutions. Adult education in the sense of educational practice we find today in many organizations and social groups: Parishes, churches, private organizations (individuals and societies), party political institutions and alternative movements (e.g., women's centers).

If we consider adult education as something historically given, we can recognize the following subsystems: 1) Fields of practice (institutions); 2) Responsible; 3) Interest groups (business, churches, parties, etc.); 4) The state education system; 5) Working people; 6) Participants; 7) Didactics; 8) Contents; 9) Facilities such as libraries, museums etc.; 10) Associations; 11) Institutions for vocational training for adult educators; 12) Science with teaching and research; 13) Judiciary. - With this diversity, the question inevitably arises which characteristics hold the structure of "adult education" together. There are different organizational structures, a versatile catalog of tasks and areas which can be assigned to the most differentiated science branches. On the other hand, we have not only structures and processes of an organization diversity but also manifold person-structures on the part of participants. These person-structures can in turn be seen in complex environmental structures, e.g., micro, meso, exo and macro systems (after Bronfenbrenner 1989). Our formation concept of for adult education will have to include this networking.

Organizationally, adult education resp. popular education is assigned to educational science resp. pedagogy. But so unchallenged, this classification is not. Kade suggests establishing an "overarching educational science" (Kade, in: Krüger / Rauschenbach 1994, 159).

Adult education opens along with vocational and general further education: Political education, life education, culture education, spiritual formation, education to maturity and emancipation, crisis intervention, life support, philosophical education, and guidance of the human to more differentiated consciousness and ethical behavior. A subdivision in educational, psychological, subject-specific, religious, spiritual, cultural, life-practical, and philosophical education is practically impossible (Tietgens 1981). Adult education is a field of action and, in this respect, for the science an action science ("agogics"). However, this does not solve the problem of science classification. Because: "(There is) neither constitutionally nor historically an original science of adult education" (Tietgens, in: Mader 1991, 47).

Adult education has gradually become an independent non-university branch. These include, among other things: Popular university education, parenting education, leisure pedagogy, mass media, youth, and elderly care. There is no scientific tradition that assigns adult education - in the broadest sense of the term - to the field of psychology. However, certain research such as learning processes of adults, socialization, interaction and motivation are mainly carried out in the psychological field of science.

The current ecclesiastical adult education is multifaceted, centered on the one hand on moral education and on the other hand on religious instruction. Of course, it also tries to provide general education and even vocational training. The practice takes place in lessons, in lectures, in seminars, in meeting events, in church services and of course in personal advisory discussions. Central educational contents of this ecclesiastical adult education are Charity and God's love, parental love, morality, sex education, marriage preparation resp. marriage and family education, conscience formation, justice, peace, suffering and death integration, will formation and life discipline, duty and fidelity, honesty and truefulness, joy and hope as attitudes of life and much more.

In this psychic-spiritual, philosophical-gnostic, and ethical-life-practical catalog of topics is mixed across a variety of doctrines and dogmas about God, Christ, and the creation. The education to faith is in all subject areas fundamental part of this adult education. If one separates these educational issues from the specifically religious teaching principles, then as rest is shown up a human education with a variety of more simplified and outdated theories of personality psychology and philosophical anthropology.

The science of adult education has been conceived as an educational sub-discipline with an interdisciplinary design since the 1960s. The term "adult education" today mainly refers to school and vocational education in the sense of further education and training (e.g., second education path; further education as a career builder); but as well hobby courses and personality development courses are included.

The term "adult education" is sometimes used synonymously and includes specialist training for professions. General education on areas such as culture, history, music, languages, religions, etc. are generally also assigned to adult education. Probably the shortest definition of the adult education is: "... (it) includes organized activities and programs that involves the formation of adults" (Siebert 1991; Pöggeler 1974; Tietgens 1981; Klafki 1971). Let us consider the practice in a few key words below.

Adult education generally means: Imparting knowledge and insights, intentional educational process, self-education in the sense of perfection, assistance in learning, rational influence for the purpose of greater ability, without striving for ideological or political thinking and behavior (at least at adult education centers). This includes an enormously wide range of goals: Imparting knowledge, solidarity, character formation, responsibility ability, life support, creativity, imparting meaning, peace, non-violence, virtues, morality, being orientation, etc.

Tietgens (1981, 30) formulated four main social characteristics for the legitimacy of adult education: 1) Environment that has become abstract for the individual; 2) A future perspective without confidence; 3) The living together suffering under the polarization of passivity and action drive; and 4) The individual handling of the right to reflect on oneself. The same reasoning topics today are actualized again with the "risk society" and the "experience culture".

Most of the responsibles are organized in a state-free manner. The purposes are defined differently depending on the institution (Mattl 1991). The responsibles of adult education are: Vocational schools and technical schools, popular universities, church institutes, esoteric associations, federations and associations, companies, communal institutions, social movements, individual persons, commercial institutes (academies), foundations, ecological movements, third world-organizations, health movements, self-help-groups, alternative education houses, psycho-centers, leisure centers, trade unions. Various mass media, in particular the television, can also be referred as responsibles and providers.

The adult educators have quite different technical training depending on the subject. Most professionals are part-time, some are voluntary. According to Jüting (quoted in: Schäffter 1993/3, 444) around 95% of all teachers in adult education are engaged in part-time jobs. The professionals are called as: Adult educators, educational consultants, teaching experts, trainers, educational assistants, graduate pedagogues, andragogues, course instructors, teachers, pastors, social workers, social pedagogues, and "experts" of all profession branches. A professionality without identity characterizes this unit group (Künzel 1991).

What are doing all these assistants of adult education? Their activities are characterized by many words: Education, instruction, training, behavior change, change of attitude, leadership, pastoral care, tutoring, teaching, retraining, counseling, psychagogics, socialization, therapy, etc. Such activities are partly based on singular learning processes and partly on holistic human education.

But this identity problem relates not only to the professionalism, but also to the subject canon. This problem is therefore evident at all levels. Means "adult education" (according to Tietgens 1981) "everything that is declared as adult education", no clear conception of science and no clear legitimacy can be developed (Tietgens 1981, 11, 18, 19, 24). The range of vocational qualifications through self-awareness (now an integral part of adult education) to hobby courses can impossibly be included in "a theory of adult education". Adult education programs to: Profession, leisure time, consumption, media, health, traffic, military, thinking, learning, feelings, behavior, sexuality, family, raising children, art, language, law, politics, churches (religions), environment; overall, therefore, contents far beyond the subject canon of school leaving examinations (Matura).

The target groups are remarkably diverse and in no respect homogeneous: Inner-office personal, professionals, individuals with specific interests, marginal groups, youth, and young adults (about 16 years), elderly / seniors, unemployeds, members of the sponsoring organization. About 10-15% of adults find their way to adult education (Pöggeler, quoted in: Rebel. In: Benning 1986, 378). The basic question is still relevant today: How can the remaining 85-90% of adult population (or at least a third) be induced to participate in adult education activities?

In adult education, educational programs are governed by the supply and demand principle. Not a theory of education, not a socialization theoretical justification, nor the participant orientation decide on the program structure. "The contribution of scientific theories to program design is small" (Siebert 1994, 315). What is realized is "what has proven itself". The "marketability" has guaranteed the survival of adult education centers in Germany to this day (Nuissl / Rein 1994, 303).

The marketing depends to a large extent on responsibles and target groups. There is a tendency for private responsibles to use different marketing strategies than institutional or municipal responsibles. The development of adult education depends largely on funding. In many cases there is no state support (however: The total costs by popular education centers in East and West Germany in 1992: around 1.4 billion DM; in: "Nachrichten",

Grundlagen der Weiterbildung 6/1993, 371). Private organizations and companies, fund often the whole, mostly a major part of the expense costs.

The business investments in in-company training are enormous. "In 1992, approximately 18.8 million people in total have participated at internal or external company continuing education measures. Included the indirect costs of continued pay, companies have spent an amount of 36.5 billion DM for further education." (Weiss; in: Grundlagen der Weiterbildug 1994/4, 177). In the same issue is marked under "Nachrichten" (p. 238) that due to difficult cost accounting options (indirect costs), the total amount of investments for further education still "significantly should go beyond that". The Swiss "Bundesimpulsprogramm Weiterbildundoffensive", a program for the period 1992-1996, has so far financially supported 550 further education projects (Schmitter, Ch.; in: Grundlagen der Weiterbildung 1994/4, 208).

Some responsibles reach their target groups with their ideologies and dogmatic teachings resp. moral obligations. The target groups of "pure commerce" must pay the service in full range what in times of recession has consequences. The principle of "work for pay" does not apply full validity in adult education.

"Further training is to be understood as a social subsystem that takes up the increasing need for synchronization between different temporal structures of social subsystems in form of personally significant discrepancies, these defined as learning approaches and finally operationalized through learning organization" (Schäffter 1993, 460).

In this network, adult education is part of the education system of a state (Isenegger 19 77, 13 and 212). The adult education has individual meaning, national importance, and international necessity. This is concordantly confirmed by all experts, including the UNESCO. Characteristic of adult education is since the '60s to today: Heterogeneity of previous knowledges and social classes, diverse and unlimited subject canon according to demand (no canonization of subjects), rejection of a single human image as orientation, no consistent education term, lack of profiling, no consistent educational scientific paradigm, diverse motivations for all age groups, various educational (forming) intentions, education proposal according to the need in the professional areas, variable local facilities, formation of the individual (professional needs and society expectations equally in the range of subjects), wide reason base resp. legitimacy.

The question about the "theory of adult education" is clearly answered: "The status of the discussion is characterized by the multitude of theoretical approaches and accesses to adult education, at best can be designated as theory-substitutes" (Dewe 1988, 25). Furthermore, there is no recognized paradigm in adult education (Dewe 1988, 16), i.e., no recognized valid models and examples for solving practical problems.

At the 14th congress of the Deutsche Gesellschaft für Erziehungswissenschaft it is stated: "The situation in adult pedagogy or andragogy (has) become very confusing"; and: "Even in the description and analysis of what is referred as 'adult and continuing education', exist serious problems"; and further: "An 'unclear identity' can be seen, for example, in the sometimes superficial differentiation of adult education as an independent practice area or as a delimited discipline ..." (Alheit / Tippelt 1994, 368-369).

Nietzsche harshly criticized the educational ideals of his time with the word "education philistine". The history of the First and Second World Wars gave rise to massive questioning of what "education" was in the years after the middle of the century (Fend 1974). None of the pedagogues - as far as the author is aware - could be called an "individuated human" or a "sage" (in the sense of Plato's model of the highest level of psychic-spiritual development).

This is a serious problem. After all, the pedagogues resp. andragogues in the education system have the most important responsibility and the greatest influence on psychic-spiritual popular education. The psychic-spiritual education of the human has been the central concern of German education for 200 years. It seems that the educational mandate has not achieved the comprehensive personality development of the humans. The social significance of the education system must reach but this dimension.

With the beginning of educational science education in the conventional understanding was pushed away of new terms such as competence, socialization, learning processes, responsibility, qualification, and emancipation. Since about 1980 new (old) topics push again for discussion: Criticism ability, autonomy, self-determination, formation of conscience, responsibility, and maturity. There is a lot of talk about "self-realization", but hardly anyone dares to set principles of valuation and norms that go beyond the existing vague similarities with others or even contradict them (Brezinka 1978, 217). The search for the "whole human"" urges the pedagogues. Their questions always remain the same: What is the human? How should the human become? How can he find meaning in life? How should he interpret his being? And: How can the pedagogy help the human, to find the right answers to such questions and to live these adequately in self-commitment?

We want to clarify this problem with a few quotations:

"In feudalism, all people were equal insofar as they were determined by their class, namely by their birth ... The civic society mediates through individual efficiency and performance promotion, the lifting of all class barriers ... The enlightening question of whether humans are naturally equal or unequal, ... to the question of whether the performance of humans is predisposed or environment-determined ... The human is neither predisposed like plants and animals, his imperfection (= incompleteness; author.) lies precisely in the fact that his destiny is not predestined. He is also not determined by the environment like plants and animals, because the world around him is a world that he has worked on, interpreted and changed ... (from this follows:) the determination of the human for self-determination ... "(Benner, D. 1993, 292-293).

"... So only the child himself can reveal to us what the natural blueprint of the human is" And further: "... There are deeper needs in which the individual has to be alone with himself, separated from everything and all, dedicated to a mysterious work. Nobody can help us to achieve that inner seclusion which makes our most hidden and as mysterious as rich and full world accessible to us ... Obviously the principle of order and development of the character and spiritual and emotional life must start from this mysterious and hidden source ..." (Montessori, M.; in Reble, A. 1992, 519-522).

"An animal is everything by instinct ... But the human needs his own reason ... he must plan his behavior by himself ... The human must ... 1. Be disciplined ... 2. Be cultivated ... 3. Become clever ... (this also includes manners, politeness, taste ...) 4. Acquire a good attitude ..." (Kant, I.; in Reble A. 1992, 319).

"... As much knowledge and education as possible - therefore as much production and need as possible - therefore as much luck as possible - that is about the formula. Here we have the benefit as goal and purpose of education ... the greatest possible profit ... the insight ... with which one knows all ways to make at easiest money ... quick education to be able to quickly become a money-making being ... thorough education to be able to become an excessively big money-making being ..." (Nietzsche, F.; in: Reble, A. 1992).

"... And just as ... the prerequisite for mental productivity lies in the racial quality of given human material, so in the individual, education must first and foremost consider and promote the physical health ... The racial state has in this cognition to focus his entire educational work primarily not on pumping in mere knowledge, but on cultivating perfectly healthy bodies. Secondly, then comes the development of mental abilities. Here, however, again at the top the development of character, especially the promotion of will and determination force, combined with the education for responsibility joyfulness, and only finally scientific training ..." (Adolf Hitler's Erziehungsgrundsätze; in: Reble, A., 1992, 579). "No human develops ... out of himself because of his disposition and his genetic potential to become a human. He can only become a human ... through education ..." (Dietrich, T. 1992, 43).

"The lack of standards of value and worthwhile goals of adulthood, which is widely noticeable today, is a symptom of a general emptying of meaning in the human being ..." (Pöggeler, F. 1970, 168).

Many pedagogues have dealt with the basic questions of the human and human education in relation to these questions. Some have achieved pioneer work and supplied valuable contributions. The school system, adult education and institutions of social education are raised, and have developed in it. We can only mention some of these people by name here in passing, for example Claparède, Aichhorn, Steiner, Lazarsfeld, Montessori, Buber, Bernstein, Cope, Weniger, Peterson.

Central concerns of adult education from the perspective of pedagogues are: Right of everyone to be able to participate in social life through education; education to be able to be active in democratic processes; opportunities of social and occupational mobility; enabling correction of the school education; orientation helps; judgment formation and rational criticism; constant new acquisition of intellectual freedom and autonomy; need to be able to cope with constantly changing requirements; permanent renewing and expanding of majority and maturity. Is the process of realizing these concerns now "learning", "socialization", "enculturation", "education" and / or "becoming human"?

Isenegger sums up the aims of school philosophic-anthropologically as follows: "It belongs to the human ... with free will that he can take responsibility for his own life ..." (1977, 24-26, 211 note 7). Specifically, he reports person centered goals like capacity for self-control, learning ability, ability for problem-solving, positive self-image, ability to non-violent conflict resolution. The failure of this educational achievement of the school is showed by sociological and psychological studies.

The sketched overview is sufficient to determine some characteristics:

The term "education" has in pedagogy with the variety of goals and concepts a versatile significance of aspects of education, culture, society, and professional training to the "emancipated human". It is essential to clearly define the term of education in connection with the "psyche" of the human.

The concepts about the human as a psychic-spiritual wholeness contain diverse elements, partly with metaphysical and partly with empirical content. The understanding of education is as different as the various conceptions of what education resp. andragogy is and should be as a science. The various positions are grouped around the criteria of scientific understanding: Hermeneutic-speculative, descriptive-phenomenological, and empirical-positivistic (Brezinka 1978, 2-10).

The term "educational science" as a delimitation from the (earlier) "pedagogy" is more of a language game. Pedagogy is the science of upbringing and education. With the expansion of scientific understanding is still no "coercion" to introduce new language forms which only disconcert and create misunderstandings. The human - whether child, youth, adult, or elderly – stands in the center of the educational mission. This mandate goes beyond the teaching of skills and abilities for daily and professional life. Pluralistic unity about what pedagogy resp. andragogy is as a science of upbringing and education must be created.

According to the understanding of education and pedagogy, there are also various term systems in the individual subject areas. The concepts of psyche, of the human as a psychic-spiritual wholeness and of human development are manifold. Ideological and religious interests still seem to shape pedagogy here and there. "Thinking styles" and "Imponierprosa" create a kind of "esoteric communities" or "competition temple" (Rössner 1992, 105-132).

The scientific nature since the 60's still causes for fierce discourses. It seems wrong to us to contrast phenomenological-hermeneutical position with empirical-positivistic understanding of science. They complement each other and are mutually integrative parts. One cannot exclude a reality from science simply because it cannot be reproduced or controlled with popular scientific methods.

The working methods in pedagogy are remarkably diverse according to their task area. Teacher behavior, educator behavior, methods of educational counseling, teacher training and socio-pedagogical intervention concepts all have their own work concept.

However, there is a lack of defined models for advising adults on "general personality development". They can be borrowed from psychological advice. But there is a lack of a clear understanding of education and didactics.

The nature of positions reveals different thinking tendencies. These in turn are characterized by their kind of scientific nature, technological interest, and humanistic commitment of the representatives resp. chair holders. More recent developments come from pioneers in practice as well as from science. From a historical-critical point of view, one should ask whether the situationally successful and dominant should be placed at the center of such an assessment (Dräger, in: Tietgens 1985, 31 f.).

The success controls vary depending on the subject area within the pedagogy. About performance assessment, the literature is hardly to overview. Similarly, evaluations concepts about the teacher behavior exist. The success of "personality development", on the other hand, has only been comprehensively elaborated cultural and social critically. It seems to us to be essential, to include the psychic-spiritual education of adults with clear evaluation criteria. The societal explosiveness may prevent some scientists from approaching this problem. However: If the pedagogy has the educational mandate from the state, it is itself also accountable what the human effects with this education in the state. If many humans daily cause great damage (e.g., accidents, illnesses), the crime continues to increase and the environment is being destroyed, then pedagogy has not been able to adequately bring its own educational idea to incorporate.

As far as we can see, the areas of pedagogy are indeed divided in individual areas, but education term and target setting are rather "spongy" than directed to variable client groups. The human with all his formed and malleable psychic forces - as personality - is not clear and not deep enough included in the conceptions of the various educational realities. There is mostly a lack of depth psychological understanding that includes the formation of unconscious forces in the model. Diagnostics in andragogy is only partially in development. The relation of educational mandate and life sufferings (conflicts, difficulties crisis, challenges, and misfortunes) of the adult human is still largely unexplored and little treated educational theoretically.

Professionalization is diverse and only clearly defined in school and educational counseling. There is no professionalization in adult education. The "pedagogue" working in adult education is under no specific requirements, concerning his own personal education and his training (including supervision). Additional studies for adult educational qualifications are now available (see "Tipps", Grundlagen der Erwachsenenbildung 6/1993, 370). A multitude of practical activities are hidden behind the term "pedagogue". What is it anyway: The "pedagogue", the "educator", the "adult educator" (Kupffer 1990)? The specification of tasks could give the professional activity of the adult educator in the field of personality development a clear identity. This professional image building is missing. There are hardly any specific postgraduate courses in this area, as have long been introduced in psychoanalysis and psychotherapy. We consider such continuative specific formation of andragogues, and pedagogues as necessary.

Those pedagogues and andragogues, the offer ways and answers to the fundamental questions of the human, be it in teaching programs, either in counseling, have first and over again to form their own in terms of personality development and individuation. Who wants to form humans in their psychic-spiritual wholeness must first form himself in it.

The social importance of pedagogy lies not only in elementary school, socio-educational institutions and adult education. The educational mandate also covers social dimensions. A broader understanding of the area of tasks of pedagogy is necessary. The situation in Europe, viewed from the painful side, reflects a huge deficit of "mature" humans with a differentiated deep psychologically cleared consciences formation. The concrete life is largely not discussed with goals of "maturity" and "emancipation". The everyday life of the collective shows a chaotic picture of immajority and a lack of "maturity". Without the categories of depth psychology, there is no sustainable and comprehensive personality development.

For the fundaments of andragogy as a science and practice, some conclusions can be drawn from:

Andragogy is according to our first definition: Personality-psychological, life-psychological, and life-practical, philosophical, and spiritual education. The andragogy deals with the formation of personality (of the adult human), and with the basic questions of the human.

We define andragogy from the side of the human, i.e., from his psychic-spiritual wholeness. Andragogy according to this definition is essentially not understood as vocational training in the sense of further and advanced training. Andragogy is not general education. Craft hobby courses are even less part of the task area of andragogy, even if the educational value can be considerable and learning objectives of human education are implicitly included. But now every kind of organized or autodidactically (correspondence course) learning process of the adult is de facto defined as the subject area of andragogy (e.g., Pöggeler 1974). In fact, the subject of training adults (acquisition of knowledge and skills) and the organization of these learning processes is considered an "agogic" subject. We place the andragogy as a science subject area in addition to pedagogy, social education, and gerontology.

Today, human education can be found in practice in adult education. So, of course, one can say that andragogy is part of the common adult education; or it is the foreign word for the German word. Theoretical concepts contrast with the manifold practice. The science has an order from the state, practice institutions announce quality need and from the everyday life people declare educational needs. So, there are various scientific theoretical and practical oriented classification criteria. We propose an initial classification based on the pedagogy, which is roughly divided in general pedagogy (upbringing / education) and in school pedagogy. Other special educational areas are: Social pedagogy, pre-school education, gerontology. Such fundamental division prove to be an advantage for teaching and practice of andragogy, for identity formation and professionalization.

In the various current studies on adult education, there are proposals for classification, all of which delimit so-called "further education" including retraining as an independent sector. In addition, the political education and the general education are each defined as a separate area.

"Personality development" is not classified as an independent sector everywhere (Klupp 1992, 12; Krämer / Walter 1994, 7-10; Winkler 1993, II; Frommer 1991, 104; Netzel 1992, 14; Dewe et al. 1988, 14-25). Following Pöggeler (1974, 20-35, 218-256), we rewrite the department of personality development in a first approach with "life education, moral education, spiritual education, being education" and separate it from the specialized courses such as general education, political education, vocational training, hobby education, leisure formation, retraining.

We therefore use the technical term "general andragogy" to include personality development and individuation; the other areas of education are areas of "special andragogy". The general education, parts of leisure education and political education can be placed, depending on the objectives of the course.

In the practice it is often the case that an institute or responsible of specialist training (further and advanced training) offers both areas in the teaching program; and that the andragogy, in its educational interest, also includes general education and practical leisure education with specifically human-educating aspects (e.g., music, painting). Albers means by general education, the "coping private life situations" and subsumes professional and leisure education also to "personality development" (1987). We consider this division to be of little use in theory and in practice and suggest a different division here. The "special andragogy" must define its educational goals or educational concepts for itself.

The academic resp. technical training is in university and technical college areas, in the pedagogy sector (new: andragogy) with degrees: lic.phil., Dr.phil., Dipl.Päd. (New Andragogic), etc. A postgraduate further education is to build on. In our view, for example, psychologists, philosophers, graduate teachers, social workers, adult educators, remedial teacher, and social pedagogues should have access to this specific further education. The problem of different levels of education can be solved through supplementary programs.

The practice of andragogy as personality development thus has clear activities that differ from adult education as specialist vocational training:

1) Education in the sense of teaching / imparting for personality development and individuation.
2) Training as part of teaching for personality development and individuation.
3) Counseling in the sense of life counseling / life support (as a supplementary part of education and training).

The responsibles of such a practice can be according to our conception: Institutions of adult education, companies, non-profit organizations, community, professionals of andragogy on their own direction (school, institute, center, practice).

The social developments that can be expected in the 21st century create a certain urgency to raise the question of the location of pedagogy resp. educational science (formation science, educational research) and its representatives (pedagogues, andragogues). If one looks at the research works from the period since 1975 to the turn of the millennium (see: Gretler, A., Die Schweizerische Bildungsforschung in der Nachkriegszeit ..., SGB, No. 1, 2000, pp. 111-142), the example of Switzerland shows that over 80% of all research activities concern the school subsystems. Just under 4% of the projects deal with general adult education. These projects deal with curricula and teaching contents, with learning objectives and learning processes, with teachers and learners, with structures and organization, with interaction processes, with assessments of learning and teaching performances, with the determinants of learning and requirements for learners, also with networked worlds. There are certainly also research projects on leisure, family and geriatric education as well as general human education. - This status of educational science tends to apply to the entire German-speaking area of Europe.

Does this topic represent the science of pedagogy resp andragogy, the educational science and educational research? Or should these tendencies even be interpreted as the submission of pedagogy and educational research to the power of economy? The Schweizerische Vereinigung für Erwachsenenbildung (SVEB) gives a clear signal in this regard (see SVEB Bulletin No. 2, 2000, p.3); the members were asked: Should the SVEB rename itself "Swiss umbrella association *for further education*"? Result: 57 votes with "yes" and 29 with "no". One goes there, consciously, or unrecognized, at a distance to the general issue of pedagogy (resp. andragogy) and becomes a service company of economic interests. A well-functioning economy is undoubtedly important. The educational science certainly has a central role here. But: *The economy is not yet the life of human being. Economic success does not make a good life nor a healthy state.* The status of pedagogy and educational research reflects a vision of economic growth, but not a vision of human education for the 21st century. Is this the end of science of human education?

Overall, we conclude from this situation analysis that the educational theory of pedagogy and andragogy should be taken to the next higher evolutionary level. The human with his entire psychic life is to be integrated into the educational concept. The social relevance of holistic education (Neumann 1949) is as relevant today as it was after the Second World War. The freedom of the individual has its limits where the "archaic" people in the sum of their behavior destroy in the long term and widespread the entire collective - that is, culture and social life. Personality development thus becomes an individual duty of life for everyone, which must be promoted by the state in the same way as general education.

"If the education system fails, the whole society is threatened in its existence" (Picht 1964, 17). People have "become barbaric" and "what is still alive shows unique brutality and emptiness", wrote Flitner in 1921 in his "lay education" (Flitner 1982, 32). The same could be empirically demonstrated today by adult education science for more than half of the adult European population. Today, the practice of adult education - and probably their science – is bound to market constraints and needs to attract the already emancipated and mature participants into the classroom with NLP-tricks and Roger's interview technique. As an action-oriented science, andragogy must respond to the situation in practice: Without a doubt, a difficult path between ruthless honesty and considerate understanding while at the same time claiming to produce correct (true?) empirical knowledges for the practice. If the pedagogy resp. the adult education cannot expand its human image and does not develop building new paradigms for its scientific recognition methods, it will remain in an impasse. Because today's concepts lead neither to psychic organism, nor to individuation. They are looking for causality where human life does not function causally at all, but rather teleologically. They want the reproducible empirical experiment, where everything is in an immensely complex network and always in flux. This is a dead end, where the love is at best given a marginal meaning, where the spiritual force in the human remains unused and the psychic-spiritual evolution can never really advance.

Holistic Human Knowledge for Human Education

We want to investigate here the question of what personality formation - and thus human development - includes, which psychic forces are addressed. The introductory key question is: Can one learn "personality"? Can one form "personality"?

Kron (1994, 119) says: "In the *learning term*, human behavior is represented in an ensemble of rationally determined and determinable goals, contents, processes and media. The functionality of the individual in the society has moved to the center of this view of human appropriation of the world". – "The center of the *education term* is characterized by the uniqueness of the human. The human is seen in his educational activity, i.e., in his discussion with the surrounding cultural world of values. The goal of this individual spiritual activity lies in the valuable personality ... The understanding of meaning is to be seen as anthropological and individual foundation for this educational process. This is not only orientated on the given cultural assets, but also on their meaning structure, which is related on a higher purpose or on a highest good, e.g., freedom, mutual respect, justice ...".

Clemens Menze formulates a core problem in determining "personality development" in the Enzyklopädie Erziehungswissenschaft (Lenzen, D. / Mollenhauer, K., Hrsg., Stuttgart 1992, keyword "Bildung", page 350): "In the respective historical interpretation of education the pedagogical insights in the essence of becoming human and the destiny of the human are summarized ... There is therefore no definition that could determine what education once and for all means in terms of content, so that everyone would have to agree to such a determination. Only a formal identification is possible, according to which education can be understood as a complex process in which a personality structure that is said to be desirable is to be produced ...".

Pervin (1993, 17-19) suggests a working hypothesis on "personality". Here are the key elements in brief: "1) The human organism has characteristic differences from other species ... 2) The human behavior is complex ... 3) Behavior is not always what it appears to be ... 4) We are not always aware of the factors that determine our behavior and we do not always have them under control." ... "At this point in time, however, there is no generally accepted definition of personality ... various definitions are possible ...".

Does the "positive personal direction" exist as an inherent dynamic of personality development (human formation)?

Rogers (1982, 42-43, 115, 168) writes: "If there is such a thing as truth, then - I believe - this free, individual process of searching would have to run towards it ... The undisturbed development always has a positive orientation ..." ... "The goal that the individual would most like achieve, the end purpose that he knowingly and unknowingly pursues, seems to be to find himself, to become himself ..." And further: "The person sets the direction himself: Away from the facades, away from the 'actually-I-should' away from the fulfilling of cultural expectations, away from pleasing others ... Development towards self-determination, being process, complexity, openness to experience, for acceptance of others, for self-confidence."

Maslow (1973, 41) presents 13 goals of human education; briefly formulated here:

1) Greater awareness of the reality.
2) Growing acceptance of oneself, the others, and the nature.
3) Increasing spontaneity.
4) Better problem centering.
5) Greater distance and longing for seclusion.
6) Growing autonomy and resistance to acculturation.
7) Greater freshness of understanding / greater richness of emotional reactions.
8) Higher frequency of border experiences.
9) Growing identification with the human species.
10) Changed interpersonal relationships.
11) Democratic character structure.
12) Greatly increasing creativity.
13) Certain transformations in the value system.

Our key questions are: How do look such goals of personality development in concrete terms? And: Are these process goals realistic? Or does the thesis of the "spontaneous turning of the inside towards such goals" perhaps only apply to morally educated people? In other words: Isn't the trust perhaps too great, far too illusory that the humanistic psychologists have in the human nature? And further: Are not millions, even billions of people, already so far removed from their "healthy nature" by their biography, from their culture, their political and economic environment, their social environment, their religious upbringing (e.g. fundamentalism) that, for example, Roger's optimism is fundamentally a wrong assessment?

To answer these questions, we must first clarify and define the "personality" as the structure of the psyche.

Composition of a system model of psychic life

Writing about the psychic system requires looking in all directions and positions, and first, overviewing the fifty most important models of personality. In addition, there are many hundred books, that deal with principal theories and individual theories. Every scientist must go through it and then tries to create his own summary. In general, a scientist then develops his new theory, which is attached to this series. Those who study all the theories again, will say: "But it cannot be that everyone is wrong except those by the science just newly presented theory." We do not want to annex a new theory in this long line in this chapter but try to collect those knowledge elements and consideration aspects that are in human education of particular importance in direct relation to personality education and individuation. We have created the new term "andragogical psychology" for these subject areas. The core of this department contains a system model that contains all the important facts and theory elements of the relevant theories about "personality" and "psychic-spiritual development" resp. individuation, which are of relevance for practical educational work. Other topics that we do not discuss here are: Teacher behavior (of the andragogue), teaching psychology, educational psychology of adults. Let us leave it open whether an integrative model of personality can be seen as a new integrative theory of personality or is interpreted in professional circles as "collection" of diverse concepts.

A first central problem when trying to create an integrative system model of personality is that some terms are so diverse, and contradicting defined that one inherits the subsequent problems integrating them into a new theoretical system. Key terms have meaning contents to the point that they are difficult to handle, e.g., behavior, motives, meaning, needs, transcendence, self, reason, intellect, drive force, attitudes, roles, factor, and the unconscious. Elementary psychic forces are addressed in all terms. It is necessary to define these terms clearly so that constructive communication is possible at all.

A second problem is that the scientists try again and again to explain with these terms the basic psychic force, to a certain extent the "axiom" of the psychic behavior. All psychic phenomena should be led back to this basic force. In some theories three or more such "axioms" can be found. It is exceedingly difficult, perhaps even impossible, to prove what can be considered as real psychic basic force. But it must be possible to talk about so concretely that the disputation act constructively.

A third problem emerged from the fact that positions claim, for example, that the unconscious does not exist, while - as is well known - the whole history of psychoanalysis refers to the unconscious; or that one of them claims that dreams are unimportant, that they are nothing more than the "garbage can" of brain-physiological processes during the sleep, while others understand the dreams as "via regia" at the center of knowledge processes about the depths of the psychic. When certain psychologists claim that the love as life force is not an empirical subject, but at best can be assigned to metaphysics, we oppose these people that they are dishonest and conduct their science ideologically. We hold these psychic basis force for just as "empirical" as the intelligence and the consciousness contents or the "spirit" that "speaks" in dreams to the "I". The same applies to all those who claim that the unconscious does not exist and that dreams are nothing as chance products or even "stupid stuff". We cannot respect this type of scientist as a conversation partner because his arguments are not factual, but only an expression of defense and thus a denial of reality.

A fourth problem is an ideological and dogmatic phenomenon. We are convinced that the development of a system model must result free from ideologic and dogmatic propositions. "Marxist personality theory" or "Christian personality theory" can be called as ethos teaching, but not as a scientific statement system. It is also dishonest if a theory is designed and presented in such a way that it can be used directly as a "money machine" in line with the market; yes, such concepts are worded hypno-suggestively and appetizingly for the market. They only serve to ensure that consumers fall again for a new trick or that psychologists resp. psychotherapists can found a new association with a new school to create work. This has nothing to do with science.

Vester (1991 resp. 1983) studies biological systems in terms of system and growth: "Qualitative growth provides for a system wide deployment of opportunities. Quantitative growth, however, only the monotony of an expanding movement ... The higher the function, the lower the quantitative volume growth ..." (Vester 1991, 66). Intelligence arises from organization and differentiation of the 15 billion brain cells. Vester applies this biological system-theoretical principle to all types of social networking. In observing biological self-organization, he also sees the solution paths for ecological problems. This organizing and structuring principle can in our opinion be transferred to the development and differentiation of the psyche as an organism. So, we conclude: The educational mandate of andragogy can only be socially and humanistically relevant resp. efficient in system theoretical and in qualitative differentiation. Andragogical psychology develops the decisive basis for this.

This chapter is a concentrated summary of our separate study "Konzept der Individuation" (2001). We refer to the literature list there. The psychic system model that we present here is the conclusion in the sense of an integrative compilation of knowledges from the individual chapters of the work mentioned. The andragogical psychology contains some significant emphases by the current state of knowledge, but it is equally clear that the history of philosophy, psychology resp. psychoanalysis (-therapy) and pedagogy resp. adult education represent the foundations and roots of our design: *Andragogy as theory and practice is more than 2500 years old.*

The construction of systems contains certainly some fundamental decisions: A subsystem is seen as a basic force of psychic life in the human. Such a basic force cannot be traced back to other forces. Our theory formations in this regard are open to discussion and revision. By working with system models, the basic understanding of a basic force is already formally defined: There is no simple variable that can be used as an axiom. There are always several factors that work in conjunction with other individual forces as a psychic base unit.

A psychic system consists of the following eight main characteristics:

1) Integrated wholeness of simple, diverse, and complex facts.
2) Inner causal and / or constitutive relation to function ability.
3) Comprehensive or partial self-regulation of the unit.
4) Manifold characteristics in many combinations.
5) Inward and outward orientated directionality.
6) Relative constancy in characteristics and dynamics with all changeability.
7) Tendency to comprehensive or limited self-contained reactions.
8) Relative stability, dynamics, activity, openness, and target direction.
   (Pervin 1993; Kleining, in: Roth 1991, 194-203).

Terms such as "personality", the "unconscious" and "feelings" are system terms, where we understand the last two as subsystems of the main system "personality" resp. the "psychic organism". The relation to reality is constantly dynamic because the reality is always more than a system and always more than the language (Roth 1969, 125; Lewin 1963, 273).

We understand the psyche as a system that demands a holistic approach. The system itself consists of several elements that are related to each other. The state of each element is also determined by the state of other elements (Becker 1982, 43). Furthermore, the system of psychic life can only be sufficiently determined when it is embedded in the habitat. Our system is transcendental together with the "force of love", and in particular with the "spirit", i.e., there are humanities dimensions involved. This also includes values, the collective unconscious, the reality of archetypes, etc. We assume that a system of psychic life must be revised and expanded again and again with new knowledges.

The humanistic psychology claims to represent a holistic concept. Characteristics are, for example: Autonomy, value and meaning, creativity, development of potentials and the "self-transcendence". The last one means acting goals that are beyond the psychic system. In our opinion this "holistic" system is missing crucial psychic components. Above all, the spirit (in dreams and imagination), the unconscious and the reality of psychic energy are missing. The cognitive representatives about themselves can certainly represent space and content of the definition of this wholeness. In fact, the human can perceive himself and to think about it. In our opinion, however, this space cannot yet be called a "psychic system wholeness".

So, if we understand the psyche as a holistic, living, dynamic and open system, then we can - we must - put this living wholeness in a process of development and unfolding. We have called this process INDIVIDUATION. Individuation is thus the process that allows to unfold all the psychic subsystems into a multifaceted, balanced wholeness. Individuation is then also a certain life form because the psyche as such a whole always wants to and must express itself in actions in the life systems.

The following sub-systems are part of the overall system of psychic life:

1)	The actions (in connection with the life fields).
2)	The psychodynamics - the psychic energy.
3)	The "I" as the center of the consciousness with its auxiliary functions.
4)	The intelligence - the cognitive processes.
5)	The feelings and their dimensions.
6)	The needs - the drive forces.
7)	The unconscious - the (pictorial) life patterns.
8)	The spirit and its functions in dream and imagination.
9)	The love as constructive life force.

The entire history of philosophy, psychology and pedagogy speaks of these realities. We have put these together to an organic structure, even dismantled some theoretical concepts and repositioned their components. The problem of the wholeness persists: Every researcher has only a limited knowledge. Who can see beyond his own limits what has not yet been recognized? Who can comb through a hundred thousand books and always correctly access what must belong in the model of psychic organism? Who can know today what the science of human education perhaps tomorrow will discover of new and important in the mysterious depths of psychic life? In this respect, the integral whole remains relative.

This is followed by two pages with graphic illustrations of classic models of the psyche and personality, as they are generally known in psychology and psychoanalysis. Then follows the illustration of the psychic organism - our expanded conception of the psyche resp. psychic life as it is used for individuation. We can certainly claim that our (didactic) model is superior to all classic models known to date.

Illustration 1: Models of Psyche and Personality (1)

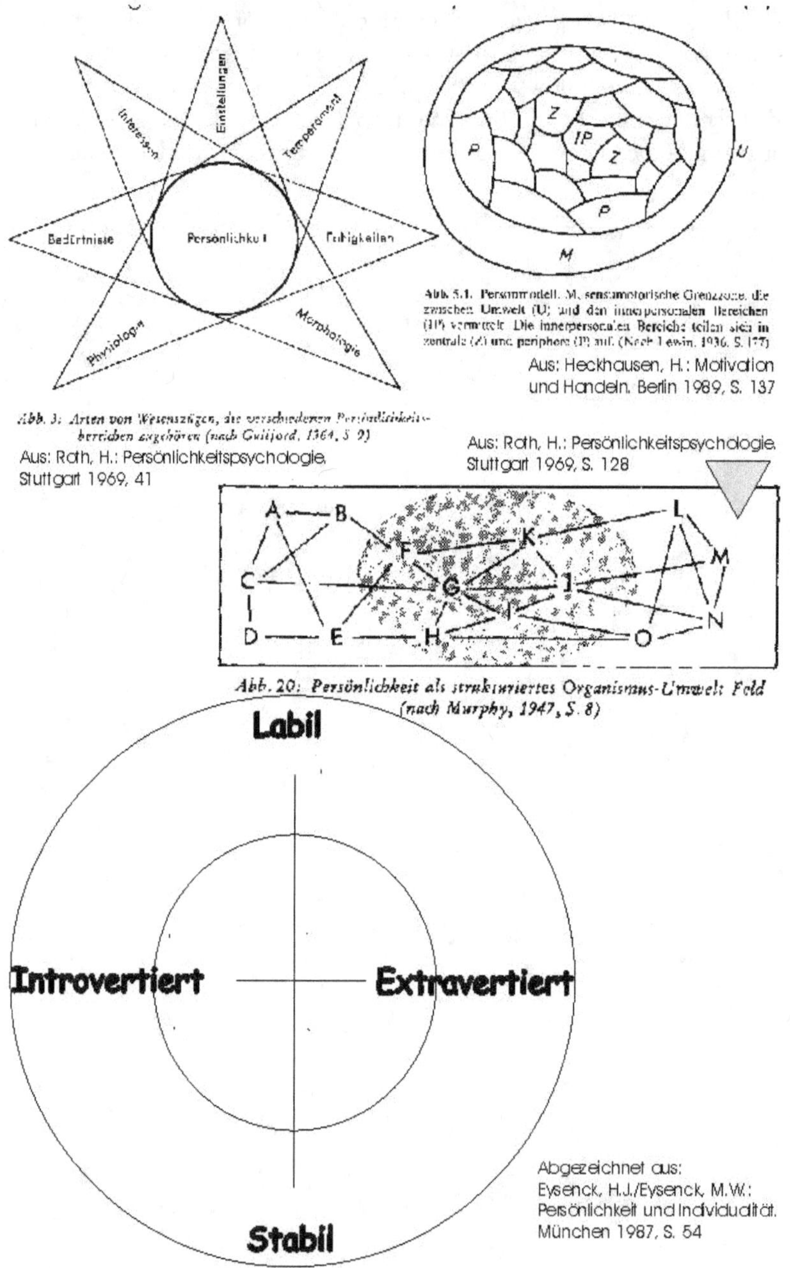

*Abb. 3: Arten von Wesenszügen, die verschiedenen Persönlichkeits-
berreichen zugehören (nach Guiijord, 1364, S 9)*
Aus: Rath, H.: Persönlichkeitspsychologie,
Stuttgart 1969, 41

Abb. 5.1. Personmodell. M, sensumotorische Grenzzone, die
zwischen Umwelt (U) und den innerpersonalen Bereichen
(IP) vermittelt. Die innerpersonalen Bereiche teilen sich in
zentrale (Z) und periphere (P) auf. (Nach Lewin, 1936. S. 177)
Aus: Heckhausen, H.: Motivation
und Handeln. Berlin 1989, S. 137

Aus: Rath, H.: Persönlichkeitspsychologie,
Stuttgart 1969, S. 128

*Abb. 20: Persönlichkeit als strukturiertes Organismus-Umwelt Feld
(nach Murphy, 1947, S. 8)*

Abgezeichnet aus:
Eysenck, H.J./Eysenck, M.W.:
Persönlichkeit und Individualität.
München 1987, S. 54

Models of Guiijord, Heckhausen, Rath, Eyseneck

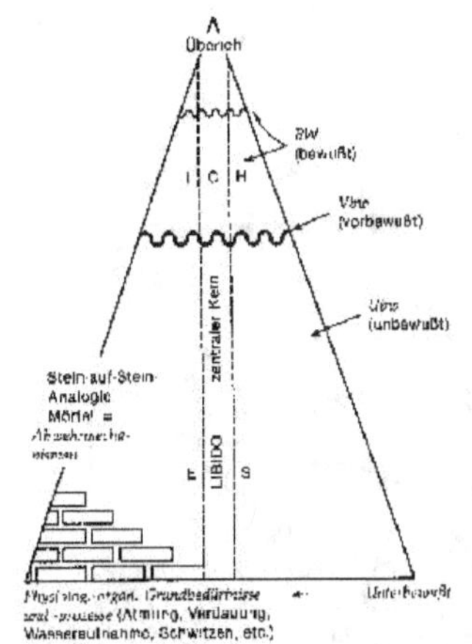

Abbildung 2: Graphische Zusammenfassung von Freuds Theorie

Aus: Bischof, L.J.:
Persönlichkeitstheorien.
Band I. Paderborn 1983, S. 98

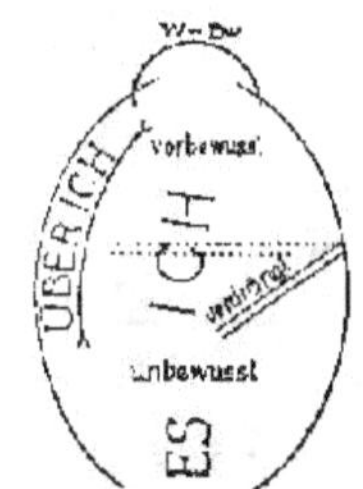

Freud, S.: Die Zerlegung der psychischen
Persönlichkeit. Aus: Studienausgabe,
Vorlesungen zur Einführung in die Psycho-
analyse und Neue Folge. Zürich 1969, S. 515

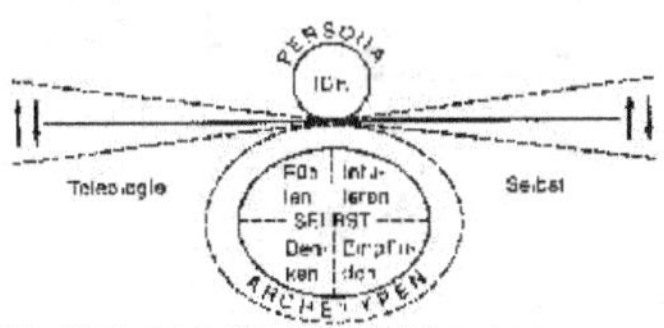

Aus: Bischof, L.J.: Persönlichkeitstheorien.
Band I. Paderborn 1983, S. 188

Abbildung 4: Graphische Zusammenfassung von Jungs Theorie

Polaritäten des Modells C.G.Jung:
Extraversion-Introversion; Progression-Regression;
Persönliches-kollektives Unbewusstes; Bewusstes-
Unbewusstes; überlegene-unterlegene Funktionen;
Psychische-physische Energie u.a.m.

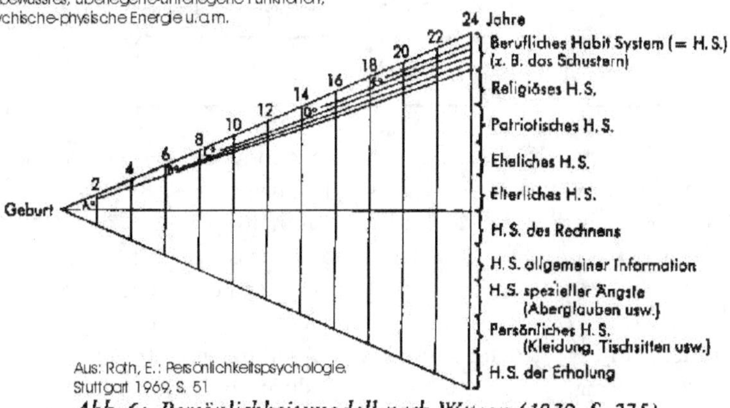

Aus: Roth, E.: Persönlichkeitspsychologie.
Stuttgart 1969, S. 51

Abb. 6: Persönlichkeitsmodell nach Watson (1930, S. 275)

Models of Freud, Bischof, Jung, Watson

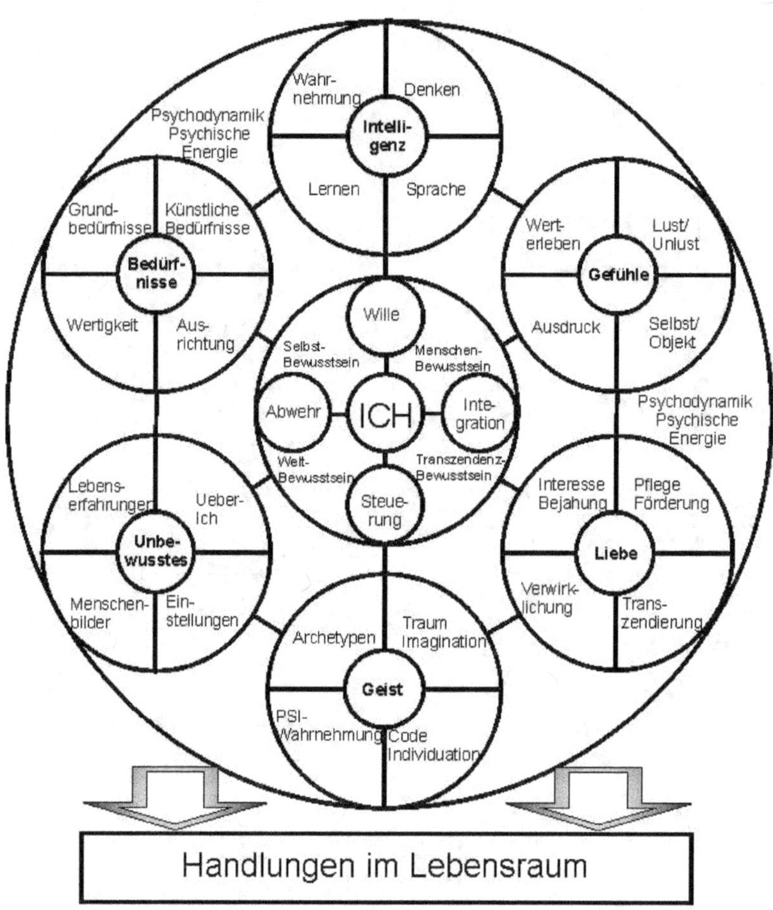

Translation: The psychic organism: with psychodynamics, psychic energy
Intelligence: Perception, thinking, learning, language >
Needs: Basic needs, artificial needs, valuing, orientation >
Feelings: Experiencing value, lust/unpleasure, expression, self/object >
I: Will, defense, integration, controls, with self-consciousness, human-consciousness, world-consciousness, transcendence-consciousness >
Unconscious: Life-experiences, super-ego, human images, attitudes >
Love: Interest/affirmation, care/assistance, realization, transcendenzation >
Spirit: Archetypes, dream/imagination, PSI-perception, code individuation >
Actions: in the living space >

We define these forces as basic forces, which are considered together to be as complex structure the PSYCHE resp. the PSYCHIC SYSTEM. As a living unit we can also conceptualize the psychic system as the "PSYCHIC ORGANISM". This system is a complex hypothetical theory, assembled into a complex whole by multiple confirmed individual theories and facts. "Personality", thus means: The individual forming of psychic organism (cf. Pervin 1993, 18). We can analyze the individual subsystems, their elements, and the whole as a unit from the point of view of development and usefulness resp. effects in the habitat. The individuation is the process that leads all these psychic subsystems into a multifaceted, balanced whole. We distinguish between two dimensions of development:

Positive development:	**Negative development:**
+ open to learning & renewal	- blocked to learning & renewal
+ flexibly available	- inflexible till not available
+ clarified & structured	- unclear, not structured
+ clear and differentiated	- diffuse & undifferentiated
+ versatile balanced	- one-sided over-, under-emphasized
+ controllable by the subject	- partial/uncontrollable by the subject
+ integrated into consciousness	- not integrated into consciousness
+ balancing dynamically	- disharmoniously dynamical
+ consciously analyzed/reflected	- not analyzed/reflected
+ integrating/building life	- decomposing/destroying life
+ predictable	- unpredictable

It has long been proven that the psychic forces begin to form from the moment of conception. In general, the process of socialization and enculturation creates inner psychic opposed and contradicting developments within each human. Everything that is formed tends to maintain itself and, like a magnetic force, controls the subsequent learning processes. So, there are two main directions in development.

The formations of the psychic organism take place predominantly in the dynamics of learning processes and external forces. For this, the science has identified many laws and relations. We understand such individual theories resp. laws as an orientation spectrum to be able to interpret arguably the actions in the habitat and the interaction of the individual subsystems for educational achievements. Transformation strategies are also based on such laws. It can generally be concluded: Life risks can be reduced, and life chances can be increased with deepened knowledges of psychic forces. This learning leads to transformations and developments.

Our human knowledge is "holistic" because we place the psychic organism in the process of individuation and consider both in the network with the life systems. It is characteristic for us that the human with all his psychic forces is more than the sum of his individual forces. We describe some psychic dispositions as "subsystems"; they only become significant from their place and their functioning in the overall system. Further is characteristic for our "holistic understanding" that the development and deployment of the psychic organism is more than a sum of individual micro-learning processes and is especially to be understood in the networking. Thereby learning is not the same as "growing" and "unfolding". This holistic understanding allows us to speak of "wholeness" though this wholeness as regards content (and maybe system) can be further expanded in the future and certainly will be. The "personality" as formed resp. grown psychic organism, and in so far as individuality, is not in contradiction. On the one hand, the human only becomes what he is resp. can become through the social and societal context, and on the other hand, he cannot live, develop, and form himself at all, detached from the community of people and the habitat. In addition, the psychic-spiritual human is tied back to what we call "spirit" and "individuation as a growth process". Insofar, this wholeness is anchored in a transcendental manner. This of course leads to the fact that the scientific knowledge about the human and his "holistic" education is more than the sum of individual facts.

The psychic organism

We now want to briefly explain the individual subsystems. All doors are open to scientific discussion to talk about whether these subsystems can really be understood as a unit. We call in memory that the andragogical interest in the construction of our system model certainly plays a significant role. On the other hand, we have endeavored to include all substantial psychic forces in the human across the many personality theories.

1) The actions:

The actions of the human are always closely intertwined with the habitat in which they happen. The acting can rarely be described without components of the environment. The living space always has a determining effect. On the other hand, the actions are tied back to the inner-psychic systems.

Of course, we can also call thinking as an action. But the act of thinking itself is not directly perceptible. That is why we separate this psychic function and generally delimit all internal psychic processes from external actions - as movement. The acting itself is the world-related expression of what is happening or has happened within. Explaining actions demands that the connections to the subsystems can be set up. The condition structure that is related to the life field is also part of the explanation context. Actions have implicitly or explicitly a goal resp. an effect. They also take place in the time dimension. Retrospective and prospective are addressed here.

Actions can be considered under the following components: a) Life system; b) The action itself; c) The aim / effect of the action; d) The psychic forces involved; e) The previous same / similar patterns of behavior; f) The actual and the optional perspective.

2) The psychodynamics - the psychic energy:

When we look at the human from the outside about how he moves, how he acts, how he expresses his aliveness in the habitat, then we can discover some elements that represent a reality independent of the specific acting. We see a person nervous or tense, vital or sluggish. Every statement is an expression of a life force. Like a melody, we can recognize many moods in the human, which express themselves in his vitality. We can also recognize stress reactions: Psychosomatic reactions, tensions in the movement sequences and psycho-physical overstimulation. Some humans react more sensitively than others to external and internal circumstances. We find this dynamic of tension in facial expressions and gestures. In acting is a force that we call "stability and lability". Some humans are more outwardly directed in their basic dynamics, others more inwardly. Here we are talking about extraversion and introversion. A quite different energy is often expressed in feelings. We call this entire structure as a unity PSYCHODYNAMICS. Its energy is the PSYCHIC ENERGY. We define this psychic energy, and, as a unit, the psychodynamics as a basic force of the psyche. Its dimensions are an expression of this force.

As observers we recognize a) Psychic energy as tension-relaxation; b) Extraversion and introversion; c) Psycho-physical reactions; d) Basic mood and its variants; e) Stability and instability; f) Sensitivity and rigidity; g) Force and intensity in the expression; h) Destructiveness and constructiveness.

3) The consciousness with the "I" and its auxiliary functions:

In general, the "I" is seen as the conscious regulation instance of the psyche and the center of the consciousness. The "I" has a life on its own, its own real image and an ideal image. These images are assigned always to values. This contrasts with contents of consciousness of the outer world. Everything that exists within the psychic systems can become a content of the consciousness.

The various psychic systems are the forces that make the "I" capable of acting. The "I", as a captain of the own ship, needs for using its own systems auxiliary functions. These include, for example, defense mechanisms and their opposing force, which we call "integration function"; the "I" also needs to perform an action a will, a control force for steering the process and a direction deliberately set or passively allowed. All psychic subsystems can be called as moving forces in the meaning of a vector. Consciousness contents of all kinds can also determine resp. influence the type and direction of the "I" controlled action. Motives are therefore not regarded as a psychic subsystem, but as a formal term that means the answer to the (formal) psychologically directed question "Why?"

Let us hold on to the aspects: a) The "I" with its self-experience; b) The self-image and the ideal image; c) The world consciousness; d) The defense functions; e) The integration functions; f) The will; g) The controls.

4) The intelligence - the cognitive processes:

With intelligence we do not mean the so-called intelligence quotient, but the complex system of reasoning processing from the recording to the result. It starts with the perception. What is perceived is expressed in language and then processed through various thinking processes. The results are: Analytical thoughts, value judgments and attitudes. The memory is another functional unit in the structure of the intelligence. As open system that not only "works" as habitually, but we can also classify the cognitive learning ability as characteristic.

In this subsystem we have a) The perception; b) The linguistic assignment; c) The thinking processes; d) The analytical thoughts; e) The judgments; f) The attitudes (values); g) The cognitive learning; h) The memory.

5) The feelings and their dimensions:

The feelings can be divided in individual classes according to different points of view. We have positive and negative feelings, which means their constructiveness and destructiveness. We refer to these aspects as "life caring and life averting". Pleasure-displeasure-experiencing can be considered a further aspect for a classification. These two aspects overlap but are not congruent. Finally, we can categorize the feelings according to their content into physical and spiritual, whereby there are feelings that can contain both aspects, such as the love. Every feeling can be weak or intense and last long or short. Feelings can be characterized on the spectrum with the opposite pole. It is assumed that the human can have several feelings simultaneously, that can be of different quality, intensity, and duration.

Criteria for classifying feelings are a) Turning to life - turning away from life; b) Pleasure - displeasure; c) Physical - spiritual.

6) The needs - the driving forces:

We can divide the term "need" into "basic needs" and "artificial needs". We call that a basic need, which has an actual driving function corresponding to the psycho-physical nature. We divide these into classes (categories) that can overlap. We can look at all kinds of needs in terms of intensity and duration. The needs have different meanings depending on the life course resp. stage of development of the human. Although the biological needs are to be placed before the spiritual needs, we dispense of a hierarchy model. We rather assume that basic needs have a claim from the nature of psycho-physical human being, from the dynamics of the psychic organism. Artificial needs are those needs that act as a compensation for basic needs as well as those that are simply conditioned, e.g., TV consumption.

Basic needs are a) Biological basic needs; b) Security and protection; c) Care and maintenance; d) Affiliation resp. relationships; e) Love and appreciation; f) Growth towards the holistic unity; g) Self-actualization; h) Achievements; i) habitat design; k) Rooted in transcendence.

7) The unconscious - the unconscious life models:

The concept of the unconscious presents a linguistic difficulty. We suppose that there is a place that can be called the unconscious; and that there is something in this unconscious that can be made conscious. The question now is: Was the content in the unconscious already conscious to the "I"? And where is the content to be placed after it has been made conscious again? We define here: All contents in the unconscious have been conscious the subject once. If we include the prenatal period, however, this awareness has different qualities. What the human does not know, so never has taken in consciousness in life, we design as the no-knowledge resp. the not-known. This does not belong in the sub-system of the unconscious. The contents of the unconscious are images that have had, perhaps still have, an experiential and factual meaning for the subject. The images in the unconscious serve as models for life orientation and lifestyle. That is why we call this LIFE MODELS.

Life models are always more or less psycho-energetically charged. If these images are particularly strong emotionally and regressively binding, we call them "complexes". These are due to specific characteristics parried of the "I" and segregated from the consciousness, so that they no longer can be reintegrated directly into the consciousness. Everything that can be impressed pictorially, is regarded as life model or as an element to a life model. During life, the human collects in more and more images that condense in complex life models in the unconscious. The different life models are structured and ultimately form a whole. The more disharmonic, conflicting, and contradictory the images are, the more chaos and disorder prevails in this image space. What the human has brought into consciousness and has corrected find a new place in the unconscious. Whether consciously or unconsciously, whether corrected and balanced or complex-like, these images always have the function of acting as a model for the lifestyle. Life models urge to be realized.

We divide the life models as follows: a) General life experiences; b) Super-ego: commands, prohibitions, punishment models; c) Attitudes and conditions; d) Human images of all kinds.

8) The spirit and its functions in dream and imagination:

The word "spirit" has many meanings in the history of philosophy and is rejected in many places. Some think: This term is no good. It is necessary to determine this basic force of the psyche concretely and in a differentiated manner. Some avoid this issue in principle, because they probably guess that if this force is real, it will compulsory. The "I" must submit to the spirit. That is why in the psychology the love and the spirit do not exist as central core themes of the psychic life.

Through many years of systematic analyzes, we have detected that a creative force acts in the dreams, which wants to guide the human intelligently, which wants to organize the unconscious life models into a new harmonious whole, which opens the access to what can be called "God" or "divine", which wants to let grow the love, which precisely directs the process of psychic-spiritual growth, which also has parapsychic abilities, and which shapes its own language. We have also found that in the imagination this spiritual force acts very intelligently according to specific basic principles and can be used for life. The "I" can come into communication with this force, but ultimately cannot influence it. It is here: Independent, only obliged to itself, directive, ordering, judgmental, but also suppressible. We call this force SPIRIT. This spirit directs the personality development from within through dreams and through imagination to the integrative process of individuation.

The aspects of the spirit are a) Language: images, symbols, archetypes; b)

Value system; c) Dream, imagination, intuition; d) Code program of individuation; e) Processing dynamics and tendency; f) Basic human-leading tendency; g) Extrasensory perception; h) Transcendental rootedness.

9) Love as a constructive life force:

This subsystem may to be new in the field of personality theories; not as a theme of life itself, but rather as a specific basic force of the psyche. We hereby set up the thesis: The human has in himself an evolutionary basic force that wants to grow, shape meaning, live authenticity and truth, take responsibility, implement interests, and maintain the value of being human. This basic force also can go beyond itself to a certain extent, i.e., to exceed individual needs and the space-time context of life to realize a higher value. The love as a basic force has a standard for justice, for humility and goodness. The love is the force that places life above the having, that includes the having as a possibility for the life of love. Although psychology, philosophy and pedagogy hardly attach scientific interest to this basic force, the love has always been viewed as the basic issue of human life. The negative opposite pole of this force means: Hatred, absence of love, denial, lies, negation, greed, indifference, egoism, Dionysian self-experience, power (in the negative sense), regression, carelessness, stagnation, and reduction of the human being to functionalism and materialism, but also ideological and dogmatic ties to life.

We record the following dimensions of the love here: a) The life appreciating values and meaning experience; b) The "yes" to life as life devotion; c) Authenticity and truthfulness; d) Responsibility, solidarity, loyalty and duty; e) Interest of knowledge, action and luck (also aesthetics); f) Transcending oneself; g) Humility and goodness (Apollonian), ability to reconcile; g) Life as being value over the having; h) The evolutionary, holistic growth and becoming in freedom; i) The back bonding to the wholeness of the own psychical-spiritual human being.

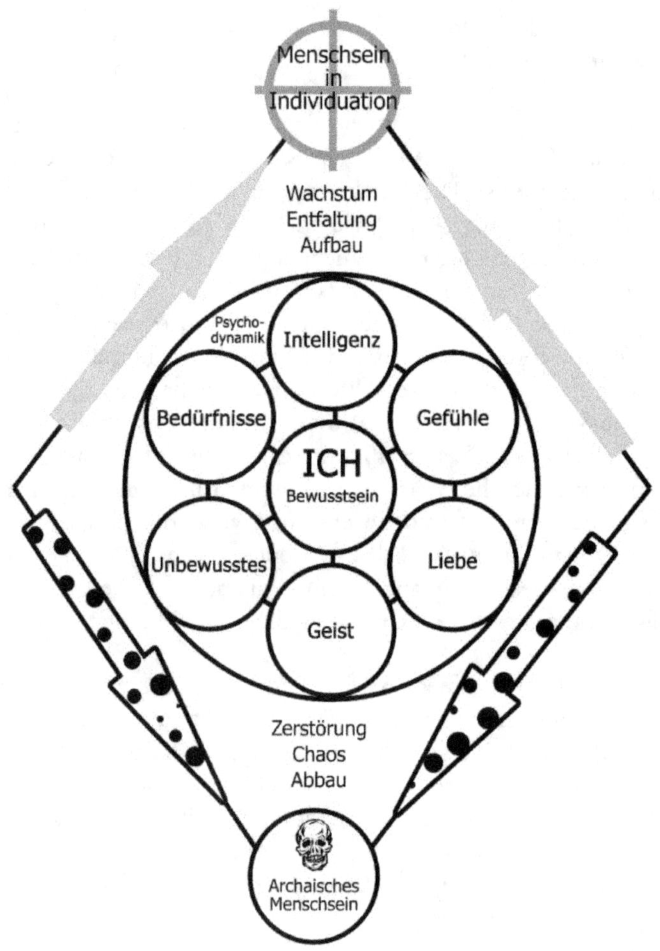

Translation:
Human being in individuation: Growth, deployment, set-up
"I" with consciousness, psychodynamics, intelligence, needs, feelings,
unconscious, love, spirit, archaic human being: destruction, chaos, reduction

The Individuation Process

We can characterize the process of the deployment of growth and the life realization with the subsystems and the into a whole included psychic system. We can also determine corrections originated by the individual life.

We divide the process of individuation into three phases:

1st phase: Knowledge of what is present in all subsystems. Understanding how the lived life created these formations. Learning how the individual subsystems work. Identifying the transformation and growth demand.

2nd phase: Transformation of the individual forces. Strengthening and developing of all subsystems. Integration into an all-round balanced unit. Understanding and using the language of the subsystems.

3rd phase: Establishing the new wholeness. Rooting of wholeness and life forms in the spirit and in the love. Updating this wholeness in the life realization. Living comprehensive responsibility and solidarity for being human.

This process takes place in the habitat and designs this space centralized in the human, i.e., in this psychic-spiritual growth process. The completion of the third phase is the highest level of human development and psychic-spiritual evolution. This is the realization of the highest archetype, which at the same time reflects in the human what "God" is. We explain this archetype as the genuine life principle according to which a world design is optimally evolutionary. The more humans work towards this basic model, in which they become inside and live outwardly what this archetype depicts, the more the society is developing in the direction of the psychic-spiritual evolution.

Individuation is the central educational area of andragogy. Because it promotes the ability to love, life responsibility, life competences and deployment. Individuation reduces crises, suffering, harm, and risks. Individuation anchors the life on all sides balanced in the psychic inner world.

Self-knowledge and personality development

Let us first take a short tour through various psychological, philosophical, and other lexicons to gain a general (historical) insight into the understanding of " self-knowledge":

Dorsch writes in his psychological dictionary (1991, 600-601) about self-knowledge (selectively): "Turning of knowledge towards one's own "I". The self as a formed and lasting idea in the experience of the human is examined for its peculiarities (own being, behavior, disposition, abilities, attitudes, motivations) ... As prerequisite for the development and shaping of the own personality, self-knowledge was already required as a basis among the Greeks of antiquity, as can be seen from the inscription on the Temple of Apollo in Delphi: "Know yourself". Self-knowledge, the perception of the self, is based on the one hand on self-observation, on the other hand on feedback, which are registered from the confrontation of the human with problems in his environment and the interpersonal communication ... Despite the justified demand for self-knowledge (Pascal, Kant) skeptical voices have never been missed (Goethe, Nietzsche), which point to the tendency of the human to mask themselves (also) from themselves.

In the international Freemason lexicon by Lennhoff and Posnier (1932, 1450) it says: "Know yourself ... (is) according to Socrates a precondition for morality, Lessing calls it the center of all human wisdom, Kant the beginning of all human wisdom. In the teaching letter "Wilhelm Meister's" the words are: How can you recognize yourself? Never by looking, but by acting. Try to do your duty and you will immediately know what is wrong with you."

Schöpf philosophically deepens the core of self-knowledge (in: Höffe, 1985, I, 154): "Know yourself ... was understood in the Socratic-Platonic philosophy in the way that the human has to question the sensual content of his knowledge and to become aware of the precondition of ideas, especially the idea of the good ... Likewise, in Aristotelian philosophy, the human could only come to a correct assessment of himself if he understood himself as a mediator between animal and deity ... What the human is he only experiences through the truth ... The meaning of every self-knowledge can only consist in "knowing you", the God to be addressed personally ...".

From a philosophical point of view, Hügli and Lübcke (1991, 525) name the following aspects of self-knowledge: "1. Self-awareness; 2. Self-reflection; 3. Knowledge of the own genuine life (as opposed to self-deception); 4. Knowledge of the own being; 5. Knowledge of the real purpose of the own life - or realizing that there is no such purpose, only the absurd."

The pedagogue Wilhelm Dilthey sees self-knowledge as follows: "What the human is only his story tells him." Gergen writes about self-knowledge (in: Filipp 1993, 75): "When the man on the street begins to 'discover' himself, when he thinks about his behavior, his moral, his feelings, the basis of his principles and expectations ... then he does none other than (what) a scientist (does) who explores the human behavior - just unprofessionally and unsystematically ... Could the layman procedure scientifically, so he could even acquire the most basic foundations of the science then his chances for self-knowledge would be considerably higher ...".

The psychiatrist and philosopher Viktor E. Frankl spoke in 1949 about "What is the human?" in the memory of Auschwitz (1975, 334-338). We take from it some thought fragments: "What is the human? ... What were the dead colleagues (in Auschwitz)? ... We got to know him, like perhaps no generation before us; we got to know him ..., where everything insignificant had melted away from the human; where everything disappeared that one had owned: Money, power, fame, luck, where only remained what a human cannot 'have' but what he must 'be': What remained, was the human himself, burned by pain and burned out with suffering, he was melted down to the essential in him, to the humanly ... So, what is the human? ... He is a being that equally has the possibility to sink down to the level of an animal or to rise to a holy life ... (the) thinking, (the) consciousness, (the) responsibility ... makes the dignity of every single human ...".

We come back to our model of psychic life. The diversity of the individual psychic forces makes clear that self-knowledge contains a whole range of useful possibilities that we want to call opportunities in life. Anyone who knows the fullness of his own forces will experience inner peace and confidence in the hour of his death: "I know who I am; I know why I have lived so; I know what my existence was good for; I know a lot about myself, about my psychic-spiritual being and about life; therefore, I also know that I will live forever".

Self-knowledge is the beginning of all opportunities in life. Some psychic forces must meticulously be disassembled and analyzed so transformations can become possible. Many renewal attempts fail if the interdependence of the forces of the psyche are not satisfactorily considered. A high input of time and work is always justified for the recognition of all forces. A central experience is that the dreams lead the human to his real psychic-spiritual being with inner experiences. There is no other force that can lead to the "highest" human being. Self-knowledge leads to himself and is an exciting self-discovery. This may perhaps cause disillusionment. But thereby it frees from illusions. Self-knowledge automatically establishes an inner anchorage. The psychic life itself determines the course of growth. Everything on the psychic-spiritual human being, finds everybody through systematic and thorough self-knowledge in himself. The greatest difficulties, however, are convenience, lack of knowledge, lack of inner education, dogma, arrogance.

Self-knowledge has many positive, valuable aspects: What one knows can be controlled, changed, corrected, formed, and consciously developed. One only sees the psychic reality in others to the extent that one knows it in oneself. The more the human knows himself, the more differentiated he can live the diversity of life: Relationships, sexuality, leisure time, etc. Those who take self-knowledge seriously take themselves seriously. This is prerequisite for the differentiated self-love and the love for life. Self-knowledgeable strengthens because: It relieves fears, promotes authenticity, animates new forces, and gives a realistic self-image. Whoever recognizes himself more and more also promotes his learning and his desires for renewal.

Our system model of psychic life is the basis for practical self-knowledge. No one is here in danger through the gate of self-knowledge suddenly to slide in some esoteric, ideological, or dogmatic impasse. There cannot sneak in hidden interests, that becloud the view or become one-sided concentrated. The theoretical principles are arguable and extensible. When we speak of "wholeness", our system provides the evidence of an honest attempt to have exhausted all possibilities in this direction. Any dispute about psychological schools and positions is superfluous.

The aspects of the fundamental positions have largely been considered, albeit in relative terms. Nice talk of self-realization, emancipation, freedom, trust, experience of transcendence, love, happiness, and success have no opportunities here. The model offers a well-founded order in the diversity of psychic life and its unfolding. The reference to life is given. The personality development has clear scientific foundations and get not lost in one-sided interpretations of existence.

First basic questions of self-knowledge, developed from our system model, are:

1. What can you say characteristically about your daily activities?
2. What is the tendency of your psychodynamics?
3. How is your average "I"-experience and your "I"-control?
4. In general, how do you use your ability to think and your (valuing) judgment force?
5. What are your current needs?
6. How are currently your feelings in the overview?
7. How do you experience your unconscious, i.e., the inventory of your lived life?
8. Which relation do you have to your dreams and imagination?
9. How do you experience your love force?
10. How do you characterize the state of your psychic-spiritual development?

The psychic subsystems enable to formulate initial questions about self-knowledge, whereby a clear order and a relative warranty of comprehensive wholeness is guaranteed. The self-observations give the grid for a clear view. Looking what is here, and interpreting what is recognized, has to do everybody for himself. Everyone can interpret learn deficits, correction needs and growth direction by reflection. The clear structure presettings allow to formulate clear first learn objectives. The question catalog of systematic self-knowledgeable should first be formulated openly. It can be applied self-taught or be used in the frame of classes. The questionnaire helps to a simple structuring in the psychagogical counselling. The scientists can, whatever they are working on, expand their point of view with the system model, keep consciously the connections and finally learn to understand as researchers their own world. Because whatever the researcher does in education and andragogy, he cannot isolate the life as a rat labyrinth. He is always also affected. At the same time, he is always researching about himself.

Based on the psychic subsystems, the psychic organism, as well as on the individuation as unfolding and growth process the andragogical psychology can include personality models (indicative targets, huge educational goals), partly as a description of certain formations of individual psychic forces, partly as a sketching of holistic character conditioning. This leads to personality ideals. The social relevance results directly and interpretatively. The legitimacy of values resp. ideals lies in the psychic forces and their effect mode (depending on the formation) and not in an ideology, nor in metaphysics, nor in dogmatics and not in a subjective arbitrariness. We want to present some generally formulated examples for discussion.

Personality ideals formulated in the context of the system model of "psychic organism" and individuation are, above all:

1) Systematic and comprehensive self-knowledge about the psychic subsystems.
2) Differentiated self -consciousness (self-image).
3) Clear, multi-layered human and world awareness.
4) Awareness of the transcendent reality through inner growth.
5) Experiencing of being in the complexity of all inner and outer living spaces.
6) Strong, dynamic, and positive "I"-experiencing.
7) Free of defense and projections with at the same time flexible clear differentiation.
8) Open dynamic integration of all life realities.
9) Strong, consciously formed, and integrated will (will force).
10) Pronounced self-regulation in the complex psychic and external world.
11) Completely liberated, processed, purified unconscious life.

12) Differentiated perception of one's own realities and those of others.
13) Creative constructive thinking with clear language.
14) Learning openness resp. continuous readiness to change un d enlargement.
15) Clearly identified and balanced basic needs.
16) Versatile balanced and used emotional life.
17) Sustainable and operational love force in all life areas.
18) Flexible and vital psychodynamics, free from cramped opposites.
19) Intensive communication with the spirit through dream work and meditation.
20) Daily acting in reflected feedback to the psychic organism.
21) Development of the psychic organism in back bonding to spirit and love.
22) Living and becoming in the direction of the living image of the highest archetype.

The pedagogy put personality ideals at the beginning of the definitions setting "education": "Self-determination, freedom, emancipation, autonomy, maturity, reason, self-activity" (Klafki 1993, 19). Derbolav, to highlight an example, begins the development of his formation theory with the "goal determination", by which he means "adulthood" and "maturity" (Derbolav 1993, 26). Brezinka is close to our approach: "Under education are understood actions through which the humans try to improve permanently the structure of the psychic dispositions of other humans in any way or to preserve his components assessed as valuable or to prevent the formation of dispositions which are valued as bad". "Psychic dispositions" he sets identically with "personality" (Brezinka 1978, 45). The problem is open, however, what the term "personality" resp. "psychic disposition" should mean. The learning areas still revolve around the three levels: Cognitive, affective, and psychomotor (Metzger 1992, 90-93). Krämer / Walter (1994, 65-67) operate on this level: "Learning objectives are differentiated according to the learning areas to which they relate (in the pedagogical tradition): Affective (feeling), cognitive (thinking) and psycho-motoric (skills) learning target areas ...". - (see also, Kron 1994, 159). - This is much too narrow for the educational concept of "personality development". We clarify this with new suggestions in our work "Concept of Individuation - Andragogical Psychology".

According to our proposal, the andragogical psychology develops on the one hand system models of the psychic life that are relevant for personality development and individuation. On the other hand, it sets the conditions for deciding on ideals and values by writing down descriptively corresponding variations as models (character images, ideals). The embedding in higher-level system relations with the living environments belongs to both task areas. On this basis, the andragogy can formulate the educational mandate and present it for discussion. Human education is thus comprehensively substantially defined. In addition to this field specific didactics is to be designed, which guarantees that such ideals resp. values as educational goals can be integrated in a "structure grid" of the concrete lesson planning. The educational mandate of andragogy can be realized.

The personality ideals mentioned are of great importance for the social life in the future. Three critical aspects are highlighted:

1) The concept of promoting talent in the professional world is largely no longer relevant today. The job market and the greed for money force many people to move in the world of work according to the possibilities. Whereas it used to be "whoever achieves something, gets anywhere", today one can see that many of those who "have" (money, goods, career, reputation, participation) do not have it because they would achieve something special with great commitment and out of inner talent, but rather because they acquire this "having" with tricks, aggressiveness, and power behavior. Where remains the inner response to professional serving with factual and social competence?

2) Just as the human is psychically shaped as a personality (person), he lives with himself, with other people and with his habitat. The dealing with the own psychic organism is shown in the dealing with nature, water, air, earth and the animal world. Just as the psychic forces are formed, so the human creates his own world, and this is how he affects the life worlds.

3) There is the renaissance of totalitarian ideology today. A lot of violence readiness can be seen. There are seen resentments towards the values of the occidental culture, emotional insecurity in the people, masses of blind identifications with political and economic "leaders", regressions and adjustments in a mass consciousness, male-aggressive life forms at work as in relationships with the woman, exclusions as model for conflict resolution, also indifference (or disorientation) in the moral issues of the daily life. Little is known how much the thinking of humans of all educational levels and social class is still steeped in the spirit of the Inquisition. Which ideology and which leaders will people attract to in twenty to thirty years?

The necrophilia, as presented by the psychoanalyst and philosopher Erich Fromm with the example of the 'Founding Manifesto of Futurism of 1909', is an occasion to think most carefully about human education (1979, 57-59). This is as relevant today as it was at the beginning of the last century. That is why we quote the central passages from it - an opportunity to make a fundamental decision:

1. "We want to sing about the love to danger, the familiarity with energy and daring.
2. Courage, boldness, and rebellion should be the essential elements of our poetry.
3. We want to praise the aggressive movement, the feverish insomnia, the running step, the somersault, the slap in the face and the punch.
4. We declare that the glory of the world has been enriched with a new beauty: the beauty of the speed. A racing car ... a howling automobile that seems to be running on rifle bullets ...
5. We want to sing the man who keeps the steering wheel in the hand, those steering axis passes through the middle of the earth ...
6. Beauty only exists in the fight. A work without aggressive character cannot be a masterpiece ...
7. ... Time and space died yesterday. We already live in the absolute because we have already created the eternal, omnipresent speed.
8. We want to glorify the war - this only hygiene in the world – the militarism, the patriotism, the destruction act of the anarchists, the beautiful ideas for which one dies and the contempt for the woman.
9. We want to destroy all museums, libraries and academies and fight against moralism, feminism and all cowardice ...".

Education research, educational science and pedagogy have failed considerably in their primary categorical tasks. They have not responded to the real needs of the human in the society. A new human education with new ideals is necessary so that in the future the humans can cope with the demands of life and at the same time with those of the psyche. If the pedagogy (andragogy) does not do this, sects, esoteric and pseudo-religious (spiritual) movements and fundamentalism will proliferate. And this is the breeding ground for fascistic thinking.

Due Turn in Science of Human Education

We have historically rolled out the three specialist areas and fields of practice that deal with human education. Characteristic of this variety of theories and practices of human education in the broadest sense of the word is, briefly summarized:

1. The scientific concepts: Different human images in terms of scope and quality; no really holistic personality theory; different scientific substance and quality; different spiritual orientation resp. rootedness; many unclear and ambiguous term definitions; considerable one-sidedness in theories and models; no clear structuring in scientific subject areas; partly technocratization of the psychic life; despite scientific claim many ideologic elements; partly religious or philosophical dogmatism; commercial interests behind term definitions and concepts; little to no constructive communication between the positions.

2. The practice-related methods and objectives: Divergence between theoretical objectives and practice; variety of vague "object"-definitions (clients, issues); variety and confusion of education issues resp. work goals; variety of quite different practices; tendency to overestimation of individual methods; little scientific innovative feedback; insufficiently meaningful success controls; extensive areas of activities without evaluation.

3. Professionalization and professional image: Competence and objectivity defined from one's own position; little innovation dynamics in the further education institutions; very different subject-specific training profiles; ideological and commercial self-interest of the responsibles; lack of didactic education concepts and strategies; variety of historically determined influences by the responsibles; lack of subject-specific clear job profiles; variety of concepts of professionalization; no postgraduate training in philosophy and pedagogy; diversity of regional to international groups.

It is obvious to deal briefly with the keyword "sect" in the overall overview. Various organizations in the psycho-religious area have this reputation for whatever reasons (Ruthven 1991; Baumgartner 1993; Schmid 1993; Haack 1993).

They all tend to have in common: No official state recognition as a church;

no recognition as a science in the frame of state structures; no social recognition as non-profit service; significant financial interests; tendency to bind the clientele for the purpose of capital increase; mostly aggressive marketing practices; creating of bonds in order to strengthen the organization; variable ideological and dogmatic teachings about the human, world and God; one-sided till strange concepts about the human psyche; unfair and illusory promises about happiness and salvation.

We do not want to enter closer to the subject here, just pointing out that several of these elements in the field of philosophy, psychoanalysis and psychotherapy can be found too. In the current "psycho-market", professionalism can in practice only be clearly delimited from elements of sectarianism in relation to the institution of science and the basic academic education. The fact that, in addition to the empirical understanding of science about the human, there are also recognized and historically significant concepts in the humanities, makes it possible to develop a multi-layered andragogy capable of discourse.

In historical overview, an interesting tendency is seen: Some philosophers and psychoanalysts, that have presented new ideas, new theories, and new concepts, got into difficult situations. They were rejected violently by their own circles, ejected by interest groups, and sometimes ostracized by the state. Such a tendency is less noticeable in education in the 20th century if one disregards the years 1931-1945. Power struggles, exclusionary behavior and ostracism are - as far as can be recognized from the literature - significantly less common. As an aside, it should be mentioned that the fields of philosophy, education and psychoanalysis have been around 90% male-dominated and still are. One example: Of 1012 full-time professors (1987), just 10.7% are women (Baumert, Roeder. In: Krüger / Rauschenbach 1994, 32). If one assumes the fact that upbringing is also essentially (if not primarily) a task performed by women (mothers / teachers at the basic level), then this statistical distribution reflects the traditional archaic patriarchy. We find this decidedly unacceptable, especially for the future andragogy.

In the individual departments, we have already formulated the first conclusions for the foundation of andragogy. In this chapter an integrative concept of the andragogy in science and practice is created on it. It is understood that some of the above-summarized characteristics must be turned off in the approach. In the planning of a concept, it is theoretically easier to design than later to implement concretely the project in practice in a constructive manner.

The starting point of our reflections is a practical life topic, pedagogically and andragogically central, always been the greatest spiritual asset: The human education. This includes elementary self-knowledge, individuation, and life counseling. We have stated that many professional groups and persons from a wide range of provenances deal with it. Vastly different scientific faculties teach and research over sub-areas, often with the tendency towards a holistic claim for personality development, which itself usually cannot be clearly identified as such. The andragogy as an independent subject area of academic teaching and research in the sense of human education (personality development and individuation) is only just in composition.

In the andragogy it may not be a development as in psychoanalysis and psychotherapy, even if a certain plurality in human image, in life philosophy and in work-technique must of course be preserved. It is on one hand to be considered positive that in the democratic societies the freedom exists to teach almost every kind of human images and life philosophy, to justify life-help with any theory and to practice this in many ways. But on the other hand, philosophy, pedagogy, and psychological counseling (inclusive psychoanalysis and the so-called psychotherapy) lose their social authority concerning the human education if they are so fragmented and cannot find a common conceptual orientation in their basis. Philosophy remains for philosophers, pedagogy for the children resp. for elementary school and social institutions and the psychoanalysis resp. psychotherapy for the mentally ill or those who are so classified. We find in all three areas well-known representatives and concepts that the humanistic human education in the broadest sense of the word, including its social relevance highlight with great dedication. The situation in relation to this interest is inconsistent without identity and without solidarity.

The andragogy in our sense is based on four interest areas. We present these in the overview, explaining them with key words:

a) Knowledge interest: Curiosity, urge to understand, attention tendency, thirst for knowledge, need for integration, awareness of creation, love for life, experiences, having an overview.

b) Action interest: The urge to work, act, shape, create, use, maintain, care for, educate, form, realize plans, develop, live consciously, live culture.

c) Happiness interest: Lust, joy, love, hope, contentment, wisdom, well-being, fulfillment, self-realization (of all one's own potentials).

d) Becoming human interest: Personality development and individuation as inner growth and deployment process in the sense of psychic-spiritual evolution.

One argumentation area of legitimacy of andragogy revolves around the "key problems" in the sense of Klafki (1985, 21). In addition, he mentions topics that we have presented expanded in the context of the social situation: Mass media, leisure, environment, peace, work resp. unemployment, ways of life, sexuality, etc. Klafki demands a "historical awareness and joint responsibility" as well as "the willingness to face these problems and to take part in the effort to overcome them" (1985, 20). The key problems of Klafki are without doubt especially important for the individual and for the society. But are there any priorities? Isn't this list already outdated? Wouldn't the meaninglessness and inner suffering to be placed at the top of the list of everyday key problems in Germany today? In our opinion, the list needs to be expanded, e.g., with stress factors (Hurrelmann 1994, 142), risk factors for mental health (Tress, 1986, 50, 69-70) as well as sociological and socio-psychological problems in our society (cf. Jungk / Müllert 1994, 30).

From the standpoint of the classical education term with the dimensions of the moral, the aesthetic, the cognitive and the practical, Klafki's list of key problems may address a nerve in human education. But if the concept of education is expanded to include the subject of the "spirit", and thus the process of individuation, then this catalog lacks the crucial theme of being human, to put it briefly in one picture: The Grail.

This would also add different psychic-spiritual key problems the list: The search for meaning, the true spiritual experience, the overloaded unconscious of the humans, etc. The absence of the spiritual dimension makes long-term any education efforts to a Sisyphean task, and any attempt to solve the key problems at the roots, to an alibi exercise. If the grandiose words such as emancipation, maturity, and self-determination as well as the never-to-be-missed adjective "critical" are not linked back to what we call "spirit", then educational efforts in such directions may create superficial happiness; behind it, however, suffering, emptiness, and destructive chaos in the inside of the human. The "experience of happiness", the "human fulfillment" and the "good life" (Klafki 1986, 455 ff.) remain - from the contemplative point of view - not achievable goals.

Closer to the "personality", Klafki formulates a long series of goals that revolve around "emancipation, self-determination and the solidarity ability": "Communication, roles, frustration tolerance, critique ability, creativity, problem-solving ability, relational ability, fear-free integration of drive and feelings, reflective tolerance", etc. (Klafki 1977, 27-29). Also, these positive goals do not reach the ground of human education, although they without doubt are "well-sounding", however the individual may fill these words with content. Thereby we indicate that some target terms have a wide interpretation scope, and that there is the danger that with these words, not is thought what also could be meant. The "emancipation pedagogy" has already been countered in the early days that there is also an educational (up-bringing) to adaption with positive values (Rössner 1972, 606, 613, 616). The transfer of certain cultural objectivations as well as the binding ability to the own culture are containing education values that are pushed back with the slogan "emancipation". In addition, there is the question of value binding, meaning and conscience binding; for us not in the sense of a "categorical imperative" or a normativism or "a priori insight", but in the direction to individuation, love, and spirit (as we have designed in "Empirie der Individuation". Schellhammer 1998).

We find a further legitimacy area in the field of the so-called "general education". Here Klafki sets in turn at the "key problems", expands these with several concerns such as: Access to different possibilities of self-realization, diversity of behavior possibilities, individual interests, and various life forms (Klafki 1985, 29). Certainly, educational goals are "answers of certain people or groups to specific historical situations under the point of view how the growing generation has to behave in the present and in the future" (Klafki 1970, I, 23-25). The ideology-critical interest is a serious concern. The factual dependence on the history is a generally recognized fact in pedagogy today. But the legitimacy of andragogy (as human education) cannot fundamentally, that is "categorically" be established with this.

Considering the immense knowledge increase, it is becoming more and more important to learn how to deal with not knowing (Treml 1994, 536). Knowing and not-knowing is an ontological and phylogenetic approach to any pedagogical concept. Responsible acting requires knowledge (Siebert 1994, 320). Who wants to form his psychic forces, to understand the interpersonal psychic life and to form it in a responsible manner, thus must acquire knowledge about the psychic life and methods of education of this (his) psychic life? Without this knowledge and ability, neither a critical-emancipatory appropriation of culture, nor a critical demarcation and progressive reorientation are possible. The education of psychic life we consider to be the central key qualification. It contains generalized available permanent competencies that focus on fundamental and always recurring life tasks. Key qualifications are defined in further education with the "triad": "Subject-specific, social and methodological competencies". Today they have been reformulated resp. expanded to the "qualification quintet" by Kaiser / Kaiser (1994, 187): Subject-specific competencies, independence competencies, team competencies, system competencies and reflexivity. In our opinion, this diversification should be expanded with "personality development". Formulated as a competence, this means: "The person is capable of continuously developing himself in all subsystems of the psychic organism throughout his life in the sense of individuation". This conclusion arises from our educational theory approach in the next chapter.

If we go one step further on, we come to the basic questions of existence and thus to the problem of "becoming human". We find the ultimately valid answers to this in the human himself, and not in the historicity of the "personality"-being today, yesterday, or tomorrow. However, there are immense dangers to slip into the metaphysical, to present with nice talk philosophical designs or even to argue theological-dogmatically. The only constructive way out that cannot be interpreted as a defense is that the andragogy researches the human as experiencing reality in a manifold especially depth-psychological and spiritual manner. Because the "becoming human" can impossibly be created in an educational process without these depths. The critical-constructive approach of Klafki (1970, III, 126-153, 1985) and the discourse of Habermas (1968, 168) receive in this dimension a new task: We have always to express in today's language, what historically and individually has a conditional expression, but inheres nevertheless in everyone as "psychological organism". The process of the becoming human (i.e., individuation) always has a historical form and is nevertheless based on inner growth principles. To formulate the temporal-spatial-bound timelessly is a difficult undertaking. Here andragogical psychology becomes "andragogical anthropology". Here are the deepest roots of the legitimacy of this science. This defines the "categorical education" and the "andragogical reference".

Thus, the andragogue is a "human educator" and not a "teacher of occupational adult education", as it is understood here and there (e.g., Pribich 1994, 4). It also seems to us that the term "education helper" or "socialization helper" (Arnold 1985, 109, 143) do not describe what human education includes and professionally demands.

Every human education aims to transform psychic dispositions. This means: In the education process, the humans are influenced to shape certain psychic forces (e.g., thinking forms, attitudes, image models) or to reshape them or to strengthen them in the given direction. Since one must ask if this perhaps could have to do with manipulation. In our opinion, manipulation wants to bypass the conscious reflection and the wake autonomy of the "I". Indoctrination asserts and sets an infallible claim to truth, usually very simplified compared to the reality of life. In this, behavior is normatively directed (Reboul 1979). An andragogy with an empirical and humanistic-critical foundation and a polytheoretical didactics (e.g., in the sense of Jank /

Meyer 1991) can impossibly create a human education that ends as a system of manipulation and indoctrination. Because the andragogy has nothing to hide, not to pretend to be 'pure' scientificness, not to cover or to distort facts, not to place seduction to stupidity into the program and not to create projective enemy images. Language always allows every kind of point of view and every argument to be manipulated with tricks. For those who master neuro linguistic programming, can perform virtuoso feats that can become for the sharpest minds to the "banana peel on the sidewalk". In our opinion one cannot yet suspect any general humanistic personality ideal of indoctrination and assume every agogic method suggestion element of manipulation. The suggestion methods in the psychagogy are not manipulation techniques. Some holistic humanistic ideals about the human and life may be mythical or illusory, but certainly not indoctrinal.

We justify our conception of science and practice of human education. In doing so, we begin with the characteristics of this practice field, the given scientific background, and the ideological-dogmatic and commercial problems. We formulate the tasks for such a science of andragogy as follows:

General task of andragogy

The science of andragogy provides to the human education, as we have sketched it out for the present: Models, theories, and practical instruments. It presents analyzes of existing implicit values and ratings and develops a system of values for its practice with the justification interrelations. The professional field is clearly to limit, i.e., clearly to define towards the bordering branches. Between science and practice there is a systematic feedback. As a science, it defines itself its scientific nature and its methodology. It is partly inter-disciplinary science, partly basic science.

Andragogy, here as human education in the true sense of the word, is made up of four main subject areas:

1) The psychic organism, development and individuation, life problems and "critical" (significant) life issues, social-cultural living space.

2) Methods of human education, diagnosis, and life counseling; didactics of life training.

3) Philosophical anthropology, ethics.

4) Scientific understanding, methodology.

This general task can be broken down into four main parts:

First partial task of andragogy:

The andragogy deals with the human as a psychic-spiritual person. To it, the andragogy develops integrative-synergetic theories, analyzes, models, concepts, and terms systems. The formulation of these subject areas is directed towards the main task of andragogy in practice. The individual areas are: The psychic organism (personality,) the psychic-spiritual development (individuation), the life problems: Crises, conflicts, disturbances, and life suffering; the interactions with the social-cultural context (social key problems).

Andragogy is a multidisciplinary science and practice. It relates its basic knowledge to pedagogy, psychology, depth psychology, psychoanalysis, psychagogics, religious psychology, social psychology, learning and development psychology, personality psychology, didactics, social pedagogy and social psychology, theory and practice of social work, educational theory, concepts of "education permanente", psycho-andragogic diagnostics, sociology, culture philosophy, counseling techniques, educational technology, conflict psychology, teaching on spirituality and transcendence, bio-energetics, eco-psychology, adult and elderly psychology.

Second part-task of andragogy:

In its basic work, the practice of andragogy is directed towards personality development, and thus towards what a person is as psychic-spiritual person and how he lives with it. The self-knowledge is followed by psychic-spiritual development (individuation). The human also experiences himself with crises, conflicts, disturbances, and sufferings in life. Because there is no life without such challenges. The human always lives his life course in the field of tension between psyche and environment. The human cannot grow without challenges. Life problems are positive part of the life course. The practical andragogy deals with diagnosis, solution, and clarification of such life challenges. The processing of life issues is understood as an education achievement, not as a technical intervention.

For that the andragogy offers instruments to answer the basic questions of life, as far as these answers can be found in the human himself. The andragogy has the task to develop theories, concepts, models, values, goals, techniques, working instruments, instruction grids, didactics, strategies, and methods for its own practice.

The practical work of andragogy is understood as: Education through teaching (imparting) of knowledge about the human and life; education through training and counseling in self-knowledge and individuation; counseling as life aid in crises, conflicts, difficulties, and suffering.

Not a psychological strain resp. a specific problem is the main motive and focus, but self-education and individuation as a systematic personal learning process. An acute psychological strain and a specific life problem can be the reason - and most of the time it is - to decide: "Well, now it is high time for a systematic personality development." Individual consultations are at best additional extensions that depending on the actuality and the specific interests may include for some time several consultations in addition to the current course programs for the education.

The responsibles of such a practice can be institutions of adult education, companies, non-profit organizations, municipalities, professionals of andragogy in own practice resp. school.

With the practical tasks we are during the "andragogical reference" and the "pedagogical basic model" (e.g., according to Derbolaw, the "pädagogische Kegel", 1987, 17; Reifenrath 1983, 24). The eleven characteristic constitutive elements are in our opinion: 1) The pupil / student (educandus); 2) The andragogue; 3) The education (goals, content, methods, instruments, etc.); 4) The historical and social context; 5) The psychic organism as the substance of education; 6) The individuation as a process; 7)The communicative interaction; 8) The time dimension of the processings; 9) The andragogy as research and teaching in expanded reference; 10) The initial situation (educational need), and 11) The target situation resp. options. Sitzmann suggests a "pedagogical square" as a methodological basic figure in adult education: 1) Personal aspect with a) Participants, and b) Adult educator; as well as 2) Factual aspect with a) Tasks and topics, and b) Organization (imparting) (In: Ruprecht / Sitzmann 1985, XIII, 95). In the following illustration we sketch an overview of the "andragogical reference" according to our concept of human education.

Illustration 5: System Model of Andragogical Reference

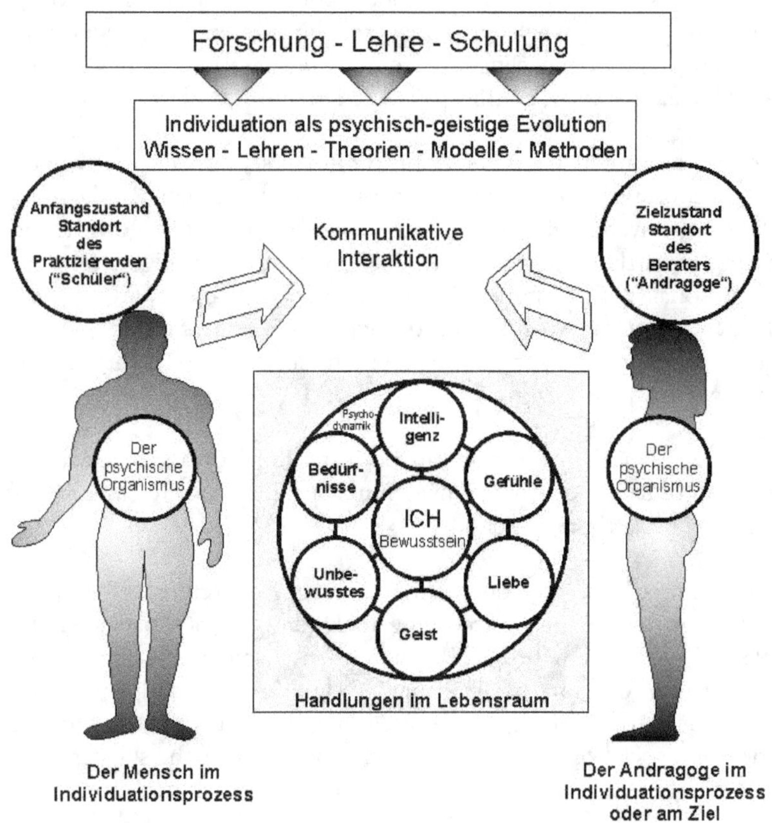

Translation:

Research – teaching- education
Individuation as psychic-spiritual evolution
Knowledge – teachings – theories – models – methods

Communicative interaction

Initial state	Target state
Position of the	position of the participant counselor
("student")	("andragogue")
The psychic organism	The psychic organism
The human in the individuation process	The andragogue in the individuation process or at the goal

Third part of andragogy:

Andragogy as theory and practice is always intertwined with philosophical and anthropological questions, with ideal reflections and with values.

The system of values may not be a political ideology, not a religion in the sense of faith, not a metaphysical resp. ontological speculation and may neither based on esoteric dogma and ideas of any origin. Because these all are subordinated to belief, power, and the play of (neurotic) fantasy. All values and justifications are to tie back to the psychic organism, the individuation, and versatile balanced utilitarian interests of a democratic pluralistic society. The value system is thus tangible, comprehensible, repeatable, and arguable. In this way, the problem of the abuse of science and research through ideology, dogmatism and pure commerce can be reduced, and solved.

Ethics is a sub-discipline of andragogy because, as an independent scientific system, it not only analyzes values (descriptive), but also formulates and operationalizes (prescriptive) values resp. goals for its own cause. This ethics is based on facts of the psychic organism, the individuation process, and the interaction between human and socio-cultural environment. Thematic aspects of this task are a) Philosophical anthropology, (human images); b) Ethics with graded operationalized individual goals (values, norms); c) Symbolism of the psyche as theory of archetypes (as a paradigm, guide).

According to Klafki (1991), goals can be created in a constructive-critical way, which includes the ambiguity and interpretation methodically and discursively. "Morality", "virtue", "maturity", "justice", "loyalty", "truthfulness", "courage" and other overall value principles, we do not determine from an "insight" or a "categorical conscience", but as a construct from the effects of the subsystems of the psychic organism and the growth principles of individuation. The scientific basis for this is provided by the "andragogical psychology" (or the: "psychology of andragogy"). The social context arises automatically. We thus introduce a rather unusual aspect to the education theory. Not a "consensus theory" (Habermas 1968) and not a "discursive validity claim" decides on the accuracy of values but the back-bonding to the psychic life and the habitat. A categorical value discussion resp. value decision becomes the more constructive the more the expertise is associated with the completed individuation. An example may indicate the reach this thesis may: An "education philistine" speaks differently about values (goals) of human education than a sage (in the sense of the highest psychic-spiritual development stage, i.e., the individuation).

"Who wants to dodge valuations, decisions, selection and commitment to the elected, can neither be conductive to education goals nor to education."

(Brezinka 1993, 259). "Helpful ideals" and "useless illusions" must be separated from one another. "We should not only know that ideals and educational goals are indispensable, but also know their dangers and observe our limits" (Brezinka 1993, 259). It remains to be added that human experience in everyday life usually contains a subjective reference to meaning and value, which also always triggers a biographical response.

We therefore consider it a mistake in education science to separate ethics into pre- or extra-scientific area and to understand a scientific-positivistic understanding of science as the only orientation of its conception.

Fourth part-task of andragogy:

The andragogy has its own scientific methodology to develop and to justify its own research practice (action research) and its own understanding of science (theory formation, system formation). The basic questions are: What are the scientific criteria for the andragogy? Which demand has the "prediction"? What is the function of systematic description, the data order and classification? What are typologies and structures? What is the meaning of the explanation of behavior? An idiographic and nomothetic scientific understanding is required from the subject "human and psyche".

The focus is on divergent systems of statements such as: a) Analytical-synthetical (descriptive, structuralized); b) Empirical-technological (descriptive, action-oriented); c) Phenomenological-hermeneutical (descriptive-interpretative); symbolic-archetypal (descriptive-interpretive, deductive-normative); normative-philosophical (ideal and utilitarian prescriptive).

As an epistemological core thesis, we can formulate: The andragogy cannot rely solely on a positivistic understanding of science. We justify this:

Firstly, the human education of pedagogy is not a "nature"-science in which all factors can be clearly operationalized and measured. Most variables cannot be removed from the context of life at all.

Secondly, the human education has its own criteria of scientific to define (scientific understanding), which must be commensurate with the "object" of the research. What is hypothetical and what has theoretical validity is subject to different criteria depending on the "object area" and experience. For example, dreams, imagination, the unconscious, and the resistance have a completely different empirical character and a different logic than nature-scientific objects. The symbolic language of the psyche is a basic fact of being human.

Thirdly, there is no pedagogy in the occidental understanding without love. Love and, for example, life happiness (or life meaning) cannot be operationally reduced to behavioral categories. Psychoanalysis and psychotherapy should also accept the love as an essential psychic force.

Fourthly, the operationalization in the educational field is basically always subjective and diverse. The problem of falsification must be clarified and solved according to the object. Language problems cannot be eliminated.

And fifthly, every scientific activity relates to valuations in every step. Here are some keywords are to be done: Selection of research questions, weighting of the probability, interpretation and association, selection in the complexity and multi-dimensionality, the practical work (e.g., choice of working tools, target definition), the practice as a value, the definition of suffering and disorders, criticism of research field and value judgments about the research results, etc.). We do not consider that a scientific value neutralization of the subject area is feasible. Any attempt in this direction leads to dishonesty and considerable threats for the human education. What applies to pedagogy also applies to andragogy. To clarify and handling of this scientific theoretical problem, there are ways and many existing approaches.

As is well known, the disputation on the positivism dispute did not lead to a result in the sense of a solution. Counter arguments have been put forward to the decisive Weberian theses (see: Stegmüller, Berlin 1973, 45-50; as well as the "Kritische Theorie").

It is no doubt useful to keep scientific statement complexes free from value judgments (Albert; in Topisch 1970, 183) and to design the normative statements systems independently. A positivistic understanding of science (Weber 1968; Popper 1969) is a decision towards rationality. This science understanding is also a decision to a certain standard of living. However, life is always more than rationality. If the science of medicine has healing as its goal, then the andragogy can determine human education to its goal. Which scientific logic can prohibit this or separate it into the non-scientific area?

The partially heavily debated discourse between the three science-theoretical main positions (dialectical-materialistic, empirical-analytical, hermeneutical) seems to have dissolved today. The idea that the human can be led to a humane shaping of the society through enlightenment must be regarded as a failure. Technocratic projects have not fulfilled the expectations. Critical-emancipatory ideals fail because of the real-life conditions. "Anything goes" is declared to be the paradigm of the so-called "postmodernism" (Klane 1991; quoted in: Jank / Meyer 1991, 126). Vinnai brings a key problem of the social scientist to the point: "... the ability of the analyst to understand his own psychic state, is essential for a correct understanding" (Vinnai 1993, 234). In our opinion, the principle applies to all psychic realities: "The scientists construct by his research the research-objective. Therefore, his approach needs the hermeneutical reflection." (Jank / Meyer 1991, 128). Thus, the "truth" becomes a subjective experience component (Musolff / Light Kamps 1993, 686-688, 699). This relation in turn calls for a methodically developed empathy: "Empathy would have to become the matrix (the reference and relation system) in which all scientific activities must be embedded, if they should not remove further and further from human life, if they should not become our inhuman masters instead of our servants and tools" (Grimmer 1993, 295) To the change of the science understanding there is in adult education today also a change in the subject of adult education and a change in the theory-practice understanding (Dewe et al. 1988, 42; see also: VSEB 1991).

The epistemological and methodological publications of the last thirty years fill shelves by meters. The result of a plethora of critical reflections and harshest polemics is: "The science theory has not been able to create in the educational science a common understanding of what the scientific is, what it has to do and how it has to be processed in the science" (Merkens, in Roth 1991, 30). That makes demands and at the same time demands modesty of the science of andragogy. Modesty means for example: "... theories (have) no general validity and no general truth value, must therefore be neither false nor true, they are only more or less helpful and useful for the analysis and possibly tended change and design of realities" (Roth 1991, 63). Empirical adult education has limits that must be taken seriously. It also has its internal problems that must be clarified in the interest of human education, such as this: "At universities is driven dizziness ... In Germany prevails at universities in the philosophical and social science faculties the Hegelian language ... What means that? It means that one cannot discuss with anyone. It doesn't come to a discussion ..." (Popper 1994, 41).

The greatest human and epistemological challenge for the andragogy arises from the fact that Freud's central sentence "There is no authority above the reason" (Freud 1974, 162; "Die Zukunft einer Illusion") is wrong. So, we do not restrict his "religion critical reflections"; because it is not the dogma that is to be discussed here. The "rationality of psychoanalysis" (Heim 1993) does not reach the human where his being is essentially founded and existentially alive, namely in the love, in the meaning and in the spirit. The force of love, the principles of the spirit and thus the rooted meaning of the being prohibit it to consider the classical psychoanalysis as a 'categorical' education concept. Life and meaning horizons extended and deepened by love and spirit are resulting real life closeness to the education theory of andragogy. Anyone who educates humans and does not reach these categories would do well to keep this limitation transparent. Otherwise, one runs danger to legitimize scientifically the transcendental self-denial and to consider scientific authority as non-existent or at least irrelevant.

This is the core problem of psychoanalysis and, for example, also the behavioral psychology, insofar as these ultimately limit itself to a human image that is based on a rationally ascertainable stimulus-response mechanism (drive and habit). The main root of the misunderstanding lies in the fixed idea: "The sexuality is motivation ground and center of our world experience as a sensual-social experience, and it is the central axis of the world experience back to the beginnings of ontogeny" (quote in: Heim 1993, 451). Certainly, the not balanced integrated sexuality causes some individual and collective dramas, with and without early childhood neuro genesis; but we see no argument to declare the sexuality to the center of human being and life. In our opinion in psychoanalysis is hidden the greatest and last of all resistances: The denial of the spirit as the central force in the psychic system. With it the experience of God (divinity of life or resp. being human) is eliminated. The constantly tried deicide happens obviously not only by the refusal to recognize the psychic-spiritual life in general, but also in the attempt to represent the drive almost as the cause of human being and as the boundary of horizon of rational experience.

If the pedagogues and andragogues can agree on what is their mandate as scientist (in relation to human education) because they themselves can systematically develop it, this is the constructive decision basis for policy as the supreme authority of science practice. The mutual communication and common target finding, then is based on the facts that both partners supply and lead dialectically to a synthesis.

As an empiric science and as humanities, the andragogy describes facts and relations in words, sentence structures and in images resp. symbols. It defines the methods for achieving certain goals in the inner and outer psychic life reality. As normative science it concludes educational goals (standards), that serve as action orientation. These valuations have an empirical justification connection and are rooted in the philosophical anthropology. The central criterion of the science is therefore: "The only important question is whether the methods used to gain experiences are appropriate for the object, the human in his historical reality, whether they are capable to cope with the unmutilated and powerful reality of the soul from its lowest to its highest possibilities (Dilthey 1894) "(Thomae 1988, 7).

The philosophical anthropology as a science cannot impose a duty on anyone. However, the scientist has for his own duty decision to take responsibility and to represent this before the public. In addition, the duty is a matter of the individual and all if of the state (Kamlah 1973, 95-98). We understand these two dimensions of scientific understanding dialectically, as parts which complement one another creatively and meaningfully. Here is neither space for ideologies nor for any dogmatism.

A metatheoretical basic problem in adult education is: "Does the theory of adult education exist?" Tietgens thinks (1986, 35): "There is a lack of theory"; and what is offered on theories is not relevant for the practice. Furthermore, we can ask: "Why is there still no theory of adult education?" But such formulations we consider as linguistic structures that create an unreal problem. These questions cannot be answered resp. their implicit claim cannot be redeemed.

The "theory of adult education" is a fiction. Because there are various understandings of "theory", versatile (accepted) subject areas and quite different institutional and individual interests. A plurality of cross-scientific networks can be constructed, for example:

Sociology, knowledge sociology, interactionism, interpretation model theory, political economy, education economy, systems theory, linguistic analysis theories, socialization theories (educational, sociological, interactionist, psychoanalytical etc.), depth psychology, educational psychology, behavioral psychology, field theory resp. wholeness psychology, history resp. theories about cultural change etc. (cf. Dewe et al. 1988; Arnold 1985; Nonne 1985; Baacke et al. 1985; Kupffer 1990).

If we consider that the pedagogy only since around 200 years is established as an independent enlightening discipline, and that there was always fashion trends and will give them again and again, that the humanity has many millennia unwritten history in front of itself (hope so we), then a long-time sustainable and directing paradigm for adult education is of greatest value and meaning; by that we mean: The human education is in its core substance, namely in the "psychic organism" and the "individuation", fundamentally defined and designed educational-theoretically and didactically for the andragogy as acting science. This is the long overdue turning point in the science of human education, that is, pedagogy and andragogy.

We would like to make a few more comments on practical vocational training:

A central message of our study is: The general human education resp. personality development can and should (must) be designed as an independent department of adult education. This includes a correspondingly specific postgraduate training of pedagogues and andragogues that is different from the "competence concepts" for adult educators in the field "vocational training", "general education" and "political education". The requirements for the competence of course instructors are different there than in our conception of human education (cf. Krämer / Walter 1993, 130-135); they define themselves primarily didactically. In the social-psychological oriented adult education, the subjective side of pedagogical action plays a significant role in the professionalization. That is why, for example, Arnold (1985, 127) requires: "The dealing with the own interpretation models is therefore prerequisite for dealing with foreign interpretation models. Autobiographical reflection, that is dealing with oneself, is the prerequisite for pedagogical understanding and dealing with others".

The "professionalized processing of biography and identity" (Winkler 1993, 143) is demanded, it appears to us, in most (all?) conceptions of adult education. We cannot emphasize enough the fact that the fulfillment of the individuation is a "sine qua non" for each pedagogue and andragogue, who wants to practice "human education" resp. personality development comprehensively and thoroughly.

The practical vocational training of andragogy consists in part of training of working methods. On the other hand, it is an irresponsible contradiction - that is a value judgment that is based on the matter - that someone practices andragogy as a professional activity without own systematic and in-depth self-knowledge and without own advanced individuation. This practical study and the own training are to be installed in a post-graduate education resp. further training. It can formally be controlled by a suitably based profession, but not from the state integrated in the science.

It is to put the demand that each university professor of pedagogy and andragogy and generally each andragogue (in human education active) should complete a substantiated systematic self-education in the sense of individuation, like the training analysis of psychoanalysts. We put the claims even higher than it is generally required in the psychoanalysis. The third phase of individuation should, in our opinion, already be developed substantially to exercise such a profession with adequate inner competence and spiritual responsibility. Instead of "training analysis" (or "study analysis"; see: Balint 1981, 328) we propose to simply speak of "the own individuation".

For discussion, we also put: The profession of andragogical practice is to enable in the same way as psychologists, graduate teachers, home educators, special educators, social -workers and adult educators (etc.). The problem of different levels of education can be resolved by supplementing programs. The practical competence includes among others: Work techniques, system diagnostics, process evaluation, case studies, supervision, and didactics. We have our own planning drafts for this, which we cannot go into here.

This outlines the key problem areas for the andragogy as a science and practice of human education:

1. Andragogy as an independent, systematic, interdisciplinary subject, including its science understanding (theory-practice-ethics)

2. Andragogical field of work: Topics resp. tasks of education, target groups; definition and diagnosis of crises, conflicts, disorders, and suffering

3. Methods of andragogical professional practice: Psychagogical and alternative work forms, counseling, teaching, meditation forms and mental training

4. Professionalization of andragogy: Education (curriculum, requirement, qualification profile, organization), stakeholders.

With these four task areas we have outlined the andragogy as science and practice of human education. Only as a personal assessment and valuation, the author can note that the placement of this andragogy should not be understood as a "sub-science of pedagogy". The human education as a scientific field should in our opinion, even in addition figure as a fully independent academic institution beside the main social science areas.

But from our point of view, we can only express an opinion on this, which others also represent: "Personality development (as adult education) is to be viewed as a separate sector" (Dominicé / Finger 1991, 63). This also enables unique opportunities for which the traditional social sciences are not yet open: A paradigm shift in terms of content and epistemology (cf. Capra 1992, 127-137; Grof 1993, 13-100).

Compared to the departments of philosophy, pedagogy (educational science) and psychoanalysis / psychotherapy / psycho-counseling, there is a division and delimitation that is already practiced in some places, but without postgraduate training. The following illustration gives an orientation about the cornerstones of the science of andragogy.

Illustration 6: The Cornerstones of Andragogy

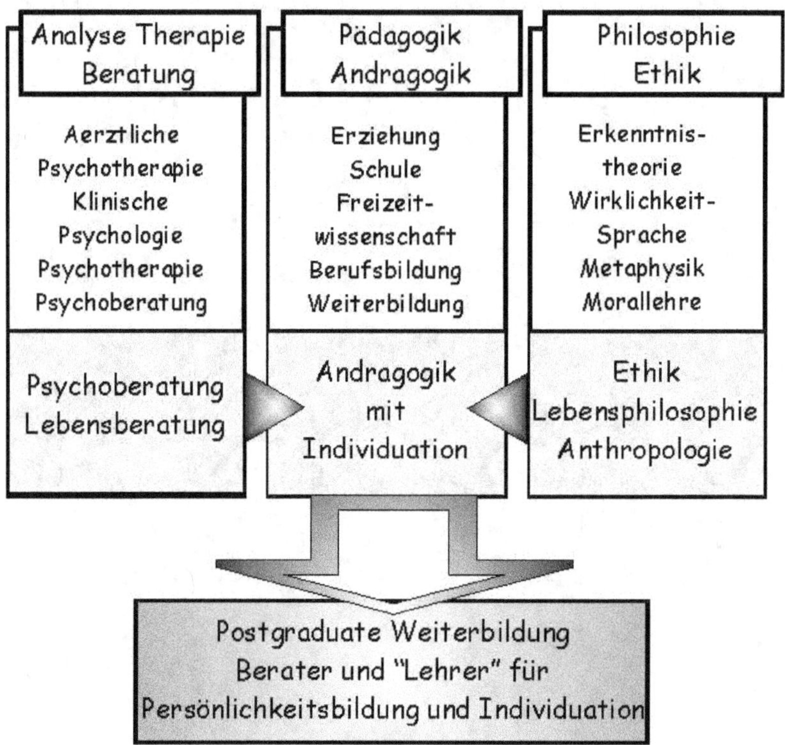

Translation:

Analytical therapy	Pedagogy	Philosophy
Counseling	Andragogy	Ethics
Medical	Upbringing	Knowledge-
psychotherapy	school	theory
Clinical	Leisure-	Reality-
psychology	science	Language
psychotherapy	Vocational training	Metaphysics
psychocounseling	further education	moral doctrine
Psychocounseling	Andragogy	Ethics
Life counseling	with	life philosophy
	individuation	anthropology

Postgraduate further education
counselor and teacher for
personality development an individuation

With this model, we want to highlight an accent, not turn the science of pedagogy on its head. Of course, there are term problems that give rise to critical discussion. In the practice of science, we see a fragmentation of pedagogy and adult education into individual sub-disciplines. We see in the term "andragogy" first an address designation, and not a construct that contains specific theories of human education (and excludes others).

We can call our "andragogy" as "general andragogy", the schooling and professional further education as "special andragogy". But that does not solve the problem. It is to be expected that the critical questioning of the so-called "general pedagogy" will be transferred to our concept. There is talk of the "fall of general pedagogy" (Winkler 1994) and of the "retreat of general pedagogy" (Krüger 1994).

The general pedagogy is reduced to "historical social science", and: "Practical claims it (the general education) will better not raise ... it will possibly be ascetic and skeptical" (Winkler 1994, 113). Such amputations we see as denigration that is based more on a protest then on critical-meditative reflections on human education. Krüger is also critical of the "loss of meaning of general pedagogy" (Krüger 1994, 116-121), but creates a new catalog of tasks based on new pedagogical basic ideas: "The term of learning becomes a central process category, education as the acquisition of knowledge about the world ... will be a trendsetting target category for educational action processes inside and outside of educational institutions" (Kruger, 1994, 122).

We do not share this education understanding. It is far too narrow and testifies a human image that is appalling reductionistic and ignorant of the categories of love, spirit and the process of individuation. Probably the reviews on the "general education" reflect above all a personal search for identity of the authors that results that the person in the (emancipatory) education science is only understood in empirical categories.

If the general education and the (general) andragogy do not achieve to develop the education of the human psychic-spiritually and practically in a new way, one will not later have to wonder if still more people become accessible to sects, for extreme political ideologies and dogmatic ecclesiastical practice. What Galbraith (1979) identifies and decries as "arrogance of the well-fed", we can, perhaps a bit hard, recognize as the "arrogance of empiricism and materialism" (the "behaviorist doctrine"; Lorenz 1993, 8) in some educational science positions. This doctrine contributes significantly to moral and cultural breakdown.

The "turning point" in pedagogy resp. andragogy also has considerable consequences at the level of experts, professors, and education researchers: Neurosis and narcissism have there no more place in the future. The completion of the own individuation will be the indispensable prerequisite for practicing the profession and characterize the professional person resp. his agogic competence as a quality feature.

Paradigm of Human Education for the 21st Century

A revised form of education category is expected by the adult education. Education is inextricably linked with emancipation and liberation from feudalism, myths, and superstitions since the Enlightenment. With the reason the chains of immaturity should be overcome for "liberty, equality and brotherliness. Education intended to abolish the privileges of nobility and clergy. And from Nietzsche to Adorno (1970), "half-education" was an often-lamented social evil, indeed the mortal enemy of education. This is how the education problems arose earlier. Today, other aspects force on: "Our endangered society requires more than ever an inward looking to reason, responsibility (i.e., being aware of the consequences of one's acting) and humanity, i.e., education" (Siebert, in Mager et al. 1991, 28).

Questions create new search movements: Aren't the previous education categories perhaps still topical? What is about the maturity in terms of advertising, TV-consumption, sexuality, sects and psycho-religious movements, multi-national corporations, banking and insurances, car and mobility, environmental behavior, consumption, and experience coercion ... just to call a few key words? It is more than questionable whether the human can develop himself responsibly and then control himself with reason alone. Apart from that: Does he even want that? Can the human want that? And what price is the individual willing to pay for his personality development? We can also ask from the other perspective: What can the science contribute to adult education, perhaps together with the responsibles of institutions, so that the humans attend educational programs to raise the awareness (and correct their models of interpretation), for example about "desolidarization phenomena, suppressions of ecological and military threats, competitive pressure, achievement ideologies, neo-conservatism with nationalistic characteristics, obedience to science and hostility to science" (Müller, in: Mader 1991, 118)? Without a doubt, the presence today puts its own education requirements to science and practice institutions with all delimitation against psychotherapy, psychoanalysis, and social pedagogy resp. social work. Incredibly special problems arise in connection with the reunification of Germany and generally with the unification process of Europe: "Are we asked?" (Lenzen 1994, 31).

Every educational theory, as far as we look back to Kant, Humboldt, Herbart, Pestalozzi, and others, is also an answer to the historical situation, in two respects: Firstly, the social conditions and, secondly, the knowledge about the human and his psychic life. Education has thus always been understood dialectically in the relation between human and world. The education goals revolve around self-determination, freedom, emancipation, autonomy, maturity, reason, and self-activity (Klafki 1993, 19). So that these goals cannot be determined as subjectivistic, they are already embedded in "humanity and mankind" (tied back to reason) by Kant, in the interaction with the concrete world by Humboldt, and rooted in practical-active abilities resp. actions in life (connected with what he versatile addresses with the word "heart") by Pestalozzi. The primary goal of humanistic education concept revolves around the value of global humanity (nations, peoples, cultures), including community.

"Self-realization", as it represents the classical education theory of pedagogy for 200 years, is more than individualism, more than subjectivism, more than psychologism and more than just rational or cognitive-emotional functionalism. Continuously, we find in education theories the connection to the concrete individual and collective life reality, to the principle of reason (goal and meaning reflection), to moral responsibility and to aesthetic dimensions, i.e. the formation of sensitivity, aesthetic judgment, ability to play and sociability (Klafki 1993, 15-41). In particular, the "spiritualization of the soul" by cultural life and cultural acting and the "contacting with the divine" are part of the formation order of education (Spranger 1973).

Our education theory of andragogy is in the sense in this tradition, with its roots dating back to ancient Greece, to Plato and Aristotle. Education already existed 2.500 years ago, reflected at different angles, including: Knowledge of life age and its chronology, problem solving, this-sided life guidance, education methods, education ability and educational neediness as anthropological condition, moral improvement as a goal, public and private interest, and the scientific reflection (after Wiersing 1986, 19-26). Again, and again, the metaphysical element of "education" is newly searched and formulated: Education should rise the human to a last instance unconditioned, to the divine, for the "pure" human being (Pleines, 1986, 35).

It remains to be seen whether metaphysics is finally abolished with so-called logical empiricism (Schleichert 1975), or whether at best new claims are to be made to the language of philosophy. Schlick, Carnap, Neurath, Hahn and Kraft (1968) probably threw out the child with the bath. With language philosophy resp. analytic philosophy (see Savigny 1970), various border problems of physics, evolution, and para psychology (see Koestler 1989) cannot be cleared, certainly not smoothed out. Aims such as "perfecting the personality", "spiritualizing of the human" or "through education to freedom" are formulations from the 19th century (Zdarzil 1986, 47, 49). They are old European concerns and are up to date again today in new words.

Future-oriented, we have revealed the main lines of the dramatic worldwide developments of the state of the world in our earlier published book "Our future in your hand" (1988). In the first chapter of this work, individual aspects of the state of our time are taken up. The education theory of andragogy is related to its social responsibility (and its engagement) in this historical reference. Personality development in the sense of individuation includes the individual, leads to community, and shapes the world from the result of its forming. Self-responsibility is extended to responsibility for others, for the democratic state, for the world and therefore also for the course of history.

Illustration 7: Education in Networking

Translation:
Exo-life-worlds in the habitat
Everyday world
From the biographic shaping to individuation
The psychic organism with the acting

Everyone of all of us has a right to adequate education to enable him to live this responsibility, that has been advocated the education theories since the 18th century. Furthermore, as we think, everyone also has the duty to acquire and realize this education. In concrete terms, this has led to compulsory schooling and vocational training, as well as to the right to "permanent education" since around twenty years. Flitner clearly formulates the necessity of adult education: "… that adult people should be further formed and educated, Herbart has described as inadmissible. It seemed to him unworthy; men and women are mature and responsible for themselves; our entire common life is based on this … In fact, we are constantly aware that the humans think dependently and 'don't know what they are doing' "(Flitner, W.: Erwachsenenbildung 1982; Aufgabe der Erwachsenenbildung heute (1966), 279). The "lifelong learning" is declared to be the principle of education, not without fears and doubts (Sitzmann 1984, 93-107): Should the human go to school for a lifetime? What is the meaning of lifelong learning? Has maturity never been reached? Does everyone always have to learn new behaviors and attitudes? Sitzmann says: "Education is in principle not to be completed" (1984, 102-103). Education is not just an external act but also an inner process that opens new aspects (life topics) in every life phase. Here takes place an individual input for the collective evolution of the human. The principle of lifelong learning receives a normative force that exceeds widely actual learning processes. The human personality is declared to be "the most important thing in life" (Samolevcev, in Benning 1986, 10). Then we can demand the same right and the same duty for personality development and individuation. The individual freedom of thinking and living may at first glance be in question.

Let us therefore briefly consider this problem of freedom. First, the freedom is addressed, which says that everyone can do with his life whatever he wants: He could also throw it away or ruin it in any way. There is another kind of understanding of freedom that cannot be integrated into our education idea: The idea that everyone could "actualize" (update) himself as it fits him and take from the resources of life what he wants and how much he wants; or indulge in "indifference of interests and lack of impulse" (Derbolav 1987, 125); or in philosophical terms: Everyone could represent ideas and live out ideas that just he likes. We have shown in various places that this decomposes a state from within and destroys it in long term. In the opinion of many critical voices, including scholars, the destruction is in full swing.

We reflect the freedom that we mean in the context of the inner "spirit" in dream and imagination. The human has the inner freedom to live the cooperation with this spiritual force or to refuse it, to make it a duty or to negate it. Philosophically and worldly this freedom could be granted till today.

In the coming millennium, it will no longer be assimilable socially and politically in the collectively. The threshold limit of collapse is too close and had become for all to dangerous. Freedom without back bonding ("religio") to spirit and love always leads to a destructive development in the collective. This is what the history and the present teach us. Inner harmony and holistic development of psychic life cannot be achieved without the spirit and the love. It should be noted in the margin that the term "spirit" has a different meaning here than, for example, for Spranger. "Spirit" means for us: The inner spiritual force that speaks through dreams and meditation to the "I" and that makes possible through inner experience of the main archetype (circle-cross-mandala and generally the archetypes) the encounter with the inner divine and allows an intelligent design variety in the inner psychic life.

The problem of freedom in relation to the inner spirit and the force of love implicitly thematizes the freedom to individuation. Concretely asked: Does the human have the freedom to live the individuation or to refuse it? If we consider the problem educational-theoretically, then the question is: Is the human obliged to form himself in all his psychic forces as the intelligence functions, feelings, needs, love, the unconscious, the will, controls, and all other psychic subsystems of the psychic organism? If the individuation with the aim to be a living image of the circle-cross-mandala is the actual transcendental and original psychic-spiritual evolution, then the question of freedom is again different: Does the human have the freedom, to live this evolutionary spiritual back bonding or to deny it? We speak in this context of the "collective guilt", i.e., we represent the thesis that this process - this "religio" ("back bonding to the inner original") - ultimately every human owes himself. From this we conclude: Freedom consists ontologically, philosophically, spiritually, and psychologically in the fulfillment of the inner being. Each suppression and escape from this self-responsibility always creates inner and external commitment. In plain language: The freedom that most people mean is not freedom at all.

Again, the term "self-realization" comes to mind. With our anchoring in the archetype of the circle-cross-mandala, the term "education" gets a Christian dimension, but there mostly in other words: Full development of the inherent form laws, realization of the divinely ordained Christian human image (Blaschek, 1986, 179). In comparison, the humanistic education term turns out to be 'purely needs-based', functional and not teleological, rooted in learning theory and without "telos" (Ruprecht 1984, 81-89). If education includes "meaning", then this term transcends the purely empirical factual reality. Braun says: "The life is the place where the question of meaning can be clarified" (Braun, in: Benning 1986, 336). But life contains more than work and leisure, more than wish fulfillment and competences, more than abilities and skills, more than human dignity and learning psychological general education (such as thinking and speaking clearly, looking carefully, and listening patiently, distinguishing, and deciding, imagining, and generalizing, designing, and valuing, new learning and relearning; according to von Hentig 1985, 151). That is the key to the problem: Who does not go through the process of individualization can never experience this "more".

So that our education theory receives a transcendental, spiritual and philosophical rootedness. If the individual deviates from this inner duty, this may in some cases be done without damage (which, however, is not guaranteed). In many cases this leads to a destructive development which is versatile verified psychoanalytically and psychologically (also "spiritual-psychologically"). If very many people avoid this inner responsibility (self-guilt), this leads with all the instrumental opportunities for lifestyle and state leadership (industry, economy, capital, communication systems, weapons arsenals and much more) soon, due to the exponential growth in all life systems to an irreversible worldwide catastrophe (Schellhammer 1988). The "education as deployment of peace" (Heitkämper 1986, 275-279) can be easily integrated here. Nuclear bombs, atomic power plants and genetic engineering as possibilities of total self-destruction makes education to a "deployment to which peace depends" .... so that "the human does not test its limits to nature and thus destroys the mankind" (Heitkämper 1986, 278).

The collective must decide which freedoms (without spirit and without love) and which self-actualization space (without individuation) should and can be granted to everyone in the community (family, group, state).

It is a fact that the education theory of the last 200 years in the implementation of its education mandate has by no means been able to bring its ideals to life. The ideals of ancient Greece (the good, the true, the inner harmony, the virtues, etc.), taken up in neo-humanism, did not take effect in the people. Neither the "eternal truths" of metaphysics, nor the experience-based foundation of values of the empiricism could record resounding "successes". Augustine's "love of God" and "love of world" have also failed, in mutual connection as expression of eternal legality of the divine in the human (Jaspers 1959, 366/367). Even Thomas Aquinas could not lead humanity to what he saw with the "ultimate goal" and "the eternal law" as the inner duty.

The core question of every education theory and didactics is: From where do we get the highest meaning resp. its legitimacy? From utilitarian considerations as an alternative to "divine laws" (Frankena 1972)? Or from criticist thinking systems (Holzenkamp 1972)? Or from a situation ethics? The reduction to lust, happiness and profit has not proven itself as a basis for education until today. Kant's categorical imperative is and remains for philosophers and those who can think of this level of abstraction as a kind of spiritual substitute: "... never process in another way than that I can also want ..." (Kant 1970, 40, 45). The reason is the "divinely working principle in the human", is an expression of God. So, the ought to be based on the reason, superior to the will (Kant 1966, 130-135). The "categorical imperative" - the "holy duty" - becomes an element of the reason and the will. Nietzsche gives us the answer later: God is dead. One puts the values into the nothing. Neither the "harmonious human" of Schleiermacher, nor the "moral human" of Pestalozzi, nor the "emancipated human" of Mollenhauer could ever reach the masses. The people have widely not become capable, to perceive individually and socially its humanist responsibility.

A problem here is whether we leave with our concept of education the scope of science and thus we move in speculative (metaphysical) spheres. Because scientificity is required for adult education: "Today we need scientific knowledge to shape our living environment and to understand it" ... "... there is the need of conveyance of science for the purpose of life orientation" (Zdarzil, in Benning 1986, 51, 54). Without a doubt, questions of meaning and value cannot be traced back sufficiently to empirical categories.

The decision to certain values is no scientific achievement of knowledge, at most a relation achievement of the scientist compared to his activity and his research results. There are target aspects of the education term that can be included empirical-anthropologically, to a certain extent in behavioristic categories linguistically and observable. We think of human dignity, virtues, love, creativity, responsibility, solidarity, humanity, etc. But never, we think, can, for example, human dignity be understood as the "origin and goal of education", as Ruprecht und Sitzmann express it from many points of view in their volume XVI of the Weltenburger Akademie (1988). Because the human dignity itself is, in our conception, in turn, an expression of the possibilities of the "living image being of the circle-cross-mandala".

The practice of education theory has previously not disposed on the today's scientific knowledges about the psychic organism and the individuation process. With our study, we have here presented the comprehensive bases. The concept of education theory of andragogy is bordered in that. The next step is to create a concept of didactics for the "human education in the group".

The human education is in formal sense "general education" resp. a constitutive part of the so-called general education (Klafki 1993, 40): It is all-sided; it applies to all people; it includes the all people common living space; it forms the basis for constructive critic ability; it aims at enlightenment (primarily about the psychic life and interactions between habitat - psychic life); it encourages the appropriate fact and action competence; and it forms the human in its psychic "basic dispositions" (cf. Jank / Meyer 1991, 177). In our opinion, human education is an indispensable part of "categorical education" (Klafki), as we outline it with our study. Kerstiens (1986, 261) defines "education" taking into account such aspects as follows: Education is the "process (or its result), in which the human forms knowledges and insights, employments and attitudes, skills and abilities as acting disposition which he needs as a person, as a participant in a culture and a member of a society, in his relation to the whole reality, in order to be able to live a meaningful life in his habitat." These include over-reaching goals such as: Informedness, judgment ability, value orientation, creativity, acting competence, relation willingness.

Klafki calls for a new general education concept as an orientation frame for the further development or reform of our education system - from the child to the adult education (Klafki 1993, 53). At the same point he says: "Such a concept ... can only be (justified) as a comprehensive, at the same time educational and political draft with a view to the needs, problems, dangers and possibilities of our present and the foreseeable future." We also find this concern also in Litt: "Clear insight (is necessary) into the interdependence and responsibility of everyone, into the system of basic democratic order and into its various dangers, for example through the attitude without me, through greed for power and abuse of power, branding of opponents as heretics, wildness of political style, dishonesty and ideology, destructive criticism, radicalism and totalitarianism, but also trivialization: It is not just about insight, but also about attitude and practicing the right style." (Quoted in: Reble 1993, 370).

In the general education, Klafki, Mollenhauer, Derbolav, Brezinka and some other pedagogues from earlier decades integrate social dimensions as well as psychological, social and ethical dimensions: Questions and problems of the historical present, the looming future, the (individual and collective) dangers and problems, the corresponding tasks, the previous approaches of thinking and solving; and on the other hand: Education of cognitive possibilities, the development of interpersonal relationship possibilities, aesthetic perception and design possibilities and the ethical and political decision-making and action abilities. Siebert (in Benning 1986, 232-233) speaks of four types of adult education: 1) Imparting knowledge; 2) Behavior change; 3) Self-experience; and 4) Professional qualification. Senzky (in: Ruprecht / Sitzmann 1986, 45-58) integrates three aspects into education: The material self (body), the social self (position, roles) and the spiritual self (values, Weltanschauung). According to Siebert (1986, 131- 136) a general education oriented towards the world of life implies in particular: 1) Differentiation, expansion of self and world understanding; 2) Self-Aufklärung; 3) Dealing with cultural traditions; and 4) Ability to act responsibly. The anthropological basic need contained therein is self-evident for him.

Let us briefly consider the term "qualification" in this context. In a narrower sense, it means the ability to perform a specific activity, especially professional work functions. Course and diploma are the main characteristics of this term. We can also look at this term in an expanded manner from the point of view of life competences. Who wants to drive a car, needs a driver's license. This implies the successful completion of theoretical and practical training with test completion. To marry and raise children, the Europeans need neither theoretical nor practical training, and certainly not a certificate. The situation is well known: High divorce rates, many broken marriages, and an enormous number of "accidents" in the upbringing of children. In a society with almost limitless modernization and rationalization, with an almost limitless mobility euphoria and with consumer options that are no longer overlookable, many people "skid". Crime, psycho-somatic sufferings, social conflicts, environmental destructions, and damages of all kinds are the consequences. We conclude from this: The human in a highly industrialized society needs special qualifications for a constructive life in the personal and community habitat. This serves to create stable livelihoods, the formation of an own identity, life mastery, constructive relationship life, raising children and the dealing with the week, and elderly.

In this way, we expand the concept of qualification from functional rationality (vocational training, retraining, etc.) to meaning elements and life practice. If the science of adult education should be a response to life practice - and that is predominantly accepted among experts - then, we find some life circumstances that urge to a qualification, according to the acquirement of certain life competences. Considering the qualification in the narrower sense as an instrument for life mastery, then the (vocational) further training does not just lead to social advancement, but it implies key qualifications (Siebert 1977) as adaptability ability and transfers effort of basic abilities (thinking, self-motivation, self-control etc.), which affect the personal life world and the existence orientation (meaning finding).

Whoever interprets shortened further training as "value increasing instrument of 'manpower'", in our opinion, underestimating the chances of a deeper and broader generalizing effect. However, this requires that vocational further training is not technocratic reduced but includes the personality development and life education indirectly (e.g., through role specific reflections). The life is also a kind of "school". The adult education cannot decline the people this "school". Nevertheless, the enormously increased complexity of social conditions poses the problem of qualification also for the living environment so that the individual can master the psychically and socially increased demands. The pragmatic variables such as economic growth, unemployment or technical change put claims on adult education to prepare training concepts for the requirements resp. competence deficits. However, the humans are also preserver of the spiritual-cultural asset. This may not be separated in education theory and not neglected in the practice. So, we see a dialectical interweaving between the professional qualification and the life-related qualification.

In our opinion there is in adult education no monopole apportionment in the processing of empirical problems to work and leisure. The question of meaning arises in all life areas, including the professional further training. The interactions, for example, always have symbolic meaning content, at the workplace mostly going beyond the purely technical action repertoire. Changes at the workplace, through new technical requirements and through subjective biographical factors are pushing for assistance through the science of adult education, whether in the context of adaptation demands, either in combination with the age-related mental development (e.g., midlife crisis and identity formation, anticipation of the third age). The meaningful reflection is part of the ability, in private as well as in professional life. Thus, the term "education" cannot be understood as "purely empiric" on the one hand and "purely hermeneutic" (with sense afflicted actions) on the other hand. Education is subject related, implies biographical and socio- cultural aspects; education in the working world includes the area of deeper networking to the subject and its life world. The adult education as science finds here enough legitimacy, to show these interrelationships to its practice, and to simultaneously introduce new aspects, where the everyday consciousness and the subjective experience in every respect contains shortened and simplified ideas (pre-knowledge, pre-theories). The achievable restructuring and expansion of the interpretation models (Arnold 1984) contains opportunities for the individual and the society.

For the educational theory of andragogy, we supplement the catalog of "general education" with: "All psychic subsystems and the individuation as a psychic-spiritual education process". This may be understood as a further development of Spranger's "typology of the soul life", especially his concern to comprehend the "whole person" (with the "objective spirit" and the divine) in an educational (forming) way. In our opinion, the individuation is the answer to the searched "final form of the mature and responsible human"

(Roth). It is free from ideology and dogmatics; it is the scientifically based factual back bonding to the psychic-spiritual human and his living space. In our opinion, this is the only reasonable alternative to an anchoring of education theory resp. the "highest goals" in the "laws of God" or in a (for example) Leninist-Marxist human image with all the corresponding consequences. At most, the status quo would remain as reality or the "nothing" as the starting point for the goals and values determination (Kraft 1 968, 101). However, we do not consider this a debatable option.

Sociologists and pedagogues paint a picture of the situation of the human in Europe that contains two main characteristics: Risks and loss of value (Beck 1986, Brezinka 1994; to name just two authors). The humans are strongly directed from the outside, released from previous constraints (also from mythologies) and tied to the "here and now experience culture" through offers and purchasing power. This leads to a strong simplification of reality and to a personality development that ignores values. The strong experience orientation (Schulze, 1992; Opaschowski; in: Klein 1993) causes instability in standards and disorientation. The "value insecure society" is caught in a "culture and value crisis" (Brezinka 1994). The value-based education is required again (Brezinka 1994), a development of the personality with sub-elements such as "critical self-concept, concrete acting capacity, social responsibility, yes to the own life" (Wollenweber 1994, 3-26) as well as "moral sensitivity, reflexivity, rational argumentation ability" (Hufer, 1993, 314-316). The adult education must be tied to values again.

Value commitment as education mandate is, in our opinion, an education task of andragogy. This differs the andragogy from today's "adult education", although certain overlaps are undoubtedly given. The professional training may intend a value binding, but in a different sense than personality development and individuation.

Learning a language, a technology, a law handling, or a foreign culinary art can educate people (e.g., to attitudes). But whoever goes to a language course wants to learn the language; anyone who realizes a computer course in his own company intends certain relevant qualifications and not "psychocatharsis", "conscience building" or "will strengthening".

We do not consider professional training resp. company training to be "categorical" in the sense of our theoretical foundations of andragogy. That is why we propose a classification in the job name: Andragogues are responsible for the human education; "Adult educators" are teachers in a particular factual area of the professional realities and certain life realities. The differences are sufficiently clear that we also consider a division into "general andragogy" (i.e., human education in the narrower sense) and "special andragogy" (i.e., professional training) to be justified.

What we set out here under the generic term "didactics" is for example in American literature called "andragogic concept", "applied andragogy" or "andragogical process" (Ingalls 1973. Cf. SVEB 1980, No.4, translation Rohrer). The seven steps of this process are: 1) Creating a learning environment; 2) Finding a structure for two-way planning; 3) Clarifying interests, needs and valuations; 4) Formulating goals; 5) Designing learning activities; 6) Conducting learning activities; 7) Evaluating results (understood also as need clarification). We mean that this process only becomes "andragogical" when it is based on an education theory for human education. Didactically, we translate the need assessment as to "start with the disposition of the participants".

The "customer orientation" as a strategic guiding principle already poses problems with advertising. It would be problematic for andragogy, and would have to be called pure commerce, if the andragogy only wants to teach what "is in demand on the market". We do not know whether it is possible with a comprehensive journalistic clearing up (advertising) to generate resp. to make aware and to clear those needs that the human education wants to address in its core. To put it bluntly, pornography in Germany may expand its sales from around 60 billion € per year to 100 billion fasters than the human education in andragogy reaches a modest billion € in sales.

Or another example: How can one make it clear to young people on the street who are inclined to violence, that they should first learn to understand their psychic situation (including the ideologization of their emotional state and their consciousness) to find, resp., go paths of solutions with love and spirit? Or: How can one bring those people who treat everything strange and different with hatred to educate themselves in their psychic-spiritual life to then be able to deal appropriately with the strange and different? Such examples can be expanded to many key topics, e.g.: Leisure activities, risk of accidents, risk of addiction, crime, gangs, relationships, sexuality, upbringing, health risks, environmental behavior, the ability to love, etc. A lot of public relations work will be necessary to motivate adults across Europe in East and West for self- education.

We have developed a concept of andragogy which, when confronted with practice, poses a crucial problem. If we ask the experts of practice, what are the challenges of adult education, we get from the European Conference "Adult Education in the future Europe", held in St. Gallen (Switzerland, 2.9.-08.09.1991), the following key words: Nationalism, xenophobia, population growth (in the south), armor, pollution, emigration, threat of war, Islamist specific enemy images, violence, archaic, dramatic changes in Europe, growing leisure, cultural encounters, nationality building and the needs of business and industry (see: SVEB 1992 , 9, 21, 42, 43, 47, 48, 60). The adult education should help to enable and to understand the political, economic, and social changes (Oglesby, SVEB, 1992, 9). The new work and life conditions are central tasks of "adult educators". The "dramatic changes in Europe" (dramatical changes) are the actual new challenges for the andragogy.

In this report (lectures, talks, summaries) the area of "personality development" is hardly discussed. It is just mentioned: "Women need to be especially trained psychologically, to strengthen their self-conscious and to learn to struggle for their concerns". (Dörig, in SVEB 1992, 83) Hoggart points out the spiritual targets, that still were alive in the 19th century in adult education:

"Insight in the personal development" (Hoggart, in SVEB 1992, 32) is a goal of adult education for him; this also includes the belief in meaning and purpose. Müller refers to the need to open new dimensions in world understanding, to revise frozen ideas and to set formation processes in motion (Müller, in: SVEB 1992, 20-27). Sporadically only appears the word "personality development".

Neither about a substantial human education nor about the vital "key problems" in the life that "hit" everyone during life, we find something in this report. If "andragogy" is interpreted as "professional further training" and the meaning "andragogical" is reduced to general didactic aspects (Dubs, in: SVEB 1992, 35), then this type of adult education will have consequences in the future. If the adult education will be focused at the principle of customer orientation, at demand analyzes in compagnies and oriented to profit-strategy approaches (of industry and economy), it remains an essential part of the human on the track. That has inevitable "long-term consequences". Because the psychoanalysis has unequivocally and proven this: The suppressed and not progressively-constructively formed (unfolded) psychic life of the human always strikes back destructively, both individually and collectively. The psychic, social, political, and ecological consequences cost many times more than comprehensive, networked human education for all ages and groups of people across Europe.

Without a doubt, this congress marks a turnaround in the direction of actual human education. Education programs that are intended to promote multicultural coexistence in a "new Europe" address people in their psychic-spiritual and psycho-social disposition. With our conception of andragogy, we go a step further to the "inner" human being: The psychic-spiritual human education through all life phases is the fundamental task of andragogy in the future. Any form of professional training and general education, be it ever focused so multiculturally and on international understanding, will undermine the psychic life in the long term if it is not shaped comprehensive and categorical.

That is why we speak of "general andragogy" if we mean human education, and leave it open, whether the economy and industry want to call their adult education "special andragogy" or simply "further education".

The key problems addressed, for example xenophobia, increasing leisure time, cultural encounters, and violence, are a topic of human education if they are incorporated into the comprehensive personality development and not just lectured as "factual topics". In the foundation of our didactics, knowledge, experience, and the processing of experiences are intertwined. This is what enables real human education.

Let us briefly review the discussion of the term 'Bildung' in the first chapter. It is well known that the word 'Bildung' cannot be translated into English, Spanish, or French. "Bildung is a German term." (Becker 1992, 13). Does that mean that 'Bildung' only exists for Germans? What the so-called German term definitions contain can be found in English, Spanish, and French literature under the words: 'education', 'educación' and 'education'. So, we can equate 'education/Bildung' with 'upbringing/Erziehung'. However, we have only postponed the problem of definition. Another problem is the perception of Germans (and Swiss / Austrians): 'Erziehung' has an unpleasant aftertaste for every adult who wants to be emancipated. The attempt to use a clear scientific language with clear, objective terms threatens to fail because of the emotional experience of the everyday world (language). That may be clarified within the science; on the front of adult education, however, it provides considerable problems: With what terms should a marketing operate, to be able to respond to the potential clients? And: How can one 'sell' a human education that the meaning locates not only in a purposeful rationality (e.g., operationalized action-oriented goals), but also in the 'pure human education', which is the core of the meaning in inner human education and not originally settled in shaping the world?

Even in the disambiguation we encounter enormous philosophical, scientific, and everyday problems. "The meaning of human existence is not predetermined," writes Lenz (1987, 160). And another example, we do not understand the education as the development of personality for its own sake, but its setting to the life in our world and to acting abilities in this world" (Becker 1992, 16). As an affront to the churchy adult education, he continues: "Adult education may never be religious proclamation" (Becker 1992, 79).

But is it allowed to be a political and economic 'announcement'? How should we solve this problem if we translate 'religious' with 'original' and mean, in this new psychic-spiritual sense, the realization of love, spirit and the process of individuation? Or: How may we use the term 'education' when we interpret 'enlightenment' (the declared goal of emancipatory adult education) also in the connection with the unconscious, the spirit principle, and the realization of the living image of the circle-cross-mandala? 'Announcing' means above all 'communicating' and 'teaching', including, also enlightenment.

Adult education is also about moral education: "Without morality in the political decision-making structures, the repetition of Auschwitz could not be prevented" (Oser / Althof 1992, 11). We can interpret this as an assignment to andragogy with a powerful emotional appeal to the conscience. Here, countless keywords can be added that also appeal to human development, e.g.: Environmental degradation, nuclear war, poverty, hunger, exploitation, psycho-social suffering, crime, unemployment, overpopulation and many other 'key issues', that probably all scientists in adult education use as legitimacy for education. Biography research expands this list of topics: Gender roles are changing; the traditional life designs have changed; the period of retirement is much longer than it used to be, the personal identity formation takes place under new learning, and development phases, etc. (see, Alheit / Dominicé 1994, 375-377). The education term has changed enormously in adult education and the steadily increasing literature sets always new accents. But what does the adult educator, the scientist of adult education know about his consumers / clients / students?

The new "biography paradigm" (Alheit 1993, 59) should here open doors to understand the human (the "black box") in his needs, plans, disappointments and desires. The relevance of biographical searching and understanding is beyond doubt: The questioner opens access to his own life story; he finds access in understanding alien lifeworlds; and with this the repressed collective history can also be processed (Schuchardt 1993, 92-98). "Every understanding of foreign meaning (bases) on the self-interpretation of one's own experiences" (Kade 1983, 43). Personality development is therefore always also biographical reflection.

"We can understand biography research as basic science for a future adult education" (Apitzsch 1993, 114). Biographical self-reflection is not psychotherapy (Gudjons 1994, 11, 20). The goals are human education through: Illustrating, sensitizing, recognizing, approaching, understanding, making fruitful for the development of one's own identity, perceiving transformation opportunities, etc. (Gudjons 1994, 18-35).

We would like to point out critically that biographical research has not presented a concept of personality to date (we do not consider the "self-concept" to be sufficient) is not oriented on any model of inner growth, only touches superficially the "depths" of the unconscious, takes the resistances too little in an educational way into account, overtakes psychoanalytical models too blanked, practices a mixture of experimenting methods from the "sensitivity trainings" of the 1970s without a theoretical or didactic foundation. Almost everything is possible that the psycho trend offers today, including reflective handling of materials such as photos, diaries, drawings, music, letters, etc. (Fuchs 1984, 170-171, 261-262). Three worlds collide when Fuchs (1985, 437) thinks: "Biography receives new possibilities for sociology ... (represents) the perfect type of sociological source materials". On the second side there is the psychology resp. depth psychology and on the third side the educational theory resp. andragogy, including its didactics.

Again, and again, we have questions to the current paradigms of adult education: What does 'emancipation' mean if the human simultaneously is trapped in his own unconscious? What is the value of 'maturity' if, for example, the humans reproduce their life patterns fixed in early childhood in new variants throughout their lives? What is to be think of the goal-oriented guiding principle "critical and self-reflective" if the human can neither properly imagine nor contemplate? How should the humans be able to solve the key problems if they cannot deal with their feelings in a constructive manner?

How will the adult education handle "self-realization" in their practice when the process of the individuation, and with it not takes even in acknowledge the dream life of the human, much less presents a concept for relevant practical education? What is the 'freedom' worth, if humans do not understand their artificial needs and at the same know only little their basic needs?

'Critical-emancipatory' is the buzzword of the German adult education. What is about the spiritual experience possibilities of the primordial in the human? Mythology is a thing of the past; a merit of the education efforts in the sense of enlightenment since about 200 years. But what is about the inner experience of primeval symbols, for example the 'Grail' or the 'mandalas'?

Must one not ask critical-emancipatoryly whether adult education might be too superficial adverse the inner humanity and the real life? We know from Freud that psychoanalysis is always primarily a resistance processing and a "fight against lies". These aspects are not on any agenda item of theory formation in adult education, neither in the pedagogy and social pedagogy. How does adult education response action-oriented to the 'everyday problems' of the human, such as inferiority, loneliness, relationship conflicts, sexual difficulties, frustrations, insecurities, stress, fear of life, depression, aggression, excessive demands, money problems etc.? The practical psychology deals with such life issues without having an educational theory. Adult education centers around education theories, but without providing substantial training concepts for such life issues of the human with exceptions such as for stress management, segmented personality development, learning how to learn, communication techniques. In fact, adult education is a young science. It has yet to form its identity. This is its great opportunity for the 21st century.

With the term 'education' we span an arc from the living space over the living worlds to the psychic inner life of the human. We understand education in this complex network. This can certainly also be communicated in German, Spanish, and French, including the philosophical question: What is all the earthly stage theater supposed to do if the deepest sense is not teleologically anchored in the transcendence? With the following, we give an overview of the dimensions (or aspects) of human education as we network them.

Biographical self-reflection means rolling up important life issues and "critical events / actions" from the present back to the early childhood.

The division of time can be determined in terms of developmental psychology as well as socialization and life course theory (Whitebourne / Weinstock 1982), or purely pragmatically, e.g., as follows: Earliest childhood (0-5 years); early childhood (5-12 years); later childhood (12-15 years); adolescence (15-18 years); young adulthood (18-25 years); early adulthood (25-35 years); middle adulthood (35-50 years); old adulthood (50-65 years); late adulthood (65+ years).

In connection with the biography research and the "critical actions", we have rolled out the important life issues in this work as well as in "Empirie der Individuation". The key words are: Relationships in the family, including educational experiences, friendships, love relationships, marriage, own family, children, places of leisure, hobbies, play, vacation, weekend, mobility, preschool, school, vocational training, professional activities, religious practices, political socialization, cultural life, reading, housing, neighborhood quality, body, sexuality (being a man, being a woman), bathroom culture, illnesses, disorders, sufferings, consumer goods, clothes, food culture, money, valuables, housekeeping, managing life, sleeping (habits), special events, current affairs.

The first self-reflective question arises: What was how? Memories through reflection and imaginations (regression), diaries, photo albums, letters, clothes, furniture, and knick-knacks provide access. Many questions about the characteristics and understanding interpretation can be asked.

The second type of self-reflective questioning is based on the model of the psychic organism. Starting from each psychic subsystem, countless questions can be mutually formulated which cover much more than the usual self-image categories (Thomae 1988, 48) and go further than psychoanalytic and psychological theories as presented in adult education. With this model, everyone who wants to develop biographically self-reflexively has a clearly structured and versatile, theoretically founded orientation. Accordingly, it also serves the andragogues.

Regarding the life systems without theoretically basing a praxeology:

■   Everyday world: Work, family, upbringing, partner, friend, relatives, friends, acquaintances, neighbors, strangers, superiors, work colleagues, foreigners, upbringing children, sport, entertainment, leisure time, household chores, car, living environment, living space, mass media, consumption / purchase, vacation, money, self-management, sexuality, health, energy, waste, etc.

■   Living world: Religion, churches, economy, parties, politics, military, social services, health care, energy, transport network, culture and art, built-up living space, public authorities, consumer goods, services, education, law, courts, taxation, insurance, police, crime, etc.

■   Exo-worlds: Life worlds of other countries, societies, cultures, etc.

■   Habitat (nature and animal world): Water, air, soil, animals, plants, raw materials, natural forces of all kinds, etc.

Our concept of "education" is complex, multidimensional, and dynamic open. Metatheoretically we demand clarity of terms, theory fruitfulness for the practice, the empirical back bonding, the clear traceability through experience procedures, that foundation in scientific knowledges while simultaneously remaining openness ("search movement"), the multi-dimensional linking human-lifeworld-history-process principles (life phases and individuation), the didactic structure of education as well as the anchoring of all aspects of the course aspects of education of the human in experiencing the spirit principle (dream interpretation, imaginations, contemplations and psycho-energetic symbolic exercises; see Schellhammer 1987, 1987, 1998).

These criteria for the basic theory of human education (cf. Ruprecht 1985, 6-15; and: Zdarzil 1985, 78-86) basically open up all levels of the common definitions of the term "education", such as: The psychic forces of the human, psychic-spiritual development, abilities and skills for work and private life, culture and society, politics and social, leisure and consumption, natural world, personal life situations, life history, key problems of society, meaning and value giving of the perceived reality. An all-round balance, concentrated on the parts with a versatile networked interplay, including the tangible and linguistically symbolic comprehensible transcendental reality, is guaranteed.

Our paradigm conveys these tools for the real life. But the perspectives are much more far-reaching: The human education of our concept leads to the "completion of individuation" and, in its final and highest form, to the "Grail King being".

This is neither literature, nor mythology, nor religion in the traditional sense, nor a fantasy of the author. The "grail" is a symbolic image of an educated psychic reality in the human. We set the standard on andragogy to create the metatheoretical, the theoretical and methodological instruments to open these realities of our educational term. We emphasize: The price that the andragogue must "pay" for it is that he has to get involved in the procedures himself if he wants to find (and understand) this "grail" as secret, to research and teach about it and to educate others, humans, the path of individuation.

And it should be emphasized again to the paradigm: Pedagogy resp. andragogy is first "holistic" (comprehensive) human education. This human education creates the key qualifications for the personal life. It forms the competencies for relationships (friendship, marriage, family, work, leisure, cultural life). It reduces many risks in personal life course and in social network of one's own life and it leads to an all-round balanced psychic organism in steady progressive development. It integrates a high level of ethical responsibility for oneself, for others, for the job, for society and the life worlds. That is individuation and this reaches the human in his deepest psychic-spiritual being, also in the most decisive meaning questions of being. Individuation forms a type of human who in the future will help shaping the image of pedagogues (andragogues) in teaching, research, and practice.

The social developments that are to be expected in the 21st century create a certain urgency to raise the question of paradigmatic position of pedagogy resp. educational science (education science, educational research) and their representatives (pedagogues, andragogues). The main trends of developments since 1968 can be clearly identified: Equal opportunities, exhaustion of talent resources, school reform, subject didactics, teacher training and the like. Every new future-oriented paradigm must orient itself to this situation and justify its expanded perspective.

If one looks at the research work from the period from 1975 to the turn of the millennium (see: Gretler, A.: Die Schweizerische Bildungsforschung der Nachkriegszeit ..., SGB, No. 1, 2000, p. 111-142), the example Switzerland shows that over 80% of all research activities concern the school subsystems. Just under 4% of the projects open general adult education.

These projects deal with curricula and teaching content, with learning objectives and learning processes, with teachers and learners, with structures and organization, with interaction processes, with assessments of learning and teaching performance, with the determinants of learning and the requirements of learners, also with networked lifeworlds. There are certainly also research projects to leisure, family, and geriatric education as well as general human education. - This status of educational science tends to apply to the entire German-speaking area of Europe.

Does this subject area represent the science of pedagogy resp. andragogy, educational science, and educational research? Or does one even have to interpret these tendencies as submission of pedagogy and educational research under the power of economy? "Further education" as a paradigmatic term instead of "adult education"?

With the term "further education" one can consciously or undetected go at distance from the general matter of pedagogy (resp. andragogy) and so this "learning paradigm" becomes a service company of economic interests. A well-functioning economy is undoubtedly important. The education science certainly has a central task here. But: *The economy is not yet the life of the human being. Economic success does not make a good life or a healthy state.* With such a "modern" reorientation, the fundamental core theme of pedagogy is evidently left to a few professors in the quiet room. - This reflects a vision of economic growth, but not a vision of human education for the 21st century. Is this the official new "paradigm" of science of human education?

What can be seen from this? The education science is reactive, not visionary-active. It responds to needs of economy (for example: knowledge, skills), to developments in new technical equipments (for example: personal computers, internet), and to Europeanization (for example: English teaching, harmonization of study programs, recognition of diplomas). But are these really the central societal expectations to pedagogy? Or is pedagogy and education research simply part of the dance around the golden calf? Of course, the "golden calf" is not the problem here. The problem is that those who dance with it do not want any self-knowledge and no holistic psychic-spiritual education.

Isn't self-knowledge the beginning of all (general) human education and thus the basis of a future-oriented new pedagogical resp. andragogical paradigm for educational researchers, experts in education, professors in pedagogy and, of course, for those active in andragogy in all possible fields of work?

Marks for Didactics of Human Education

Didactic foundation:

The andragogy works on two levels: Education and training as well as counseling to individuation and to current life challenges (crises, conflicts, failures, difficulties, life sufferings). The counseling as intervention is predominantly based on theories from the field of psychology and psychoanalysis resp. psychotherapy. However, the adult educational counseling is neither psychotherapy nor psychoanalysis (cf. Petersheim 1993, 165-204), but it nevertheless opens all (!) "depths" of psychic life. We cannot bring up the topic of "counseling" here, just as we have to forego as regards content systematic of life challenges (life problems, "critical" actions). With the working form of education and training, we are during didactic problem statement.

Building on our educational theory, we want to highlight some central features of didactics of andragogy resp. the human education. "Didactics" means "the entirety of teaching process". Klafki calls ten characteristics of humanist didactics (1993, 87-89), of which we will highlight excerpts: Target decisions, dealing with decision-making instances (social forces), competence of the state as responsible, demands of the learner (actual and future-oriented), methods in the context of content decisions, expertise teaching knowledge, practical interest. Klafki complements the historical understanding of didactics with his critical constructive approach: "Didactics (is) the general term for educational research, theory and concept formation with regard to all forms of intentional (goal-oriented), systematically considered teaching (in the broadest sense of reflective learning aid) and this in connection with such teaching performing learning" (1993, 91). "Critical" refers to the permanent reflection on the obstacles to achieving the educational goals and their implementation. "Constructive" places the emphasis on current and prospective practical relevance (Kron 1994, 128-136).

"Curriculum theory" interprets Brezinka (1978, 214, 232), as part of normative pedagogy because it is the decision on personality ideals, so on value judgments. Curriculum resp. teaching theory we summarize under the term "didactics".

Didactics is not only empiric educational science. It is also normative philosophy and implies anthropological categories.

In all parts of the didactic practice, its arguments and its material are based on empirical, including introspective, facts. The "critical" dimension of Klafki can be extended understood as a critical reflection on all decision-making processes and decision-making contents, to some extent the permanent openness to renewal and amplification. For our conception of andragogy "critical didactics" means in the approach: The reflected control of back binding of educational processes resp. training (formation) to the psychic system and life reality. The social critical and emancipatory task of pedagogy we see among others especially in Mollenhauer, Blankerts, von Hentig, Giesecke, Gamm and for example, in a particular image as a "praxeology" in Derbolav (1987, 22).

The didactical practice thus relates to: Goals and objective decisions, selection of contents (life links), structuring of target and subject program (stages and steps), methods of teaching and learning (teaching as experience space, exemplary learning), activities of teachers and learners, media of teaching and learning, evaluation control to promote learning processes (in class and in life), requirements for teachers and learners as well as social relationships between all those involved. The instruments for developing individual subject areas and for own evaluation is the teaching research (Ingenkamp 1970, I, 272-442; Klimsa 1993, 121-203; Kron 1994, 102-193).

This short opening of didactical questions of human education illustrates that andragogy as pedagogy resp. the educational scientific field includes a unique tripartite division (Brezinka 1978): Empiric (and humanistic) science, philosophy of andragogy and practical andragogy. The development of subject-specific theory of didactics (curriculum theory) can make extensive use of the research, and experiences of pedagogy. Here some simplifications, some special features, and above all, other structurally organizational conditions arise. The "didactic planning of ecological adult education" (Müller U. 1993) is a comparative example.

The initial situation: As far as we know there is no scientific or practical andragogy resp. human education in Switzerland and Germany as we propose here as science and practice as well as social organization and professionalization. The problems of "curriculum reform" (school reform, syllabus reform) omit. Instead, there is the practical political problem of introducing an educational organization for human education resp. individuation. Whether this will once happen in the frame of existing structures of "adult education" (organizationally in Switzerland, for example, with "Schweizerische Vereinigung der Erwachsenenbildung"; SVEB) or from the ground up independent and new, cannot be decided by us and not be forecast. We let open this problem and generally all aspects of the external organization and decision-making processes. This must be developed by those who want a conception of andragogy in the sense proposed here and institutionalize it in concrete terms, entirely in the sense of "co-determination - co-responsibility" according to the current educational guiding principles. In democratic processes, the society has a say in what kind of human education it wants to integrate into its education system (especially the adult education sector). Or the unpredictable forces of free market economy alone determine.

The subject canon is simplified compared to school didactics. The andragogy is thematically limited by the subject areas of psychic systems, individuation, and its life practical relevance (life systems). A first "law" of curriculum theory (according to Derbolav 1987, 124) requires that the tasks of educational world (here: psychic systems, individuation, and their personality ideals resp. educational goals) must correspond to later life tasks (actions in the habitat, social relevance). We have highlighted these connections. Its didactical integration into our personality development can only be achieved here in the beginning. It is a central task of didactics of andragogy. Klafki mentions five "epoch-typical key problems": The peace question, environment question, social inequality, technical dangers and possibilities, the "I"-you relationship (Klafki 1993, 56-60). In the introduction we have set out the spectrum of social issues. Biography research as well as social psychology (Hurrelmann / Ulich 1991) and the sociological analyzes of social life (cf. Eggers / Steinbacher 1977) provide further topics.

The second law (according to Derbolav) concerns the layer structure (elements of levels and steps) of curriculum. A first approach is the structure of science, for example according to the "psychic organism" and "individuation". Our taxonomy of learning objectives (Bloom 1972) builds on the system model of the psychic organism and is thus much farther regarded as the division into "cognitive, affective and psychomotoric" performance activities (see. Kron 1994, 159). A second approach is the order of the inner psychic-spiritual development, the individual phases of individuation. Here it arises the question to the inner interdependence between learning psychological conditions and possibilities in adults on the one hand and the inner growth and development sequences on the other. The learning psychological processes resp. forms and steps have versatilely been explored in psychology and pedagogy (see Gage / Berlinger 1986). The personality ideals resp. their educational objectives, as we have presented in brief (see also: Empirie der Individuation 1998) are to differentiate assimilative to the nine transformation stages of individuation (ibid). A third approach is praxeological: The current and future expected life situations of the human in democratic industrial societies are a criterion for selection and structuring of the material resp. the training exercises. Personality goals are to be developed in the context of life reality. Social relevance can be built in directly here. Its main difficulty lies in the theoretical connection of developed psychic forces with the various life situations (cf. biography research).

A central didactical task is to guarantee the educational goals through organized knowledge transfer and systematic training. The curriculum theory of andragogy is also linked to the evaluation of educational performance in teaching and in life. Across all above mentioned, didactical problems also it is to see the question of appropriate methods and media of this personality formation. There is already an abundance of literature on practical design of courses and seminars (cf. Müller KR 1994; Klimsa 1993; Frommer 1991). As the superstructure results finally the concept building of the professionalization (Sagebiel 1994, 284). We found over 500 titles on the topic of "professionalization in adult education" (Pädagogische Arbeitsstelle des DVV, literature research).

"Didactical activities in adult education have to promote progressive solution strategies if it would take seriously its social mandate" (Siebert, in: Mader 1991, 21). According to the statements of Siebert, progressive solution strategies are linked to reflectivity ability about oneself and the key problems. This includes processing forms such as: Overcome, master, develop, solve, renew. The scope is only really apparent when we keep the opposite in mind: Not reflecting includes trivializing, turning away, fleeing, resigning, becoming estranged, disfiguring, dispensing, stagnating. As a result, the everyday consciousness is correspondingly narrow, the perception reduced, the models very simplified prejudices and the adaption cut in. There is hardly any constructive-critical learning, neither about oneself (self-reflection), nor about relations (psycho-social networking), and not about life problems. "Adult education is just there for effect, provokes only their mental processes, where the imagining of reality interpretations and readiness for the processing of reality interpretations fit" (Tietgens, preface in: Arnold 1985, 7).

We conclude: The non-determinism by instincts (Gehlen, Portman) is replaced by the determinism of stupidity, i.e., the absence of reflection ("post-modern" feature, Vester H.G. 1993). One cannot take responsibility realistically without an all-round reflection. Personality development as education to self- reflection opens e.g.: Discourse ability, learning capability, solidarity ability, human-centered value and meaning formation, socio-psychological aspects such as action and communication abilities including processing capacity in the everyday life as well as flexibility of "I"-identity, interpretation model revision, ampliation of everyday knowledge through experience (Arnold 1985, 13) and the individuation (cf. Winkler 1993, 141). If the didactics of human education is founded on an educational theory with personality, individuation, life history (biography) and everyday life, then this kind of adult education can redeem its humanitarian demand, otherwise not, or only partially. "With the strong emphasis on rational achievements, an abundance of other development opportunities is excluded" (Meueler 1993, 159). It is actually a difficult question how experiences of what we call the "functioning of the spirit" and the "living image of the circle-cross-mandala" can be included didactically (and thus operationally). The difficulties begin with the subject of the unconscious, which we largely "disenchanted" and "demystified" in "Empirie der Individuation" (1998). We think that there are methodological ways to combine meditation (imagination and contemplation) with creative-analytical thinking.

Our didactical position is sufficiently anchored in the educational theory (cf. Klafki 1993, 251). Our education term is integrated into the didactics. We have defined the centering, superordinate orientation and evaluation categories for all andragogical individual measures. The roots of this pedagogical (andragogical) understanding of education go back to the culture and society critical position of Rousseau, Herder, Kant, and others (see Lehner 1989). Let us differentiate some specific didactic problems in a few further sections to our educational theory foundation.

The general didactics of pedagogy (Kron 1994) and andragogy (Pöggeler 1974; Raapke / Schulenberg 1985) provide us the scientific systematic framework for practical educational work in groups (lessons). For personal development and Individuation results in some specific elements that must be threaten as "special didactics". Our own experiences in this regard are not enough comprehensive to be able to formulate scientific statements. We outline roughly the crucial tasks or problem settings:

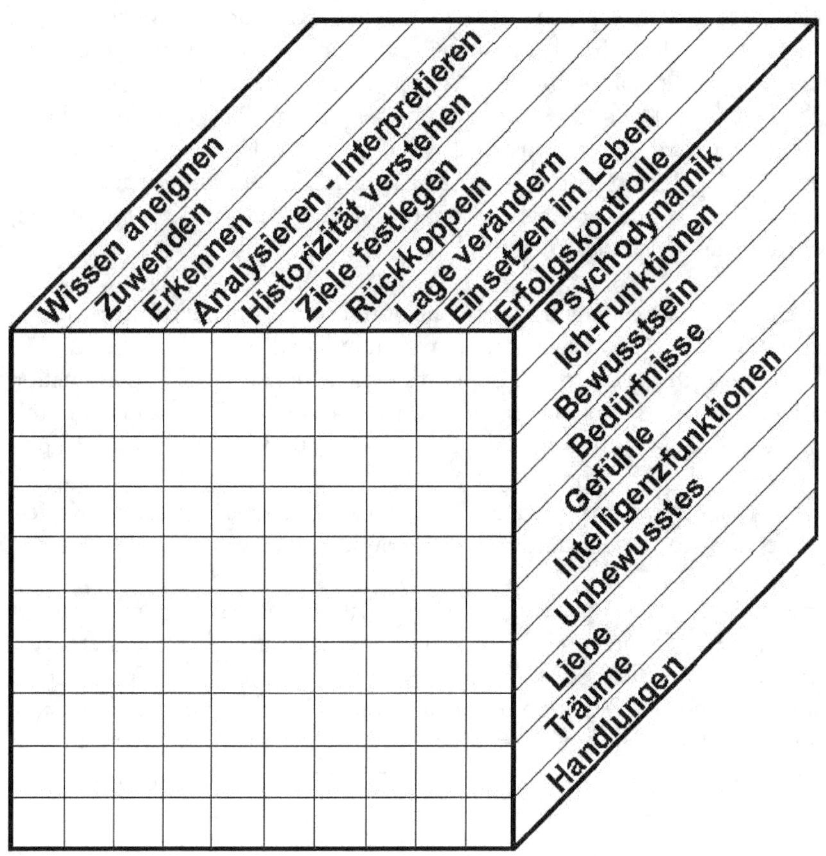

Translation:
Acquiring knowledge; turning to; recognizing; analyzing-interpreting;
understanding history; defining targets; back bonding; changing situation;
inserting in life; evaluation control
Psychodynamics; "I"-functions; consciousness; needs; feelings; intelligence
functions; unconscious; love, dreams, actions.

Didactic problems:

1) Theoretical approach: The various theoretical approaches are to be combined into a new systemic theory unit; this includes such as learning theories, information theory, communicative interaction, educational theory etc. (Peterssen in: Roth, 1991, 664-667; Pöggeler / Wolterhoft 1981; Mader 1991; Dewe among others 1988).

2) Level didactics: The age-specific teaching and learning (Beckmann, in: Roth 1991, 675) requires specific considerations, especially among the older generation. A question is, for example: How can and should be created age homogeneous groups? In other words: Can young people be guided didactically in the same way with older people (about 60 years) (Whitebourne / Weinstock 1982, 134-154)?

3) Open curricula: How and when can a co-decision of participants be installed to the selection of materials, instructional design, and involvement of "personal material" (Schorch, in: Roth 1991, 707; Müller K. R. 1994)?

4) Transparency, ideology criticism and discourse (Klafki, Habermas): In which forms can participants be included in decisive "critical-constructive" processes (so-called "participant orientation")?

5) Lesson situation as learning room with exemplary life reality: What can and should be the "experience subject" in lessons? In which relation are student prerequisites and contents (Schorch in Roth 1991, 710)?

6) Experience and rationality: In which relationship are rationality, experience, and evaluation resp. qualification (Peterssen in Roth 1991, 668)? Specifically: Which qualifications of self-education can be determined today for coping with life in our society and for leading people in all possible professional fields?

7) Interactions: In which relation are individual persons in the study group to each other and at the same time to the content (thematic centered interaction; Kohn 1975 160-175)? This question also concerns the adult educators themselves (Wahl 1993).

8) Evaluation: How can and should the social and life historic implications scientifically be recognized, evaluated, and feed back in the education program (Klafki, 1985; Dieterich 1987)?

A didactic model contains various elements from the most varied of related sciences, in particular socialization conditions (Kaltschmid 1986, 210, 219). We limit our discussions to subject-specific problems.

Some aspects we want to unroll below, to limit the subject topic. Our practical works for elementary and advanced stage individuation are an attempt to implement the here discussed educational theory and didactics in practical teaching tutorials. For a more in-depth understanding of the following section, it is helpful to have a look at these practical educational documents.

Standardization of personality development:

We drafted the "educational idea" of andragogy and sketched didactical cornerstones for personality development. The individual sub-areas of personality development and the integrative educational process of "becoming human", which lead to the highest level of psychic-spiritual human being, we have outlined in our "andragogical psychology". Personality development is not simply "life help". It is more than "psychological popular education". It is not just "self-experience" or "humanistic psychology". Individuation is much more than a "sensitivity training" or a course with "topic centered interaction", more than an "analytical group therapy" and not to be compared with the majority of offers of the esoteric market. The public courses offer of further education in the subjects of "humanities" (e.g., at adult education centers and private training institutes) are based on a different education theory than ours. Of course, these training opportunities can be understood and integrated as part elements or "Additum" of the comprehensive personality development.

With the process of individuation, the general andragogy becomes a scientific "teaching system" about the "highest good" of the human. This "good" cannot simply be "sold". Its educational value can also not "create" a need in the human with sophisticated advertising. Interest awakening advertising, introductory lectures, introductory weekend courses and objectively interestingly designed documentations are sure andragogical useful effectively a forming preparatory work.

The andragogues as we understand them, are "administrators" of this "good"; they are also "wise", at least on the advanced way. Because they also have the professional task of paving the way for the human to find answers to basic questions of the being. They have the comprehensive educational mandate, the life course - especially after the life center - to transcend, i.e., to expand with meaning and spirit, with love and value for the life -fulfillment, and, also in the view of the finiteness of life (Pöggeler 1970; Pöggeler 1974, 284; Dienelt 1984). We have set out and justified the vital need of the comprehensive personality development under many points of view. Pöggeler already in 1974 clearly pointed out: "The un-adultness of some adults is one of the greatest dangers for in freedom living society ... The fate of the democratic society will depend in the future on whether it will succeed to keep awake the spirit of freedom and responsibility through lifelong education" (Pöggeler 1974, 288).

The participant of education programs of individuation is a learner. He must learn a lot. There is no personality development without self-knowledge. There is no holistic growth and development process without comprehensive self-knowledge. The learner must acquire different processes of renewal, transformation, differentiation, integration, the increasing unit. This does not happen in andragogy by dogmas and doctrines or mythical stories. The educational path is the inner experience and inner education, with substantial knowledge transfer, training of the experience methods and integrated life relation (self-reflective biography). Individuation cannot be achieved on a "weekend course". A program of three months (e.g., weekly 2 lessons) may certainly impart an in-depth introduction or roll up a section of a psychic subsystem. How small a block unit is organized, always every educational unit is in a plan of the process and in the anchoring to the educational idea. This is our guiding principle for organizing the material in personality development.

Those who want a holistic and comprehensive personality development in the sense of individuation today have a huge selection of different directions. Everyone must judge for himself what kind of "wholeness" he achieves where. He will have to choose a "direction". Or he creates his own plan for the entirety of personality development and looks for appropriate building blocks on the market.

Such an attempt is likely to be quite difficult. How can an interested person plan without having the necessary knowledge? How can he organize a structure, although the building blocks on the market do not contain a common standard of the "holism" of psychic life and the process, i.e., are not coordinated at all? How should someone be able to put blocks from different directions of personal development together without the presentation of a didactic foundation? In the following section, we want to propose a solution based on an initially rough subject organization.

Some inner processes will be dealt with by the individual alone or with supplementary individuation advice. In the following considerations, we will concentrate on the educational process that can be designed and planned.

Organized lessons are suitable and necessary for this. Many learning processes can be organized through lessons. In the organization of lessons, psychological theory, action theory, value theory and didactic theory are combined with the educational idea and concept of the overall process (Mollenhauer 1972, 17-18). Individuation, however, implies a growth that cannot simply be created with learning (material) units, such as a computer course.

The scientific structure of the individual psychic realities, the habitat structure and the structure of individuation process provide the basis for designing a standardization of constitutive educational units. The standardization of central educational processes enables an interested person to acquire the various educational units at different locations with different andragogues. In this way, everyone can long-term individually plan and implement his own education according to his possibilities and wishes. We remind to this: This andragogical personality development is above all a life form and not a "training to be completed as quickly as possible". For this purpose, anyone interested can keep a so-called "education booklet", such as the one offered by the "Schweizerische Vereinigung für Erwachsenenbildung" (SVEB) for the entire field of personal further training. All courses, lecture series, congresses, teaching units and training programs attended can be entered here.

Does this kind of educational organization lead to "schooling and infantilization" (Dewe 1988, 56)? We see no weighty indication of a serious risk. The infantilization happens in life, in experience culture and in advertising. Twenty hours of television per week infantilized adults more than four hours "school desk", to name just one example. We find regressions of all kinds in abundance in the daily life of the collective.

The defense mechanisms for example are for Freud the core issue of any psycho-analytical work. Many expressions of defense reflect developmental psychological early stages. The defense mechanisms are primarily a psychological-anthropological fact, not a psychopathological characteristic, as the psychoanalysis often gives the impression (cf. Wurmser 1993).

We experience the reality. We act in it. We use language to describe the reality, we create knowledge, and we make "sense" (Biller 1994, 126-127). Knowledge is elementary component for experience and action, for understanding and giving meaning (Biller 1994). If an "integrative education" wants to reach the whole human, then comprehensive knowledge of psychic life is an indispensable prerequisite to be able to provide practical personal development at all. This can never be done through self-awareness training alone. The knowledge has a central position in the didactic functional model (cf. Lehner 1989, 187) and it is impossible to imagine today's concept of qualification without it (Merk 1993, 44-47). The media didactics (Klimsa 1993; Müller 1994 etc.) cannot create personality development and individuation if the basic knowledge is not prepared scientifically, in a practical way and learning psychologically. That is why we consider material processing to be an elementary didactic component for the acquisition of material in practical education (Kaiser 1985; Kade 1983).

In addition to the standardization of the educational program, personal educational planning also requires organized professional practice in andragogy. Every teacher and learner in Switzerland, Germany, and Austria (to limit here the German-speaking space) can orient himself at a recognized standardized educational program. The andragogy (as educational institution) can comprehensively set a basic program and propose resp. let open an "additum" to teaching units.

Our curriculum development is open according to our theoretical foundations of didactics and allows a great individual variety in the inner planning as well as in the external organization of extended educational units. In this way, individual inclinations and interests of teachers and learners can be considered. Because individuation creates neither a "unitary human" nor a "uniform" program.

Let us first look for an orientation for the standardization in the material. Here we are concerned with the essential features and not the detail elaboration. The representatives of andragogy will have to work out these together in the future. It is also an interdisciplinary work (PAD 1993) with crucial sociological components (Eggers / Steinbacher 1977; Dewe et al. 1988).

Organization of subjects:

We assume that although the subjects of personality development are inspired by the individual sciences, takes the essential, but do not represent this knowledge volume. We also set out that the selection criteria in addition to the "base-material" is over all the life practical relevance. The science orientation goes as far as it is necessary for the concrete life and growth process orientation. A certain extension is specially to let open where the cultural good appeals to a personal enrichment and a personal interest of participants. Elements for thematic areas resp. focal points of interest are, for example: Ways of life, family, sexuality, leisure activities, cultural services, environmental issues, religions, literature (including mythology and fairy tales) as well as questions of value and meaning (Biller 1994).

Hence follows a basic structuring criterion: At each educational level are expertise (psychic life) and life issues (life links, biographic issues, "critical problems") to be split in a "basic material" and in free disposable "additive materials" (Klafki 1993, 182-184). The total volume of basic material and "additum" depends on the criteria of relevance and need for the individual educational processes, graded in the three phases of individuation.

As per our system model of psychic life (see illustration 8), we can according to the individual subsystems make the following subject division (block units): 1) The actions; 2) The psychodynamics; 3) The "I" and its auxiliary functions; 4) The intelligence functions; 5) The feelings; 6) The needs; 7) The unconscious; 8) The spirit in dream and imagination; 9) The force of love.

We have placed these psychic subsystems in the process of individuation in an overall and comprehensive manner and defined three stages or phases. These correspond to the course of growth resp. education, whereby developmental psychological models (cf., e.g., Flammer 1993) can (must) be scientifically significantly differentiated. We call the first phase as the "basic level", the second phase as the "intermediate level" and the third phase as the "advanced level" of the educational program (phase units); in key words: 1st phase: Self-management and life education; entry into self-knowledge; 2nd phase: Systematic self-knowledge; main transformations and dissolution of the opposites; 3rd phase: Development and creation of the new wholeness.

In relation to this "material" we have systematized the habitat into a first rough division with the following areas: Relationships, encounters, family, goods, food, capital, work, world of work, school, education, entertainment, culture; environment, nature, religion, ethics, philosophy; society, politics.

To a certain extent, all psychic forces are in an empty space if we do not relate them to the habitat. "Eco-psychology" has opened a wide range of topics for this purpose (Kruse 1990; Roszak 1994). Every psychic force finds a radius of action and an expression in many life situations. Conversely, all these life realities form the psychic forces of the individual. In this respect, the "psychic-spiritual matter" cannot be separated from "life reality". The selection from the abundance of life realities is based on the laws of learning, according to the present meaning of "critical" life story and relevance for the future. "Life links" also enable favorable learning processes and create increased motivation. The material for teaching personality development includes thus in the core the psychic areas, by extracting various elements of biographical life realities as frame and life expression.

Based on our explanations about self-reflective processing of the own biography as well as about the material organization for the education of the psychic organism, we want to present a practical example of the material organization "psychic organism versus lifeworld" for discussion.

We consider the "lifeworld" from the point of view of biographical self-reflection and structure it in three steps:

Step 1 - Getting started: What was when and how?

"The following exercises aim to get the start to self-reflection on your own life story. Describe in key words or with a sentence 5 significant salient characteristics for the main question: *What was when and how?* At the beginning of a description, first set your age in the appropriate situation (in brackets). Go back in your thoughts year after year in your life as far as you have memories. Let the thoughts and memories run wild. Write spontaneously what comes to the mind without selecting. It doesn't matter whether you forget important things and have many or few memories."

Variation: You can first read through the individual topics and formulate 3-5 specific questions before looking for memories based on the main question. This is a stimulating, creative and exploratory introduction, especially for group work.

We place this first step in the reflection on the own life story in the general "personality development", i.e., in the "1st stage individuation" and at the beginning of the "2nd stage individuation".

The subject areas of the self-reflective biography are:

1. Family: Parents, stepparents, siblings, relatives, style of upbringing, education, work, social conditions, absences (separation, death).
2. Relationships outside the family: Acquaintances, neighbors, work colleagues, pastors, doctors, counselors, teachers, ethnic groups, etc.
3. Friendships, love relationships, marriage.
4. Own family, children, partner's family, relationship patterns.
5. Living, living atmosphere, quality of living, quality of neighborhood, removals.
6. Body, sexuality, education, being a man / woman, bathroom culture, pregnancies (course, termination), menstruation.
7. Nutrition, eating and drinking culture.
8. Illnesses, disorders, sufferings, operations, therapies, addictions (alcohol, tobacco, medication, drugs, food, play).
9. Pre-school, school, advanced training, learning, education, school

subjects, certificates, change of school, school career.
10. Vocational training, work, occupational activities, working place, unemployment.
11. Leisure locations, leisure activities, hobbies, games, vacation, weekend, mobility.
12. Religious practices, beliefs, philosophy of life, esotericism, sects, psycho-religious movements
13. Political socialization, political events, activities, ecological movements.
14. Cultural life, reading (newspapers, magazines, books), music, art, film, theater, television.
15. Objects, consumer goods, clothes, money, valuables.
16. Psycho-social aid organizations: Unemployment fund, welfare, counseling, rescue stations, homes, insurance benefits.
17. Households, life management.
18. Sleeping (frame, habits, dreams).
19. Crime (victim, perpetrator).
20. Ecological environment: Air / water pollution, traffic, noise, radiation, poisons, overpopulation, poverty, waste, degradation of nature, cruelty to animals, energy consumption, disasters, armed conditions

Step 2 - Effects of the own biography: What has had a formative effect?

We place this first *deepening* in the own life story partly in the general personality development, partly in the 1st and 2nd phase of individuation. Central life issues also belong to the first awareness formation. Important key questions here are: "How have the biographical circumstances influenced your psychic force systems?"; or: "How do you live privately and at work?"; or: "How do you deal with your dreams? How do you meditate?"

A basic occupation is: "Go through your information on the 20 biographical topics and try to feel how your life experiences on all these topics have shaped your psychic life. In each case, note the effect characteristics of the individual subsystems in a short sentence:"

1. Action ("critical acting", habits, roles, schemes).
2. Psychodynamics (tension-relaxation, intro- / extraversion, life force).
3. The "I" (I-experience, awareness, defense, integration, will, control).
4. The intelligence functions (perception, thinking, language, learning).
5. The feelings (the experience of meaning and value).
6. The basic needs and the substitute needs (artificial needs).
7. The unconscious (experience models, human images, attitudes, values / norms).
8. The dreaming and imagination (meditation, fantasy).
9. The force of love (humanistic, transcendental, creative aspects).

10. The psychic-spiritual development (individuation).

Step 3 - Complex networking with the psychic system: How are the "micro-networks"?

We place this very systematic deepening in the own life story in the 2nd phase of individuation. The processing is always done in small steps. It is beneficial if the first step of biographical self-reflection is repeated after the 1st phase of individuation. It can be expected that after this education, far more and more differentiated information will be given on the 20 biographical topics. In the meantime, the student has learned to perceive more attentively and more clearly what previously was insignificant and to thoroughly review life with precise questions. The elaboration of the analysis sheet "educational needs" with many individual questions on psychic forces provides further assistance (see the study book: Empirie der Individuation, Appendix). On the one hand, the student has a differentiated biographical situation analysis and, on the other hand, a differentiated picture of his currently formed psychic forces. This material is the starting point for this thorough biographical self-reflection.

One working level is the precise perception of formative interconnections of biographical conditions with all individual forces of the psychic system. The other level of work relates to the question: "What do I want to create new, to differentiate and particularly promote?" This implies precise formulations of educational goals and graduated steps of self-education to achieve these goals.

A valuable subject amplification is the self-reflective analysis of coping strategies (Halsig, in: Brüderl 1988, 37-75; Thomae 1988, 79-110). According to these authors, the main coping strategies include performance (cognitive, active, action, ability, realization, responsibility, assertion, and implementation, pick up opportunities); adaptation (to situations, personal needs, demands, correction of expectations, seeking and using advice and help, identification); escape (delaying action, leaving, restricting, delegating / rejecting responsibility, distraction); as well as defensive, depressive, resigned and aggressive strategies.

When working on coping strategies, the focus can be on two areas: 1st: How does the student cope with his biographical elaboration? And 2nd: Which coping strategies can be identified in the 20 subject areas in the biography and in the present? With our didactic suggestions, many variants of dealing with such forms of reaction can be creatively developed and implemented in groups.

Apart of substantial educational goals of self-reflective activity with the own biography in the way we present it here, group work in this context has the following effect: Humans get into conversation; one learns to understand each other better; imagination is awakened; the perspective is expanded; cooperation and solidarity about life destinies are promoted; the awareness is broadened; similarities are discovered; isolation is broken; courage in self-reflection is encouraged; self-knowledge becomes an objective discourse; potentials are discovered; hopes in possibilities of transformation are raised; intuition is promoted together with the analytically-reactive thinking; independence and autonomy in practical self-knowledge and self-education are built up in a substantially sound manner; competences about human knowledge and dealing with others increase; communication about psychic life is differentiated; a positive self-affirmation is gradually built up concretely; and last but not least, everyone forms his own attitudes about psychic-spiritual growth, free from manipulation, indoctrination, emotional "flights of fancy" and "empty words".

The autodidactic development of this in-depth and thorough self-reflection and self-education is relatively difficult and arduous with the scope of material. We dissuade from getting in this "adventure" alone and without help. In addition, more than "questionnaire work" is possible and useful here, as we have shown in connection with biography research (cf. also: Gudjons 1994). The work forms can have workshop character, are partly meditative and constructive-creative. Role plays based on biographical facts are also conceivable. The andragogues have a wide scope to use their creativity as well as their inclinations and experiences in designing. We have developed three workshops for this purpose, each with a workbook of 40 pages: A) Self-knowledge and individuation; B) Dream interpretation and meditation; C) Social competence and life skills.

We organize the educational program based on the three phases of individuation: Basic level, intermediate level, and advanced level. Each level consists of a firmly structured education program and a detailed flexible training program. The educational program consists in the core substance, which can be created in a versatile, realistic way, and with individual knowledge. We expect that the participants of the training program further develop themselves through reading and freely chosen offers from the psychagogical adult education. A fixed structured standard program can only involve the core structure of knowledge. Life practical, psychological and life philosophical issues may widely be designed. Our standard programs do not claim to cover all knowledge that is useful for the respective level, but only the fundamentally necessary knowledge with many flexible (open) amplification options.

For the duration of the individual phases must be emphasized that many individual factors determine this: A life history of 30 years in general must work up much less of "material" as one of 50 years. A loaded childhood and youth as well as heavy blows determine the duration. Not all persons have the same amount of time per week for their education. It is also normal that one can or want to work less intensively on oneself at times. Individual life events can cause interruptions. The pace of learning differs between the humans, which is considered 'normal'. Everyone is at a different starting point, if he starts with the education program, brings his own experiences with and lives in situations that can profoundly shape the course. Everyone has different pre-experiences and a different knowledge about the human.

The training program is structured with variable block units. This includes in our opinion in a learning unit for about 2 hours (weekly, for a year course):

- 20-30 min.: Analysis of "critical event situations" (CES): Presentation and processing of 2-3 actions experienced as "critical" (from 2-3 participants) with a focus on analysis, goals, and approaches to transformation.
- 20-30 min.: Dream interpretation: 2-3 participants can present a dream, interpretation, and discussion, discussing life relation (decisions).
- 20-30 min.: Relaxation, mental training, contemplation: Alternately train different exercises and reflect on their results systemically.
- 20-30 min.: Imagination and analytical-reflective processing: Alternating exercises on the subsystems: Unconscious, love, needs, feelings, intelligence functions, "I" system.

Addition: 10-20 min.: Due to our special knowledge and inclinations, we end each time with various psycho-energetic exercises and rituals (see Schellhammer 1987).

The training program is flexible for these reasons: All psychic subsystems are repeatedly processed in regular rotation, always looked at new aspects and placed in the current and biographical life context. The educational program gives the andragogue a frame in which he can design his exercise program. The exercises are partly imaginative, reflexive, creative, discourse etc. The andragogue can here use in full his inclinations and particular abilities, without the program risks to swim in an aimlessly "feeling and adventure bath" or to be restricted in a single theoretically well-founded view and action manner. We hereby propose a structure for the training design. The educational program sets the path, subjects, practical methods, and goals. This enables the andragogue to work constructively and systemically.

With psycho-energetic and mental (meditative) methods following experience goals can be achieved: Relaxation, psycho-energetic centering, revitalization (strengthening), psycho-catharsis, activation of processes of transformation, completion of main transformations, experience of archetypes, harmonization of cosmic energy in rooms and experiences on the effectiveness of psychic energy in general. Additionally indicated: We judge the healing promoting effect by all the psycho-somatic strain to be extremely high as result of the depth relaxation effect (Schellhammer, 1985, 1987).

A training program can be offered varied in terms of time. In general, educational programs in adult education are offered quarterly, every six months, or as an annual unit with 2 hours a week on one evening. However, it is also possible to hold block units (Saturdays, weekends, educational weeks) at regular intervals.

Our material organization is based on many years of experiences which are not yet been evaluated scientifically. Certain intuitive, personal decisions certainly play with in the drafting. The author worked on the first phase of individuation with a few hundred people. We still have too little experience in organizing materials from the middle of individuation process. Our elaboration of this area therefore needs to be expanded in the future.

Theoretically, the delimitation between the phases can only be defined in terms of focus. According to inner developments some like to process deeper certain areas of psychic subsystems than another, but at the same time other areas are still little understood, while another here has processed. Such differences in the educational processes are unavoidable. So, the transition from the first to the second phase and from this to the third phase is fluid. We see the transition itself as a process that can take a few months.

The educational programs of the basic and intermediate level, the theoretical material of the first and second phases of individuation, can be completed as a learning process without any major interruptions. Everyone is free to study the educational program III at an early age to know what is to be expected. However, the inner educational process can never be completed at this speed. That is why we understand these educational programs as "work material" that can be used again and again in the training program and must. We, however, dissuade to complete the education program III just followed up the educational program I and II. A practical training program should be interposed.

The material organization that we present here is based on the practical works on the basic level and advanced level individuation, which were prepared in parallel, as well as on the scientific study "Empirie der Individuation - Andragogische Psychologie".

In the overview, we can organize the material and the educational program as follows:

General basic education (small block courses / seminars / workshops):

Topics: Self-analysis, psychic life, biographical processing, evolutionary human being, individuation, social competences, dream interpretation and meditation. Our practice: Freely designed in seminars with a total of 40 subject units.

1st level individuation: Development

- Dealing with the concept, methods, life issues, educational needs, etc.
- Knowledge and experience of the psychic systems and the individuation
- 10 units, an effort equivalent to at least 100 lessons

BASIC LEVEL: TRAINING PROGRAM:
1-2 years; 2 lessons per week (or block units at intervals)

2nd level individuation: Growth

- Systematic self-knowledge and thus initiation of all transformation processes
- In-depth education about every psychic system, the process, and its methods
- 10 units, an effort equivalent to at least 100 lessons

INTERMEDIATE LEVEL: TRAINING PROGRAM:
2-3 years; 2 lessons per week (or block units in intervals)

3rd level individuation: Fulfillment

- Inner growth up to the consolidation of unity and wholeness
- Furthermore, this phase of individuation includes selected individual topics on philosophy, religion, culture, mythology, society, symbolism, life topics, etc.
- 10 units, an effort corresponding to at least 160 lessons.

ADVANCED LEVEL: TRAINING PROGRAM:
Standardization is not possible. This level lasts until the goal is achieved.

We remind: In the human education, a separation of environment (life world), biography, and personality (psychic organism / individuation) is neither theoretically nor practically possible. The human image on which our "material" is based contains a clearly structured dynamic model that fulfills the demand for a "new conception of the human" (Dienelt 1984, 103, 132, 152).

Tragetings:

The formulation of goals is a crucial basis for lesson planning. In pedagogy resp. educational science, the main guiding principles are emancipation, self-determination and co-determination ability, maturity, ability to solidarity, the ability to act autonomously, etc. (Klafki 1993, Brezinka 1978, Derbolav 1987). These are the tragetings at the most general level. For the general andragogy, we can define the following descriptions as the primary objective: Holistic, comprehensive, inner versatile balanced, harmonious, and educated psychic forces. This highest inner goal definition (the individuation) implies the external aspect: Implementation (actualization resp. realization) of this inner wholeness in the habitat for oneself, for fellow humans, for society and habitat design (which means that Plato's idea of inner harmony and the harmony in the state is updated in a new form). This goal orientation sees itself as a lasting further development and differentiation for a lifetime. To this target level belongs also: Disposing and handling of all methods that concern the formation of psychic forces, for example, relaxation techniques, mental training, dream interpretation, meditation (imagination), analytical self-reflection and the abilities to use constructively these newly formed psychic forces in life.

The adjacent target areas contain targetings that relate to several psychic subsystems and not to the wholeness. Individual techniques of self-education and self-experience are included here. Such goals are, for example: Complete elaborating of the lived past, living sexuality in an integrated manner, flexible and considered handling of the own feelings, integration of cooperation with the inner spirit (dream interpretation, meditation) in the daily life and in the further development, balanced living basic needs taking into account the force of love, back bonding of value - and meaning experiencing to love and the inner spirit, appropriate implementation of inner forces in the daily life, goal-oriented speaking with self-critical thinking, use of intelligence abilities and creativity in all matters of life, implementation of the individual transformation steps of individuation, etc.

The subsequent target level (the starting point of all learning processes) relates to the individual psychic subsystems, their inner subsystems with the individual forces, for example:

Being able to recognize and deal with the individual psychic forces; ability to develop these forces constantly, to free blockings and to integrate them in the "I"-guidance as constructive forces; turning to and taking seriously the own psychic inner world, realized and practiced step by step in all subsystems; understanding the relations between the individual psychic forces and the outer lived everyday reality, especially its history of origins; developing the own values and attitudes, life models in general, to all life issues, and above all to every single goal: Transferring self-knowledge and self-education in all possible life situations.

At all target levels (see illustration 8), the goals are always oriented on the one hand to the inner world and on the other hand, as acting goals, oriented to the daily life. We cannot do a detailed structuring here. This is a too extensive task. Since the goals are tied back to the psychic organism, they have a fixed basic structure. Nevertheless, a curriculum can, (and must), be structured in an open manner. Every organization of learning process must be kept flexible, but without "losing the thread". Each student (adult) brings himself and his life (with the biography) into all learning processes. The andragogue himself is not outside of the topic, which means that the teaching and learning processes always run as interactive processes. What all participants bring in such a learning process, is "living life material" and therefore conflictive for group dynamic processes.

Exemplary learning processes can be carried out here. In addition to imparting basic knowledge, the life inventory of each participant and the practicing of methods have of central importance in the tuitional processings. Each topic that is subject of teaching processing, includes as part of the methods of experience and of processing with these psychic realities (design forms, techniques, procedures). Knowledge without back bonding to the inner experience and to the own concrete life would bypass the educational goals. The lesson planning and designing integrates at the same time: Target level, inner psychic topic, habitat, design options and methods, inner experience, and group dynamic processes. Lesson planning in andragogy is based on the principle of openness: In the target formulation, in the participation, in the media and methods choice, in the learning strategy and evaluation.

The current personality development on the free market offers goals such as "self- realization", "holism", "self-development" and many more. The humanistic psychology and all those who use its vocabulary label their practical programs with such highest goals. As far as we overview, a large part of practice of personality development (self-experience, psychotherapy, encounter, etc.) has not attached any constitutive importance to didactics. Thematic exceptions are based on the recognition: "Emotional attention is a basic human need and promotes learning" (Tausch-Tausch 1971, Rogers 1973, Maslow 1973). The cognitive-emotive psychology confirms this fact (Hoffmann 1979, Foppa 1981). An important task of educational theory and didactics of general andragogy is the many individual goals and values to incorporate into a taxonomy in such a direction that on the one hand the actual comprehensive wholeness can be formulated, and that on the other hand it really includes all psychic subsystems and individual forces.

We consider this to be an extremely important condition, since otherwise well-sounding goals such as "away from the facades, from fulfilling cultural values, from pleasing others, from actually-I-should and towards process-being, complexity, openness to experience, acceptance of the others, self-confidence" (Rogers 1973, 167 ff.) cannot lead to the intended educational achievement. Similarly problematic goals and values formulates Maslow: "Perfection, completion, effortlessness, wholeness, goodness, legality" (Maslow 1973, 94). The positive human image of Menninger includes among others: "Impartiality, benefit of the creative talents, ability to stress adaptation, optimal need balance, identification with ethical values ..." (Menninger 1968, 148). Such formulations make it clear: Goals are value judgments, partly in the sense of "that is good" (judgmental), partly in the sense of "you should do the good" (imperative) (Hare 1972, 21).

In addition, a back bonding to the everyday reality in the target formulation is essential. This work process contains decisions about being and growth values (Maslow 1973, 41, 94-95, 160) and decision in the hierarchy (Frey 1971 166; Meyer 1972 15). For this purpose, target level models (ZEM) (Aregger 1972, 78-79, 110-120) are to be created: Kore ideas, disposition targets, operationalized learning targets.

We have formulated personality goals and ideals at various points, regardless of a differentiated learning organization. We want to address these approaches and present formal criteria for the subject organization in a target-oriented manner. We start with the educational theory of our conception of andragogy. The following illustration 9 sets the individual components resp. levels in relation to one another.

Illustration 9: Learning through Realistic Motivation

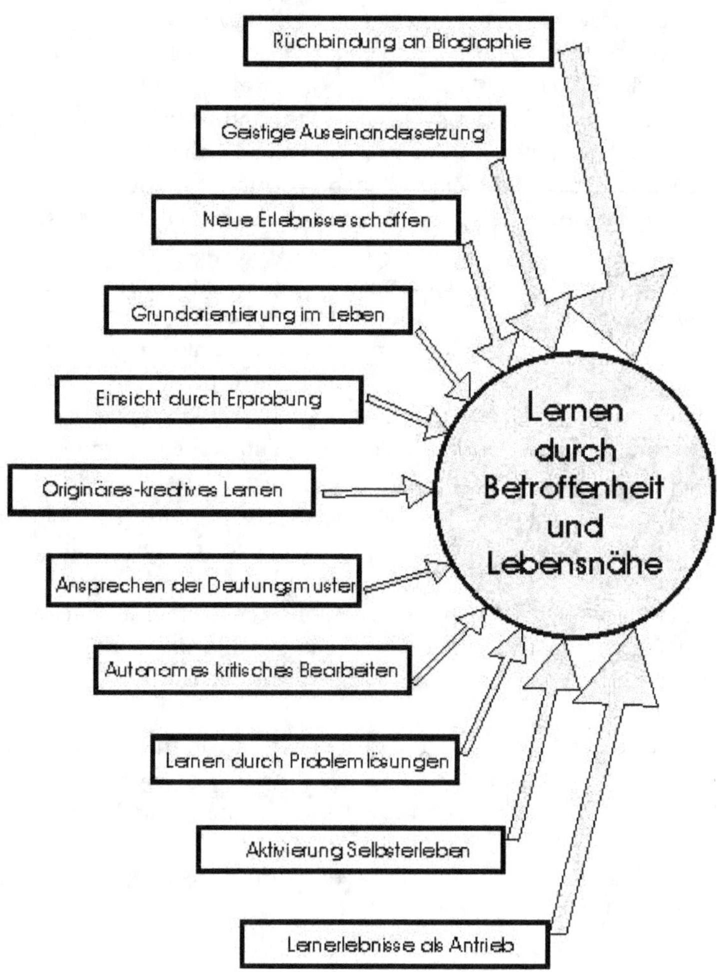

Translation:

Back bonding to biography > Mental dealing > Creating new experiences >
Basic orientation in life > Insight through trial > Original-creative learning >
Approaching of interpretation patterns > Autonomously critical attending >
Learning through problem solving > Activating self-experiencing > Learning
experiences as motivation >

Learning by concerning and truth-to-life

The fact that the "crisis of our time" is also a central crisis of meaning and value ("Meaning is an irreplaceable element of education", Biller 1994, 228), a moral-ethical and spiritual crisis (Habermas 1992; Oser / Althof / Garz 1986; Maier 1986; Dienelt 1984), urges us to attach the greatest importance to the problem of determination of ideal and goal in context of psychic and at the same time real external life. Horkheimer (1968, 81) asks: "Is there just one outrage that has not already been committed with a clear conscience?" We think that a real ethical-intellectual education with obligatory back bonding to the inner spirit and to the love is possible if this is built into the process of individuation as structured and planned comprehensive educational program.

At all the target levels, various characteristics can be called in the target formulation (Schorch; in Roth 1991, 710; Peterssen; in Roth 1991, 670-671). Formal differentiating, macro and micro goals can be distinguished. Macro goal means: Orientation, sketching, entrance, introduction. Micro goal means: Consolidation, micro-systematization, clarification, differentiation, mastery.

The classic categories are: 1) Knowledge: Psychic forces, subsystems and their parts, overall system, life realities, relations with habitat, experience methods; 2) Ability: Recognizing, experience methods, transforming, unfolding, inserting, regulating, anticipating, interpreting, communicating; 3) Values: Comprehending, interpreting, weighting, setting, justifying deficits and meanings (sense) and assume responsibility (as an ethical principle); 4) Deciding: At the level of knowledge, abilities and values, recognizing, justifying, realizing decision possibilities. - These classic categories can be divided into macro and micro targets (level).

The goal formulation contains ethical, psychological, secular, methodological and educational elements (Brezinka 1977). If we connect a goal with the concrete habitat, then this becomes concrete (as regards content) and therefore always part of our conscience, our responsibility, and our concern. We formulate a goal because we consider it "good", justify it in context with human-psyche-world (i.e.: life-relevant) and expect democratic consensus. In this consensus process, the clarifying of terms is important. Everyone develops his own system of "good-bad", "right-wrong", "meaningful-meaningless" and "useful-useless". A certain "standardization", i.e., general recognition of value standards resp. the acting norms, is part of a socially recognized and scientifically justified educational program (Albert 1972, 127, 148). The language is the level of target discussion and target formulation. Some conditions facilitate the communication: Simple, clear, applicable, logical, justifiable, thinking operational accessible, free of contradiction, able to develop, able to build up (Leinfellner 1967, 14 -17; Brezinka 1977). The (normal) difference in symbol formations must be clarified in the exchange process. The common from the sum of different formulations shall become an orientation for the individual in the future. If the focus is on the detail and the whole does not fall out of consciousness, but rather the whole is always recognized, then in the andragogy of future, a super-individual catalog of goals can be created as a working document. It is part of the educational idea of andragogy that the formulations are always congruent between human and habitat. The consideration of present and future interests also results from the educational idea. No goal should be set at the expense of any other goal. The decisions and formulations result in the concordance between science orientation and life orientation (see Tietgens 1981, 33, 185, 195, 199; Mager 1970). The target organization (sequence, structure) occurs further with consideration of general learning laws and the growth principles of psychic life (developmental psychology of adults).

The didactics of pedagogy has developed considerable theoretical and practical contributions in the last twenty years (for example: Blankertz 1971/1977 (10); Klausmeier 1978; Schulz 1980; Reich 1977; Petersson 1983; Heursen 1984; see also the overview in Kron 1994, 117). The didactics of andragogy can develop its own didactic "structural grid" (goals, contents, methods, media, etc.) and strategies based on this.

This is a guarantee of a truly holistic and comprehensive education to the "inner harmonic human" and for the individual and collective life design as an external reflection of this inner new created reality.

In the general survey of didactics (including adult education), mechanistic models predominate, a thinking in terms of dimension such as control and domination, efficiency, and benefit. It seems to us that in adult education, especially in human education, the subjective side should be given more consideration. Teachers and learners are the central active designers with their (learning) biography, their life and coping style as well as their character. Both should have fun in learning (teaching) and educating themselves. To creativity should be given just as much space as the personal language and the individual inventory of images (from life experiences). An input-output system with clearly defined goals, instruments and ways does not achieve these subjective aspects. New dynamic, self-regulating learning cultures are to be developed for the andragogy.

Lesson design:

In this section, we touch a few more elements on the didactic problems of personality development and individuation:

Element: Learning principles

The relation to learning psychology in lesson design is always decisive for learning success (Koskenniemi 1971; Kron 1994, 230-292). Each learning process has its own course, e.g., "warming up" (initiation), development and then design (Schulz 1972, 25-26). Clear target formulations enable a success experience and a success control. However, it seems to us that we can only separate so clearly in didactic structural grid what is theoretically or scientifically founded. We cannot specifically separate psyche, language, values, and world. The lessons themselves can be organized as an experience space (von Hentig 1973, 25; Gudjons 1994; Aebli 1994/8). Applying learning laws implies the inclusion of teacher behavior (Wahl 1993).

In our seminars, we have made the experience that interested persons represent a very heterogeneous population, even with extremely specific forms of contact (advertisements, program presentations). The lesson planning must take this into account and to plan the inner differentiation accordingly. Our guidelines from these experiences: 1) All participants should individually optimally be supported; 2) The independence in learning activities is to be activated; 3) The different dispositions apply as starting point for learning processes; 4) The cooperation is to install in the organized learning and to support 5) The individual life topics are to be used as life links; and 6) The motivation must be kept awake and supported individually (Frommer 1991; Raapke / Schulenberg 1985).

The principle "respond to the human, where he is" (so-called "participant-orientation") applies to all planned learning activities. Thus, the learning requirements are to be considered in lesson planning for each stage resp. phase. This means that in a learning unit in small groups according to different learning principles can be worked and possibly must. We cannot edit here the learning principles in details. But we want to recall: Cognitive internalization, linguistic repetition, discrimination learning, motor-behaviorist learning, exemplary learning, symbolic-associative learning, emotional learning, problem solving learning, formative structural learning, operant learning, interaction learning, term learning, hermeneutical learning (meaning comprehending), repetition learning (already processed in the current literature on didactics).

Only with keywords we can here indicate on the implications of a self-reflexive personality education. The justification contexts are first in the field of anthropological education categories. We indicate this with some historically known terms such as enlightenment, openness, autonomy, spontaneity, letting grow, independent activity and self-responsibility (cf.

Gieseke 1991, 81; Siebert 1991, 19-32). When reversed, these pedagogical guiding principles indicate dangers. To mention are here, among others, external determination, control, apathy, half-education, facade, adapted routine, alienation and, as a result, inhumanity. Secondly, self-reflexive learning allows the evolvement of a wide anthropological potential. This has some trend-setting consequences for didactics. The personality development is didactically to design so that this potential can be produced, promoted, and used. Banal this means, for example, "helping to self-help" through suggestions (impulses) for independent learning activities (repetitions, links with known issues, experience exchange, confrontation, learning planning, identification, etc.). These general didactic elements include, in our opinion, further practicing of meta thinking (thinking about the own thinking) as well as reflection on the links between knowledge and individualized acting steps (see Wahl 1993, 72). This also includes the diversified aspect of coping strategies. That is practical self-knowledge.

The teleological character of all learning steps acts centrally as a learning support factor. This is to consider in the lesson planning in the context of learning processes. The experiential learning on the own life inventory includes this aspect. The "problem-solving learning" on the material is over all other learning principles (e.g., operant conditioning, cognitive learning, design-structural learning, motor and language association learning, discrimination learning and conceptual learning). Meaning connections that reach the learner's everyday life promote learning and motivation. The success experience can thus arise directly in everyday situations. The andragogic teaching is to be designed as a structured, protected habitat. Here one learns, experiences, and practices what should become reality outside of the lessons. Role-play and topic-centered interaction get a goal-oriented and life-relevant function. The protocols for recording "critical event situations" (see in: Empirie der Individuation) include the current "critical" life inventory of the participants.

The 20 biographical topics can also be presented didactically in the protocol form for creative and reflective discussion. Experience related examples from the everyday reality to all psychic subsystems apply as the "material" for problem solving oriented learning. The step from experience to insight and then to duty can neither be conditioned nor forced. Successful experiences on living material (we also refer the self-experience as "life inventory") created in class promotes the integration of what has been learned into everyday life and supports the motivation to continue learning resp. to educate oneself.

According to Krämer / Walter (1994, 35-37), the following requirements must be considered for adult learning: "Adults are not a 'blank sheet' ...

Adults are critical learners ... As a rule, adults are voluntary learners ... Very many adults have clear goals, they link with learning ... Adults learn application-oriented and goal-oriented ... Adults learn at best if the subject is logically comprehensible and allows an intellectual debate ... Adults achieve the best results then if they can individually determine the pace of learning". We would be due to our experience in personal development apply for certain limitations, particularly what concerns the "clear objectives" and the relation between (rational) knowledge acquiring and experiential learning. However: Not everything in human education through individuation can be operationalized and "didactically grasp". Regardless of this, the didactical important question arises: How can such frame conditions, requirements of participants, be considered in human education resp. in didactic construction? The following sequence of steps has proven itself: From first experiences to basic knowledge and targetings; and from this new foundation in turn to experiential learning; then again to targetings and, based on this, target oriented knowledge amplification, which is the structural basis (as organized knowledge) for new experience-oriented experiences.

This stage control cycle promotes motivation and creates new motives for motivation. The occupation with results of experiential learning and simultaneous reference back to the everyday world of the learner and to the biography of his interpretation models (Arnold 1985, 101) could satisfy these learning psychological conditions once reflection and steady knowledge amplification effect directly learning processes. Educational processes are in interaction of identity work and reality work (e.g., self-concept-approach of Winkler 1993). Such an educational process certainly follows the line of the basic postulate "higher development of humanity" (Benner 1983, 297; quoted in: Arnold 1985, 119). "Participant orientation" means for us on the one hand, "start where the participant is", and on the other hand, the educational mandate realizes realistically from the actual given educational needs. Very many know nothing at all about the psychic-spiritual life and the evolutionary human being. And when we talk about teaching, we should not overlook the fact that learning processes should lead to success in life. There are also other factors at play that are outside the educational process.

Element: Lesson design

The learning steps (appropriation process) are planning element for the teaching design: Elaboration of theoretical knowledge, dealing with concrete case studies (model-like illustrations), linguistic realizing of outer and inner experience, intellectual internalization and linguistic repetition (consolidation through experiencing and repeating), practical application of linguistic units in action units, and transfer in various personal and collective life realities (flexible availability) (Bönsch; in: Roth, 1991, 719-723, 729; Horney, among others 1970, I, 7 57-763). Elements for the practical lesson design are: Getting to know, case study discussions, brainstorming, exercises, experience exchange, plenary discussion, panel discussion, dealing with topics, performing / presenting, cooperation and feedback, integrating communicative competence, creating consternation, perceiving emotional processes, processing group conflicts, discussing learning inhibitions, imparting information, instructing (training), arranging abilities, orientation in the habitat, orientation in the psychic space, discussion in small groups for dealing with, role play, projects (applying, implementing, learning), "preheating" (initiating, unfolding, designing), impulse method: Theses, keywords and questions for reflection and discussion (cf. Müller U. 1993, 229; Klimsa 1993, 305-320).

At adult education centers, events with an often considerably large participant number of 50 to 80 people are not uncommon. This means that there are certain limits to the choice of method. It is usual here for something like: A short presentation, then a group discussion and finally a final plenary discussion (Pöggeler 1974, 209-210). In our didactic treatise, we orient ourselves on group sizes of 8-15 participants. Larger groups (up to 40 participants) require an organized subgroup work, for which different work schemes are available: Small groups of 6 people ("method 66") with one leading participant each, then a panel discussion with the leading persons who present the group results and finally the summary by the andragogue. Variants are couple talk and round table. Planned directing can make the classroom interesting and lively. Individual abilities of participants can be built into these work forms (Tietgens 1981, 45-48, 198-199). The social work forms are an important planning tool the larger the number of participants. The entire organization of teaching and learning processes is to do for each teaching unit resp. per overall program according to this planning aspect. So, we consider the different performance dispositions of participants in terms of: Amount, complexity, expenditure of time, motivation, degree of self-employment and ability to cooperate.

Element: Media and materials

Many working materials can be used to design lessons. These are specifically: Knowledge units, theories, models, information, quotes, individual facts, statistics, case studies, documents, images, tests, checklists, photos, slides, films, graphics, keyword lists, exercises, experiential material, thesis units, etc. For the presentation are at disposal the known instruments: Blackboard, molloton wall, overhead projector, video equipment, network browser, and other more. There is a large amount of literature on this (cf. Langner-Geissler

/ Lipp 1994; Weidenmann 1991; Will 1994; Müller KR 1994; Brühwiler 1994).

Element: Evaluation

A particularly difficult aspect is the verifiability of a completed acquisition and examination process. On the one hand, knowledge and methods can be checked operationally (multiple choice test).

We mean a reduction to behavioristic and cognitive learning processes. Expanded (hermeneutic and symbolic) criteria for transcription of the educational level to be recorded can also be included (Derbolav 1987, 129). The completion of inner forming processes and realization (probation) in the habitat are to be included in a success control (for learning motivation). The learner's self-assessment plays a central role. It is a learning objective in itself for all learning objectives (levels). Nevertheless, objective resp. extended criteria must be defined that can substantially include the status.

Due to its decades of experiences, the depth psychology (of all directions) may express objections and restraint particularly critically and seriously. Indeed, through all analytical processes of experience, a person can hide a deep-seated unconscious problem from himself and from everyone else. There are also people who construct dreams to "look better", or who can imitate resp. act out something perfectly, without having formed resp. newly and expanded developed in the depths of the unconscious resp. in the root areas of all psychic forces. The "finite and infinite analysis" (Freud 1940) reflects this problem in a somewhat different context. There are certain problems in the unconscious, which can only be resolved with extreme effort and the most thorough self-reflection (with introspection), but which in our opinion cannot yet be declared as a "disease", for example Oedipus / Electro complex, strictest and rigid super-ego-constellation, psycho-social suffering experiences, rigid ideological and dogmatic attitudes, layer-specific self-experience, etc. There are also fate experiences (as victims and culprits), which consequences require several years of most intensive self-education to become able to live those internally constructive, and accepting (e.g., disability, economic collapse, divorce). We think there are clear orientations for the target levels, so that the "problem of the infinite analysis" does not arise in andragogy in this form. We have also made the experience that effects of disfiguring and covering unconscious resp. still unformed forces are always self-evident in the long term. Here the qualification of the andragogue is addressed, who must be able "to recognize in the melody the wrong notes".

As a solution model, we refer to our own professional experiences: A person's dreams and imaginations inform very precisely about the level of inner education (in one or more psychic systems). If the success control is oriented parallel resp. at the same time to the inner world, to the outer world of this person, to the inner experience (dream, meditation) and to active participation in the classroom (as a learning and practice field), then a differentiated picture can be created about the status of the completed individual learning steps. The andragogical psychology can construct checklists as a network for registrations of "educational needs" resp. the achieved goals.

In general life-related adult education, the following standard items are suggested for the evaluation of a seminar: 1) I liked this seminar; 2) My expectations and goals were met; 3) I learned a lot of new things in this seminar; 4) I now have a deep insight into my ... behavior; 5) The seminar was helpful for my daily work; 6) The working atmosphere was pleasant; 7) I am satisfied with the seminar leadership; 8) I can recommend the seminar to others (Klupp 1992; Wahl et al. 1993, 44-45). Krämer / Walter (1994, 86-87) recommend further aspects: Time design, media use, professional expertise, understandability, participant orientation, methodical safety, the work of the lecturer and other questions about outer frame (kitchen, conference center, etc.).

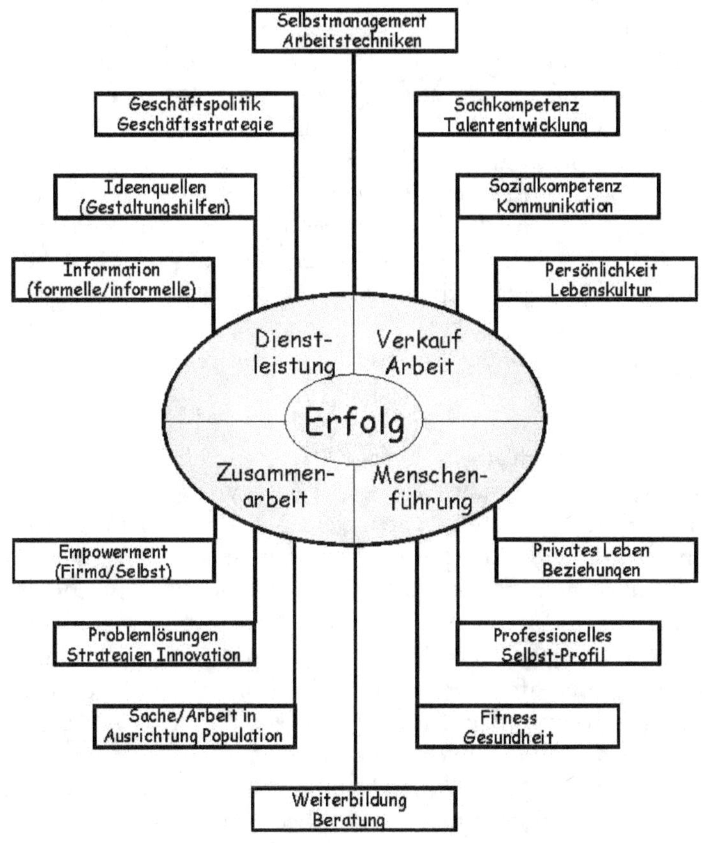

Translation:

Self-management/Working techniques

Business policy/ Business strategy   Fact competence/Talent development

Ideas sources/(designing helps)   Social competence/Communication

Information (formal/informal)   Personality/Life culture

Service   Sales/Work

Success

Collaboration   Human guidance

Empowerment/(Company/Self)   Privat life/Relations

Problem solving/Strategies/Innovation   Professional self-profile

Fact/work in direction population   Fitness/Health

Further training/Counseling

Element: Modular system and educational units

We have in the subject organization made a subdivision in step resp. phase units. We have emphasized that this educational program as modular system is part of "education experience". Anyone can use modules at any time, interrupt or break off the education. Nevertheless, the (often asked) question arises: How long does this educational process take to the goal of individuation? In other words: How many teaching units are necessary to include the whole process of personality development and individuation? That depends on many factors and cannot simply be determined with thematic learning units. The most interested persons for andragogical education should be (as the experience of the author to date) between 30 and 50 years old. The range of actual life experiences and current life realities is enormous wide in quantity and quality. The motivation is also hugely different.

The individuals differ greatly in terms of education, life standard, professional responsibility, previous knowledge, experience with self-education, current conflict and crisis, psychological parents etc. Many have first to learn that self-education needs a significant personal commitment (reading, keeping dream dairy, daily relaxing and meditating etc.). Apart from these preconditions, the inner growth process needs its minimal time. The inner process is also spiral and cyclical. That means: The individual psychic subsystems must be dealt with repetitively one after the other always deeper; and: The inner growth process has its own dynamic that cannot be accelerated at will. Every human has his own individual rhythm of "growth pushes".

We estimate the duration of the overall process to an average of about seven to ten years to achieve the goal of individuation, with regular moderate use. It should be emphasized here, that the vital educational goal of andragogy is not at first this highest goal, but rather "living in the process of individuation". So it makes little sense, if not detrimental, to create a curriculum that strives for the highest goal in the best possible way and best possible time. According to our experiences, it should also be pointed out that very many humans who are over 50 years old can hardly find the openness and motivation to tackle this process. In many of them there is also an increasing hardening of the overall character with increasing age. Finally, it should be emphasized: Life continues 'normally' after the goal has been achieved; new life challenges require new, different educational processes.

Element: Requirements for the participants

The teaching planning in the andragogical education theoretically must consider a wide range of individual dispositions of learners. De facto, the demand determines a course realization. A course is advertised, and the number of registrations is usually not predictable. We want to disregard this problem here and discuss it under "advertising". The andragogical practice is neither a high school, nor a university, nor a subject-specific (professional) further education. The participants come from the real life and are in many cases already over the half of life. They have their history and fate, their suffering and distress, their guilt and responsibility (Pöggeler 1974, 214). The conditions can partially be channeled in the announcement of a course but are rarely homogeneous able to schedule. However, they have a considerable influence on what happens in the classroom (Tietgens 1981, 34-35, 102, 125-127, 184, 189, 197-198; Ebner 1991, 218-227).

Diverse, different aspects of the possible requirements are: 1) Biography: Age, gender, cohabitation, living standard, occupation etc. 2) "Critical" life situations, life history, societal frame; 3) Prerequisites: Knowledge, methodological abilities, course experiences; 4) Motivation: Concrete motivation, potential of motivation; 5) Learning experiences, learning habits, learning attitudes and learning abilities (learning stress); 6) Cognitive-emotional abilities: Abstraction, transfer, absorbing, processing; 7) Problem situation, problem recognition ability and problem solving capacity; 8) Willingness to transformation, ability to transformation, resistances; 9) Openness and tolerance threshold (ideological-dogmatic ties); 10) Ideas, expectations, hopes and demands on the "education"; 11) Cooperative ability, initiative, utilizability of creativity and intuition; 12) Language code: Association schemes, forms of thinking and interpreting, ways of speaking; 13) Responsibility, conscientiousness, moral character.

Planning element before the lesson is carried out: Advertising.

The adult education in general, but also the personality development as it is offered today, is subject to the market principles of supply and demand (need). The "fragility" is a serious problem (Tiegens 1981, 76-77, 192-193). Various market factors play a role here:

Population, economic development, current social affairs, and the media. There is for this andragogical education no urgent key motif, such as in psychotherapy.

The central active factor in the demand is the motivation, because "the path to a free spirit is effort and hard work" (Meueler 1993, 175). The question remains open: Who wants this "service to the human" (Kurzdörfer 1981, 177)? For the offer the question arises: How can be addressed the existing motivation or even be created motivation (Siebert 1991, 154-164)? And then expanded: How can this be obtained and promoted in the teaching process. The extrinsic motivation appears to us to be secondary. The personality development offers little opportunity for worth and recognition. Individuation is hardly in demand in the industrial market economy process and does not represent any standard, neither in leisure nor in consumption. There is still no "compulsory education" for human education. Thus, the intrinsic motivation is of particular importance for those who are interested and for any activation of a demand. Tietgens and others suggest that advertising should already contain an (pedagogical) educational mandate.

The short-lived nature of our time is opposed to some didactic principles. "Weekend courses" are often in demand, which should lead to love, happiness, wisdom, and wellbeing in one big step. The pleasure-oriented consumption and entertainment "zeitgeist" and the characteristics of "postmodernism" also oppose to andragogical educational program. With long-term-oriented usefulness arguments, it is not possible to motivate people to learn new things regularly over a longer period in addition to the "troubles" of everyday life. Also, to be considered are lack of joy in learning and openness to learning, defense against the unconscious, disinterest in spiritual issues, lack of responsibility consciousness for the own "fate" and the fact that this education does not fulfill any direct capital interests. It seems to us that these obstacles cannot be solved with a theory of didactics. With the begin of the learning program, however, these factors can be integrated as "life inventory" in the problem-solving learning as "exemplary learning" to counteract this "short-lived nature", "pleasure orientation" and this "defense against the inner life".

For advertising, we suggest in key words: Addressing the imagination syndromes; responding to pre-knowledge; awakening needs; finding and addressing needs; target group determination (targeted offering); addressing education readiness; anticipation of learning success; attracting attention; catching (controlling) of reaction variants; understanding (information through verbal communication); informing contacts with supporting organizations; transparency of the scientific and anthropological basis.

We have pointed out the various problems of psycho-esoteric market on several occasions. It outweighs exaggerated promises, dilettantism, sectarianism and spiritual-religious ideologizations. Most of the offers are neither "comprehensive" nor "holistic". The "compulsion" of the market situation demands "quick education" and "experiences". The outdoing of the rivalry urges some to deceptive formulations about programs and goals.

But andragogues are neither advertising experts nor "clothes sellers". One the one hand the social development with increasing collective problems and loads create a comprehensive demand, is expected. On the other hand, the andragogy can create a new professionalization identity in its own ranks (associations, clubs, organizations, professional groups) and jointly design a market strategy and handle this step as educational task (education). We think: The andragogy should not put its valuable "good" under the table.

Overall, when planning an advertising strategy, a certain degree of realism must be maintained. There are population groups that are hardly accessible for this andragogical education. Through all social classes and occupation groups there are many individuals who would not think to educate their personality holistically. We think that the general andragogy can give older people, even those who live their twilight years in rest homes, much of personal enrichment. However, in addition to the expected resistances, there are also certain learning problems. Many people in our society are no longer able to read a book. They also seldom write and are not interested in things that have "spiritual" value.

The prejudices against self-knowledge and self- education are massive in many ethnic groups. Then there are groups of people who first need psychotherapy. Not to be underestimated are, in our opinion, those large circles in the society, that the elementary human values disregard and often create great harm. This group of people can hardly be motivated to develop their personality. Finally, it can also be seen that many people must pay enormous attention to their monthly budget and hardly have any flexibility in setting priorities. This, however, must not tempt to squander personal development as "cheap goods". Those who are not willing to take smaller or larger constraint upon himself for several years in favor of psychic-spiritual development and life enrichment, will never achieve the individuation.

Element: Implementation in practical educational achievements

It should be emphasized again here: Andragogy is neither psychotherapy nor psychoanalysis, nor psychological counseling in the sense that is used today. In andragogical education process the student must complete a significant education achievement. This requires certain teaching achievements on the part of the andragogue. We would like to suggest some practical aspects in the context of learning principles for the lesson design (cf. Klimsa 1993, 204-274):

The learning processes start with the level of knowledge (awareness) of the student. Whatever of knowledge is to be acquired about the psychic life and to be achieved in terms of education, we consider the assessment of the initial situation to be a fundamental didactic necessity. In it also roots the motivation and personal involvement. This can be initiated with the following questions resp. work tasks the sense of the classic "brainstorming": "What first questions arise for the students from the topic? Which keywords can the students initially give? What associations, the students have on the topic in general? What does the student want to know about the topic in particular? What everyday relationships can the student spontaneously establish? What practical interests does the student have on the topic?"

Once the topic has been rolled out in a short presentation as well as with theses, key words, and questions (so-called impulse method), the student can in turn make his own contributions that have an educational psychological effect through reflection: "How does the student experience the topic? With which own ideas can the student expand the topic? What topics elements have currently an actuality for the student? Which keywords to individual aspects can the student add?"

Again thinking, for storage and control, for reflection on the subjective perception and processing of the topic, learning activities can be organized, for example with the request: "Summarize the essentials! What are the open questions on the topic for you?"

The promotion of intuition and creativity is didactically and methodically elementary in the elaboration of the own life story, but also in dealing with the "material" of psychic life. We primarily mean the following aspects: Imagining, turning scenes into the opposite, reformulating problems, adding new values, solving polarities, and creating further focal points with fantasy, extrapolating into the future, creating analogies, inventing a fairy tale story from a problem situation, interpreting coincidences, adding new scenes, formulating from a problem the positive, in describing changing the central terms of everyday language, putting spontaneous ideas etc.

The educational performance of the student relates on the one hand to the processing of the subject, on the other hand to the target direction. Every student must formulate his own educational goals for each topic. Some of the goals are short-term resp. related to the current situation. The extended goals set a perspective of a few to several months: "Formulate short-term educational goals that are important to you! Formulate medium-term educational goals that you want to achieve!"

With the goal setting, the student has a high right of co-determination and a high degree of autonomy in the educational performance. To structure these processes learning psychologically and not to underly the hazard, we set further questions as learning stimulation. In this way the student can establish his personal life relation and find his own values. In addition, this is where the implementation in everyday life begins: "How do you justify your short and medium-term educational goals? Formulate some guiding ideas for your everyday life!"

Furthermore, the individual topics can be reflected under different aspects and be discussed in the group. The student's situation can be recorded with small checklists. This also includes an aspect of practical application of knowledge. These also include the context of habitat, social relations, the own life history, and the experience methods:

"How do you experience this topic in you? How can you deal with this topic (as your reality)? How do you see this topic with other people? How do others deal with this topic? What significance does this topic have for the social life? What educational needs do you experience on aspects of this topic? How do you manage access to the reality of this topic? How do you experience the personal meaning of theses on this topic?"

With such questions, a wide variety of learning processes can be activated and the learning processings can be controlled. All questions result in a sense of achievement and interactions (with the others in the group and with the andragogue). The knowledge is transformed into personal knowledge and inserted into the personal life context, even in the time perspective (past-present-future). Diverse, balanced educational achievements are guaranteed in the group, while at the same time every student learns to organize his own goals, reasons, adaptations, and applications. Some of our questions resp. requests can be processed in a playful way (role playing, interviews, small survey etc. in the sense of "project teaching"). We call this the actual educational achievement of the student. In addition, it is ensured with this didactic structuring that the learning activities not sheer in a psychological self-experience group. We have used this type of implementation resp. introduction of educational achievements in our works for basic level and advanced level individuation.

Element: Quality criteria for the professionalization of andragogy

Following the quality concept by Arnold (1994, 6-9) for further training, we can adhere in the overview on our didactics resp. educational organization:

1. Input quality: The concept is explained and justified from an adult pedagogical perspective; the planning is scientifically based, needs-based

and participant-oriented; the offer is transparent and continuously form
variant.

2. Throughput Quality: The proposed infrastructure is learning supporting
   and supplying; the professionalism is fundamentally competent in our
   concept, advisory as well as pedagogical; the didactics contains motivating
   elements, includes experiences of the participants, enables actions (in life)
   and the learning is largely reflexive.

3. Output quality: The material units are contained with clear goals and can
   be used immediately in life; the satisfaction of the participants can be
   adhered privately as well as at work; the educational goals create basis for
   life competences that can certainly promote a career; the personality
   targets are clear and unambiguous in a stabilizing and key qualifying
   manner.

As a target group for our human education, we can consider all role areas,
whether leisure or work, teaching or advice, sales or living together, the
human is always in interaction. And where it is not about social competence?
In what kind of interaction is subject competence irrelevant? From all
previous aspects it is clear: Over 50% of life is psychology, be it as theory, as
facts, as prejudice, as subjective theory or as life knowledge. This may well be
a guideline for the conception of human education in the future.

Illustration 11: The Human in Interaction

Translation:

I	Factual competence	You
Life partner	Product/thing Action/process	Life partner
Colleague	Work Goal orientation	collogue
Principal		Principal
Vendor	**Social competence**	Vendor
Collaborator	**Social behavior**	Collaborator
Client	Interaction Communication	Client
Personality		**Personality**
Behavior	**Human Knowledge**	Behavior
Biography	**Personality**	Biography
Psycho-social	**Life culture**	Psycho-social
environment	**Life knowledge**	environment
Empowerment		**Empowerment**
through:	**Over 50% in the Life**	through:
Interest	**is psychology**	Interest
Motivation	(Theories, prejudice, facts	Motivation
Resources	Life knowledge, life experiences)	Resources
Peripheral systems		Peripheral systems

Foundation level:
Philosophical anthropology and ethics

Finally, an overly sensitive aspect of quality protection of andragogic work should be emphasized: Which professor of education still teaches "wisdom" and "love"? Which teacher and which expert in human education is really a pure pedagogue (andragogue) in his heart? Which educational research and adult education attend still to psychic-spiritual education, with the love, the spirit and the truthfulness? Such questions are truly relevant for pedagogy. They hit the lifeblood of the science of pedagogy resp. andragogy. And they hit each individual pedagogue resp. andragogue personally:

1) An andragogue who does not work through his own biography is nothing but the living result of his biography. He is the sum of everything that he has absorbed from the prenatal period. In this way he certainly does not live and practice the all-round balance of all his psychic force systems.

2) An andragogue who does not clear resp. integrate his unconscious (e.g., complexes) and his shadows is dominated by these forces, and these are reflected, among other things, in his projections on his educational work field. If repression and defense work inside, so also outside in the work.

3) An andragogue, trapped in neurosis resp. narcissism, cannot pursue an andragogy that forms the human all-round balanced. The psychodynamics of his educational activity is subject to the unbalanced psychical development of his overall person. This results in a considerably disturbed andragogical reference.

4) An andragogue who is not very capable of loving, who does not take his dreams seriously, who does not have deep access to his inner life, who does not meditate regularly, who deals inappropriately with his feelings and basic psychic needs, who does not integrate and balanced form his inner opposite-sex psychic pole (anima, animus), can neither convey these psychic realities nor build them up in others. He only forms the outer human.

5) An andragogue who does not thoroughly pursue self-knowledge (self-analysis) and individuation - and thus does not implement the archetypal transformations of psychic-spiritual development - has not yet understood the essential of the psychic-spiritual human being. His human image does not "grasp" the comprehensive psychic-spiritual human being, his conception of andragogy remains, and his agogic practice is correspondingly reduced.

Imagine: The psychoanalyst works without his own training analysis. Unimaginable in teaching and practice! From these five briefly outlined aspects it can be concluded that the andragogue - from the level of teaching and research to the front in everyday life of the society - must complete his own individuation as a form of training analysis by profession. Only this fulfillment qualifies him as an andragogue (pedagogue, education expert). *The*

Now it remains to add to the andragogical vision that the presented catalog of topics about the psychic life will have to become a subject of instruction in elementary school from elementary and advanced level to high school at some point in the distant future. Developing this program didactically will be the task of educators in the 21st century. *Appropriate psychological knowledge and abilities are necessary so that the human can adequately realize himself in the future.*

Driving the Philosophical Anthropology out of Educational Sciences

What is the human? What should the human be? What is the meaning and value of human being? These are the core questions of philosophical anthropology, along with the knowledge question: "What can I know?" These are the basic questions that have preoccupied philosophy since ancient Greece. Every kind of religion tries to give answers to these questions of existence. These are also the unpleasant questions that nobody likes to hear in the "horse racing stables" of educational science. In the post-modern age of educational science, one plays the game with the language: "Anything goes; just take nothing seriously". Nobody wants to conjure up liabilities. So, there is a "wild growth of many high-level theories on high-level theories", says Benning (1982, 13). Confusion about the case of the human and values is hidden behind it: "The blind tumbling from one pedagogical fad to the other" (Kern 1978; in: Benning 1982, 13).

Let us first take a brief look at the diversity of human images in philosophy resp. philosophical anthropology:

Plato: The human belongs to the world of ideas and appearances.

Aristotle: The human has a life-giving principle, a psyche with reason.

Epicurus: The human's happiness consists of moderate life enjoyment, in the control of desire through the mind (through insight and wisdom).

Augustine: The evil of the human is the turning from the higher to the lower, away from God to the "I".

Thomas Aquinas: The one person is bad who prevents the full development of natural possibilities.

Luther: The human is sin, weakness, dark shadow.

Hobbes: The human is the man's wolf ("homo homini lupus").

Sartre: The human is "condemned" to freedom and can always design himself, but also lie and deceive.

Machiavelli: The human is inherently bad, just looking for personal gain.

Leibnitz: Ultimately, the human is of a non-material, psychic nature.

Descartes: The human is a machine in which lives an immortal spirit.

Rousseau: The human is degenerate in the hands of men ("animal corrumpu").

Herder: The human is the linguistic creature. He is the first freed of nature. In the processing he becomes the purpose and goal of himself.

Fichte: The human only becomes a human among humans.

Bergson: The human has a creative consciousness, and a creative will and lives in creative development.

Goethe: The unconscious is the greatest creative source of the human.

Kant: The human is capable of self-determination, has a free will that is determined by the laws of reason.

Marx: The human shapes his life through work and through his possibilities to develop and realize himself but is mostly alienated through work.

Schopenhauer: The human is the animal that can beat.

Feuerbach: The human is what he eats. His God is his projection.

Nietzsche: The human is the sick animal that has not yet been identified. Much is still worm in the human; he is an "incident" of the nature.

Swedenborg: The human is essentially spirit.

Descartes: The human's soul is consciousness.

Pestalozzi: The human basically consists of reason, feelings, and creativeness.

Bolk: The human is an infantile ape with disturbed inner secretion.

Schiller: The human is the being that wants and does not just have to.

Pascal: The human is the weakest reed, but a thinking one.

Kierkegaard: The human stands between nature and God, can relate freely to himself and to the life.

Scheler: The human can say no.

Gehlen: The human is a deficient being, a being that creates culture.

Monod: The human is a coincidental product of the evolution.

Schelsky: The human released from the compulsion of nature submits to the compulsion to produce.

Jaspers: To be human is to ceaselessly create oneself.

Weber: Depending on the last statement, the one is God, and the other is the devil for the individual.

Lévi-Strauss: The human is carrier of unconscious structures.

Heidegger: The human can become a shepherd of the being.

Hartmann: Religion destroys the human as a moral person.

James: The human's ineradicable, biologically valuable belief is in the feeling.

Dilthey: The human's soul life is teleological.

Dewey: The relative freedom of the human is limited in a biological, psychological, and sociological-historical interplay.

Buber: The human becomes human through a relationship with the human.

Haeckel: The human is the highest development of organic protein.

Ortega y Gasset: The human has no nature; he only has history.

Portmann: The human has a hereditary ordered organization of orientation as the task of his reason.

Bloch: The human can hope; his utopian potential lies in his imagination, his daydreams, and his wishful thinking.

Marcuse: The human lives and dies rationally and productively, as a replaceable object of technical organization.

Uexküll: The human is infinitely more open to the world.

Plessner: The human can laugh and cry.

Lorenz: The humans live in a progressive infantilization through over- and under-functioning of their instinctual systems that have become ancestral history.

Teilhard de Chardin: The evolution takes a spiritual turn in the human. In this spiritualization process he opens himself to the divine, whereby the love is the human (spiritual) force that leads to completion and even the freedom is in this function.

Guardini: The human is given the task of shaping his unique, unrepeatable life.

Freud: The human consists of a psychic apparatus: "I", id, and superego.

Fromm: The human can destroy for the sake of destruction and hate for the sake of hatred.

Jung: The acting of the human is co-determined by supra-individual forces.

Koestler: The human is a stray message of evolution.

Rogers: The human is naturally a positive social being, with strong positive direction tendencies and this despite destructiveness, fear, regression, defense, and cruelty.

Maslow: Each human has the natural potential for creative, healthy self-realization.

Watson: The human's psyche is objective, experimental ascertainable, predictable, controllable, and manipulable.

Frankl: The most human thing in the human is the unconditional meaningfulness of life.

Langevelds: The human's life story is a story of meaning; persona genesis (= becoming human) is the realization of meaning.

Roth: The human needs education and is capable of being educated.

Zdarzil: The human has four essential characteristics: Reflexivity, self-determination, self-creation, and self-expression.

Murphy: All abilities of the human, if normal or metanormal, physical or out of body, are subject to the limitations and distortions created by our inherited or socially conditioned nature.

In self-knowledge as idea and concept, there is always a human image:

Clement of Alexandria (Gnostic, dead 216): "It is then, as it seems, the greatest of all teachings to know oneself. For if a human knows himself, he will know God" (Jung, CG: Olten 1978, 238).

At most it is said today that one cannot make universal statements about the human nature. "Its universalist claim does not withstand a historical, ethnological, constructivist perspective ... Anthropology criticism has made it clear: Anthropology can only be practiced meaningfully as historical anthropology", says Wulf (1994, 7). Zirfas vigorously replied twice in the same book: "Today, the anthropology can no longer take on the function of justifying ethics (for the pedagogy) ... nor can the anthropology be regarded as a normative interpretation of ethics" (Wulf 1994, 142). Can one not do that? Is it so that no "common human image" and no "generally binding ethics" can be developed (Kamper 1992, 311)?

The criticism on philosophical anthropology is massive: The philosophical anthropology has produced no coherent human image, created no generally binding ethics, and presented no acceptable meaning for human life; it has lost the overview, got stuck in eclecticism, failed in its completion, and therefore cannot claim any special status (Kamper 1992, 311-312). Perhaps the "humanum" is ultimately unfathomable (Bollnow 1980) and a "secured human image "will never be possible" (Zdarzil 1980). But what is the leaning of "secured" mean? What is "ultimately secured" in physics? The modern physics has to do without the material objectivity of nature" (Kraft 1968, 44). The behaviorism must learn here!

Eclecticism also reigns in educational science. There are hardly any compatible theories and concepts in (empirical!) educational science as in anthropology. They all talk about the human and educational goals, not seldom in Babylonian, postmodern linguistic confusion. Some reject anthropological human images (models); others demand them. How can one still understand that? In education system, "a crippling pessimism and skepticism has evidently spread" (Pöggeler 1970, 170).

What does the educational science offer as alternative? "The distorted picture of a human appears that can be caricatured as a functionally governing apparatus" (Löwisch 1982, 18). From some sides (not from all sides!) the end of (educational, philosophical) anthropology is announced (Kamper 1992, 311). At the same time, however, there is neither a psychology nor a pedagogy without an implicit human image (Thomae 1991, 109-121). In addition: "No adult education is conceivable that does not follow some anthropological models" (Pöggeler 1970, 175). Also, no model is a model in human education.

As early as 1970, Pöggeler warned: "The lack of value standards and worthwhile goals of adulthood, which can today be widely registered, is a symptom of a general meaning emptying of the human being and an anthropological insecurity that reaches into the foundations of existence" (Pöggeler 1970, 168). One cause of this crisis in anthropology is certainly to search in the language. Kamlah / Lorenzen (1967, 24), among others, oppose the "linguistic creations" of metaphysics, which have produced above all "mythical creatures". "The philosophy (is) due to the lack of critical reflection on the own speaking gotten into wrong tracks" (Kamlah 1973, 12). A clear rejection on the metaphysical language of anthropology is given by the Wiener circle (Kraft 1968, 26-38). "Value-saturated world and human images ... serve to control emotional behavior" (Topitsch 1970, 20). These are e.g.: Natural law, value order, creation order, divine world law, primary ground, the unconditioned, God, objective spirit, the thing, etc. The philosophical and religious metaphysics is a "dangerous narcotic that destroys reason" (Carnap 1975, 176). Carnap (1975, 149-176) therefore calls for the "overcoming of metaphysics through logical analysis of language".

However, this does not eliminate the question of the "psyche" of the human. And even if the "macabre theologian joke" mentioned by Beck (1994, 232) is true, "I shouldn't have to laugh badly if our whole religion were a lie", all transcendental questions of philosophical anthropology remain open. Everything may be true that Deschner's investigations (1988) on "falsified beliefs" reveal; the question of the "microcosm human", integrated into the macrocosm of the universe, becomes more the core topic of philosophical anthropology. The spiritual traditions of all cultures and religions teach us that without the "inner path" the answers to the being and existence of the human cannot be found.

The human may be "the measure of all things" and "everything is in the flow of the history", an existentialist anthropology does not lead to where real answers (rather: fragments of answers) can be found (experienced). The "secondary nestling" (Portmann) is without a doubt an educationally relevant issue (Gerner 1982, 132-147). For the human education (of adults) we can at least recognize philosophically and anthropologically that every human must start his own psychic-spiritual evolution again and again under the conditions of parental attention (love!), and that every adult thereby in the following generation himself can reflect himself as a request in this sense. Isn't the life story of every human a "story of meaning" (Langeveld 1968)? The "being-in-the-world" is the fundamental constitution of existence with its central phenomena such as work, love, domination, play and death (Fink 1979).

"So, it is important to see in a philosophical anthropology at first through the illusions of modern profanity, to recognize the situation of the human, then to inquire in ethics what we can live in the midst of suffering, guilt and destruction and what we have to do." With Bock we mean: Despite all changes, the basic features that constitute human being are to be sought (1991, 100). The language rules for avoiding "truth romance" are formulated: "The truth that we arrive in the best possible case will therefore also be statement truth, a truth that is always open to scrutiny by the sensible and knowledgeable interlocutor" (Kamlah 1967, 148). Kamlah (1973, 16) also considers the colloquial language to be more reliable than "educational language". If the philosophical anthropology wants to enlighten and determine goals for practical life, it must speak in an understandable way. For us, the following applies: The clean analytical development of basic concepts is the foundation of all sciences (Seiffert 1973, 8). However: "The idea of the ideal exactness is a chimera" (Savigny 1970, 65).

Philosophical-anthropological speaking contains irresolvable problems: If we talk about "love", for example, then we have a complex meaning content in our background (see in: Empirie der Individuation 1998), while the listener resp. the reader brings his own ideas in the understanding process. If a thought line about "love" is integrated by the reader (through his cognitive activity; "accommodation" according to Piaget), then his state of consciousness is transformed in some sense, not simply in the sense offered by the thought line, but first as an expanded construction of the before existing consciousness contents on this topic.

In our opinion, this applies to all central themes resp. terms of philosophical anthropology. We therefore think: With its statement system, the philosophical anthropology cannot create a fixed new order in people's "heads"; that can't be its goal. However, it can expand states of consciousness through new knowledge elements, in the sense of its concern, namely more and more in the direction of a holistic human image, that let integrate the biography of the reader, his life reality, his consciousness contents and his experience of being. Only in this way anthropological knowledge can affect processes of self-reflection and value responsibility. This is also a prerequisite for intercultural understanding about human being.

The philosophical anthropology collects knowledges from various individual sciences and tries to draw a unified overall picture. The individual sciences include psychology, sociology, biology, ethnology, culture, and history. Now there are many anthropologies today: The sociological, the biological, the psychological, the philosophical, the Marxist, the theological, the pedagogical and nota bene also the andragogical anthropology. There are difficulties: What makes these different anthropologies different? And: What standards can be set to be able to say: "This is now a coherent overall picture"? And: Which philosophical-anthropological knowledge inventories are andragogically relevant? In fact, the range of human appearance and expression possibilities is enormous (Bock 1991, 99-108). In tings of culture, Gehlen (1971, 22) thinks: "There is nothing that does not exist". It is not easy to crystallize the timeless and the invariant. That is associated with considerable methodological problems (Schöpf 1991, 93). In the pedagogical anthropology, signs of fatigue and disappointment spread; we quote in combination: "The efforts to reach a consensus on their question and task ... have passed their zenith"; "a coherent understanding of pedagogical anthropology has not been found" (Benner 1994, 115-116). Does everything have to be "uniform"? We recommend understanding "unity" and "wholeness" as something organic that we try to include according to an open methodical principle.

A further claim is made on the philosophical anthropology, whereby we also want to include ethics (from the human image to models and values): The anthropology is the basis for establishing meaning and values. "Giving meaning (is) a prerequisite to succeed a human existence for the individual as well as for the group" (Portmann 1965, 249).

This is countered by scientific theory that one cannot logically formulate a target statement (SOLL-Aussage) from an actual statement (IST-Aussage, Brezinka 1978, 92-104). For the science as sentence system, value judgment freedom is required. Max Weber asked for this as early as 1917 (Weber 1988, 489-540). We must therefore keep to a clear separation of normative sentences from statements of fact. What Brezinka formulates is problematic: "The ultimate standards of value of a person ... cannot scientifically be proven" (1978, 101). What do "scientific" and "provable" mean? What sensory experience does Brezinka have? In addition, his assertion that these value measures "depend on the worldview, the beliefs, the conscience of the individual" is not at all clear. We think that there are facts in the human life which on the one hand are facts, which on the other hand always contain a value (to a certain extent the reverse of the coin). The problem is not primarily whether there are values in a human's life regardless of his conscience and worldview, but how the human responds to "values of being" of certain facts and how he formulates resp. deforms them. Let us again take the example of the love. Can we empirically adequately describe situations resp. behaviors of love without revealing the value aspect? Today we know empirically what the lack of love causes in life, namely: The deficit of emotional affection leads to considerable development deficits (Spitz 1967). We can address another example: The construction of an atom bomb can be described purely empirically; likewise, the consequences (e.g., Hiroshima). Let us add: According to empirical, probabilistic analysis, a "GAU" ("worst-case scenario"), i.e., a nuclear power plant damage of immeasurably far-reaching damage effects, should only occur every million years. Perhaps, according to these calculations, we now have "rest" for the next million minus 75 years. The damage and suffering of Chernobyl (1986 and Fukushima 2011) are enormous. It was not yet the "worst case", although increased radiation was measured in all of France and in Switzerland fishing in Lake Lugano was banned for some time. Can we separate empirical being from value and meaning where it hits the human? The "mature whole conscience of humanity" (Derbolav 1980) becomes a question of responsibility for everyone who is "hit". This can be linked back to knowledge (Kraft 1968, 102-110).

Closer to the andragogy are general educational goals resp. values such as: Virtue, critical ability, emancipation, diligence, seriousness, honesty, maturity, morality, responsibility, and others. So, the first question to be asked is what the specific conditions in the habitat are, that clearly express such values. If the unequivocal answer is not possible, then such terms are nothing but empty formulas that mean something like metaphysical soap bubbles. We conclude: Being and value are two aspects of the same reality of human being. Portmann warns: "If the danger of a human image that is limited by reduction to scientifically comprehensible data is already great enough, it becomes even more threatening through the dominance of value-free scientific findings. With such dominance, important dimensions of inwardness shrink to the insignificant" (Portmann 1965, 249-250). Models and ways of becoming human (personagenesis) with reference to finding meaning are to be developed. That is a philosophical-anthropological task!

Overall, we want to formulate the following thesis: The justification of educational goals is ultimately rooted in ethics and this in turn in philosophical anthropology, i.e., in the established human image. The variety of philosophical-anthropological questions and statements about the existential being illustrates the complexity. Some theses on the topic of the "last (highest) educational goals" are presented (taken from Löwisch, D.-J., 1982; numbers in brackets correspond to the pages):

- But what can and should the individual human hope for? (p. 168)

- What is the human life worth today? (p. 162/164)
- Not to accumulate a possession of philosophy but deepen philosophizing as movement (Jaspers) (p. 173).
- The curse of unstoppable progress is the unstoppable regression; the freedom in the society (is) inseparable from enlightening thinking (Horkheimer / Adorno) (p. 158/159).
- Everything rationalized is de-spiritualized; the individual is devalued, even de-spiritualized (Cohn) (p. 155).
- Enlightenment is the exit of the human from his self-inflicted immaturity (Kant) (p. 139).
- Happiness, health, justice, peace, freedom, and maturity contain an imperativistical element (p. 138).
- "Emancipation" wants to free us from constraints that cannot be rationally identified and shown (Hartmut von Hentig) (p.132).
- An act of self-reflection that changes a life is a movement of emancipation (Habermas) (p. 130).
- Freedom is an ultimate reason that can no longer be traced back to another reason. The freedom of the human, however, is not unrestricted, arbitrary freedom, but autonomous freedom that is giving its law itself (Annemarie Pieper) (p. 116).
- Without obligation to the laws, values, yes 'basic values' of the human being, freedom is an illusion (Heinrich Rombach) (p. 117).
- Confession and way of life in love, truth, conscientiousness, individuality, freedom, subjectivity cannot be proven scientifically (p. 114).
- The human must learn to establish hopes himself (p. 110).
- Pedagogy (here: human education) must be normative ... if it wants to help the human to find a way of acting that stands out of laid tracks and foreign-set points, that is free of routes and route regulations with built-in substitute routes (and is allowed to thereby) not to end up in indifferentism, anarchism, skepticism, nihilisms, criticism (p. 109).
- Human education means: First and most noble task ... to let a human to become (p. 72).
- The free human: Only wants what he can and does what he likes (Rousseau) (p. 72).
- All our wisdom consists in servile prejudices (Rousseau) (p. 69)
- The light of reason is given to us by God; the human is released to bond with God (Thomas Aquinas) (p. 59/60).
- The divine light (is) the origin of knowledge capacity of the human and his ability for insight (Augustine) (p. 53).
- The human does not know about the real and does not know about his ignorance (Plato; here the thought in brief) (p. 48).
- Due to his undeniable fundamental spirituality, the human is a being free

to decide and open to act, to whom it is tasked, through his spirituality, to achieve himself in his deciding and acting, thinking, and willing to create his world and to prove his spirituality in all his thinking and acting completions (Löwisch) (p. 35/36).

- Personal morality cannot be determined by the act as such, but only by the quality of the will on which it is based (Höffe) (p. 174).

Let us imagine the following situation: All the great enlightened humans of human history - these are: Rama, Krishna, Hermes, Moses, Orpheus, Pythagoras, Plato, Buddha, Confucius, Laotse, Jesus, Mohammed, Meister Eckhart and probably a few more - would live today. They would all have studied philosophy, psychology, pedagogy, sociology, social psychology, psychoanalysis, and science theory and would together be professors and researchers at a "Scientific Institute for Philosophical Anthropology". They would be the great teachers of the "royal science", for example in Berlin, Frankfurt, Vienna, or Zurich. What would they teach? Perhaps they would prove on ten thousand pages that the human should make no name and no image of God, that there is an eternal life, that there are cosmic-spiritual order principles, that the human in his soul should become a "living image" of the circle-cross-archetype (of the great mandalas), that there are human (obligatory) values, that there is no transcendental argument (and thus no spiritual legitimacy) for the death penalty, that the life of a human has consequences in the afterlife, that the creation 'earth' is planned and created by the Grail Kings of the spiritual world, that the whole humanity history has to realize a creation plan. - Let us assume that these great figures of history would teach and explain all of this in a comprehensible manner, free from any earthly religious standpoint and quite interculturally diverse with different value priorities. Let us further assume that they are quite appalled and angry, how the humans destroy the creation, how they are at war with one another, slaughter, exploit and sadistically torment one another and how they stifle the psychic-spiritual evolutionary process of humanity with their way of life. Let us continue to imagine in free imagination that they would therefore announce that new laws had been enacted in the spiritual world (perhaps they all dreamed that) so that after death the souls could finally brought to justice for their actions in the spiritual world. They would also say that the billions of souls in the spiritual world do not hang on spiritual trees, like bored bats, but must take their place in an organization regulated by law, as it is common on earth. Just as birth is the gateway to an earthly organization (family, community, state), death is considered the transition into a spiritual community where there are rights, duties, and responsibilities. These are philosophical-anthropological statements as we know them in many forms, images, and words since the early advanced civilizations.

How would scientists in pedagogy (educational science!) and adult education react to their teachings? We imagine some reaction models, in key words: Criticizing, dismantling, deconstructing, being jealous, wanting to have more right, wanting to be better, wanting to put a crown on oneself without performing the corresponding psychic-spiritual achievements, to rebel against such "concentrated" authority and ultimately saying: "We do what we want; we practice value-free science; none of this concerns us". Some would probably act like Cinderella's two stepsisters. Politicians would fire these "enlightened professors" because the economy complains that they are ruining some businesses. The esoteric "popular papers" would slam the door in their face (because their editors-in-chief are more papal than the Pope) and the specialist book publishers would send back their manuscripts in thanks: "We regret that our program is 'purely' scientific" (or 'purely' popular). The press would label them as "crazy metaphysicians", probably rather keep themselves silent (out of guilt, of course!), because they have neither gas bombs, nor weapons, nor capital, nor television stations, nor do they indoctrinate, nor manipulate, nor force, and unfortunately also cannot deliver hair-raising sex affairs. It is also unlikely that one of these scientists could perform any miracles. That makes their thing completely uninteresting. Their thinking processes and contemplations would be boring on television and therefore not in demand (a reduction in the number of viewers means a reduction in advertising income). The project of these gentlemen (unfortunately the women are missing) would be doomed to failure. They would be driven out of the educational sciences. Education and further training for the economy is in demand, not psychic-spiritual human being and not a social life with transcendentally anchored fundamental values of individuation. If personal identity and moral integrity are mutually dependent (Oser / Althof / Garz 1986, 361), then the life meaning, and human values fall by the wayside if the human refuses his inner education.

We have on the search of the current titles on anthropology of pedagogy found several journal articles and books articles whose authors are around 28 to 35 years old. They are research assistants, senior / assistants, instructors, directors of adult education institutions, etc. They write about human images, educational theory of adult education and goals of human education. Who are those people? In memory of our own experiences in the scientific institution, we imagine:

They are single, or "double-single" (and thus double earners), spend 2 weeks of vacation in Mallorca or on the coast of Greece, they drive an Audi or Golf, their living varies between an alternative style or the lifestyle of "living more beautiful", in the evening they go to the pizzeria or the 'pub' in the old town, the one or the other does a "psychotherapy" or takes part in a self-awareness group. What do these scientists know about the human being? With this question we are not suggesting the demand that they have to be a customer in the red light district for a few years, to belong to criminal circles, to go to Bosnia as a mercenary, to be serious about action research as an ethnologist and live in the bush for a few years or in slum areas for a few weeks, to travel to China, to stay in Islamic circles for a while, to look after the homeless, to go to a monastery for several months, or whatever. We have enormous doubts, however, whether a young scientist who has never been challenged by the "world" to the core and never to his extreme limits can be able to write profoundly competent on human education in a philosophical-anthropological way, to deconstruct Plato, to set up theories about "understanding" and to drive philosophical anthropology out of pedagogy resp. educational science.

Strangely enough, the Swiss pedagogue Johann Heinrich Pestalozzi (1746-1827; an expert in human and popular education) is the long-running favorite in pedagogical-anthropological research. Evil tongues say this is not because of knowledge interest, that this "lemon has long been squeezed to the last drop". It is because the teaching professors and the entire academic cadre in their environment feel unconsciously an irresistible educational urge to follow Pestalozzi, and to make such a tremendous human achievement for the humanity, but since the television program about the work of Mother Theresa in the misery of poverty in Calcutta, it is impossible for them to let arise this urge in consciousness. "The fulfillment of the own destiny" leads their existence as an abstract scientific object of reflection. Perhaps this is some sort of "sublimated calling", or a postponement of the suppressed calling.

Our field of reflection is the human education. So what interests us is not the human upright walk as an anthropological characteristic. The rather narrow view of some earlier anthropological concepts is certainly outdated.

The human is much more than just the product of social relations (Marx), more than a zoological being (Haeckel), not just a spiritual being (Hegel), and everything else than a coincidental product of evolution (Monod). The andragogy determines the question:

What are the generally valid (universal) statements about the human, i.e., "the today and always true" (Kamlah 1973, 11), which is of constitutive importance for human education? That does not exist; at most, it can be a question of examining the "human appearance and expression manners under certain historical-social conditions" (Wulf 1994, 15). "Pedagogical anthropology is constructive anthropology (as if all previous anthropological research contributions had not been 'constructive'), i.e., it does not assume that the 'essence' of the human can be included in anthropological research and reflection" (Wulf 1994, 17).

Even in a rough overview of the criticism of philosophical anthropology, one can discover very human aspects: The German education scientists are afraid of authority, of introspection, of commitments and ties, of binding values and models, of everything that is transcendent, i.e., transcends the empirical material. To ask the question about God or wisdom - that is, the "knowledge of the essentials, the ultimate reasons, and goals of the being ... of Gods rule and the divine order of all things" (Brugger 1992, 453) – to articulate as educational topic, is more than suspect of an education scientist; that means disqualification. They want to pursue "pure science" (Benning 1982, 19-31), not sheer the "horse racing track" of educational technologies and always evoke at the forefront of fashion trends (currently postmodernism) with virtuoso and complicated rhetoric including computer, media, and the age of further education. A unit creating reason has recently been rejected; "language games" are "in". A lack of perspective, criticizing and destructive thinking take up space; self-realization and emancipation: "Yes", but please not with spirit, not with love and truthfulness; every certainty of knowledge is denied; there is no "supreme principle", and horizons of meaning can hardly be recognized (Hamann 1993, 170-175).

"What is shown as honest scientific modesty in the positivist business, namely only allowing a certain type of subjectless empirical knowledge, is in truth a failure in relation to the real problems of the human" (Vinnai 1993, 18).

The empirical research is a form of adapted denial of reality. State and economy finance them, with a few exceptions. Isn't that also a failure of these scientists to the own human being? Could it be that these "pedagogues" avoid the question of the "essence of human being" in order not to have to investigate their own depths, to be able to evade certain life-world-related value duties? This reminds us of the great Protestant theologian Dietrich Bonhoeffer, who suffered deeply for his value ethics and was hanged on April 9, 1945, because of his involvement in the resistance against Hitler. One must ask oneself whether Bonhoeffer (and countless victims with him) was not the one who was duped, whether people "deserve" such historical figures at all. The saying "Oh Lord, forgive them because they don't know what they are doing" is probably a demagogic twist; it must probably read: "Oh Lord, punish them because they know exactly what they are doing". Perhaps that would create a protected space for courageous humans who dedicate their life to the meaning of life and values from the depths of the psychic-spiritual life. Realizing a calling (being a teacher is a calling, it was said earlier) would be possible again without fear. Because there are not many pedagogues in the science who dedicate their lives to the highest values of being human. One cannot profile oneself with that, at most one can burn the fingers and become a loser. One must know that when one read books on pedagogical anthropology and think forward searchingly (and always critically) on this topic. If only all those who propagate the "emancipatory-critical interest" in their scientific methods were so meticulously and astutely "critical" with themselves!

So, we try to come closer to the human image, to include the human being in a larger whole and to arrange the knowledge areas from the individual sciences to prepare a model for the general andragogy that contains general validity and andragogical relevance. Our position is clear from our educational theory and from our concept of individuation (see in: Empirie der Individuation 1995). We imply psychic-spiritual dimensions when we formulate basic statements about the "essence of human being". Certain terms are central here, which the neopositivist, the experience-plagued and the human fixated on money and power avoid "like the devil the holy water": Love, spirit, truthfulness, inner experience of God, grail, wisdom, eternal, transcendence, back bonding to the spiritual principles, realization of God, contemplation, dream interpretation, archetypes, life after death, psychic-cosmic energy, personal and collective unconscious and much more.

The expulsion of philosophical anthropology from the educational science is understandable, but not acceptable. Philosophical anthropology is an indispensable reference science to pedagogy and andragogy (Böhm 1988, 30); it is also for politics and economics.

The question of the wholeness of a human image contains a methodical (and of course an epistemological) problem and should not be interpreted absolutely. In our study books and workbooks, we have tried to collect a wealth of psychological individual knowledge and, over the years, have concluded that the human being in his psychic disposition is a meaningful cohesive structure where the individual parts (forces, dispositions, subsystems) have a tangible meaning for the whole (cf. Lassahn 1993, 51). If the philosophical anthropology would be able to develop a definitive holistic human image the chair holder could retire: "Job done, goodbye". We interpret "holism" not as something final and complete (Kron 1972, 251-257), but as an ongoing task. The ways to do this are phenomenological, hermeneutical, transcendental and, above all, symbolical. All facts, be they biological, empirical, or contemplative developed, always require interpretation. A purely rational knowledge would be a mutilation of the human being. Objectivity as a basic methodological attitude (Hengstenberg 1972, 65-83) means "turning to the being for the sake of being", not "thinginess" or "usefulness". Methodological principles determine the question forms, according to Bollnow (1972, 19-36): 1) Relativization of all non-temporal spheres of meaning (e.g. culture) and tracing back to the human; 2) Understanding the human life from the perspective of objective structures; 3) Paying attention to the forms of experiencing existence (e.g. fear, guilt); 4) Interpretation of the individual phenomena in the direction of a whole according to the principle of the open question, i.e. the openness towards the individual phenomena.

Regarding the theory understanding in adult education, Siebert (1981, 100) thinks: "A theory should make empirically substantial, logically coherent statements about the description, explanation, justification and objective of a reality area and thus facilitate a well-founded action orientation". For the philosophical anthropology, the question arises in what characteristic way the elements of a human image differ from a "theory of adult education".

We cannot pursue this epistemological problem any further here. As far as we know, it exists a no metatheoretical or epistemological concept for philosophical anthropology. The experiences in education give us reason to a certain skepticism, at least caution: "The assessment made by Giesecke in 1982 that the epistemological debate had not only brought the pedagogy (!) no benefit, but it also hindered it to fulfill its "actual tasks", seems to have become the widely shared 'common sense'" (Pollak / Heid 1994, 3).

From the brief overview of the critical aspects of the situation, we can formulate some science-oriented guidelines for philosophical anthropology:

1. The philosophical anthropology develops holistic human images and values that serve as guiding principles for the human education, the self-education, the life design, the deeper understanding of life meaning and for the cultural and intercultural coexistence. That is much more than "integrative data processing".

2. The statement systems of philosophical anthropology are life-world-oriented. They are accessible to external and inner experience and, insofar, stand within what we have incorporated in the "psychic organism". This means that general and abstract statements in the life context must be concretized without getting caught up on socio-historical and biographical facts or even being taken up by current fashion trends.

3. The statement systems are pluralistic. By this we mean: They consider the facts that different words can say the same thing, that different models with different accents can include the same facts, that the same facts can

assume interculturally different expression forms, that there are versatile life forms, that every culture and social situation in its own historical development and constitution can set different priorities and value accents, and that some models of human images interlock, sometimes overlap.

4. The philosophical anthropology integrates the diversity of subjective individuality (personal concreteness) in its general statements in such a way that everyone can complete the psychic-spiritual evolutionary process in his own way without being curtailed in his evolutionary potentials. The evolutionary transformation potential exists in all cultures and in all humans.

5. Philosophical anthropology also formulates statements that include the human being in the light of transcendence, without excluding in principle other religious teaching systems through the vocabulary of a specific religion. Insofar, philosophical anthropology is neither theology nor tied back to dogmas of any religion or esoteric life view. The question of human continued existence and its cosmological placement (Nickel 1973) is also an andragogical and thus a philosophical-anthropological challenge.

6. Philosophical anthropology processes individual knowledge into an overall view of psychology, pedagogy, psychoanalysis, depth psychology, humanistic psychology, transpersonal psychology, social psychology, sociology, parapsychology, biology, mysticism and from every form of contemplatively (symbolic / archetypal) experienced knowledge (especially wisdom). It also tries to develop the human being from the knowledges about the processes of education resp. individuation.

7. Philosophical anthropology formulates universal statements in such a way that the reference to the individual, the psychic organism, the individuation, the life situation and to actions is recognizable and preserved. In the highest abstraction (we suspect) this is only possible through symbol teachings (with application instructions) and thus requires a hierarchically graded and system-theoretical target level model for language and images / symbols.

8. Knowledges of philosophical anthropology should help the individual to better understand his life and existence and cope with. This also includes the meaning question of being human, those roots are transcendental and not just historical-situational or technological-practical. Furthermore, philosophical anthropology should achieve its expert contribution to

master the "great problems of humanity".

9. Philosophical anthropology integrates the inexplicable and the non-rational in such a way that with such issues can nonetheless be dealt constructively. We think here in particular of all kinds of border psychic experiences. In a certain sense, the knowledge through contemplation (archetype experience) is also an area of reality that cannot be "explained" in the sense of empirical- rational science. But aren't the symbols an indispensable key to understand humans (Cassirer 1991 and 1923-1929; Kessler 1977)?

10. Philosophical anthropology formulates values, norms and meaning aspects from its human images, which are founded in the overall context and tied back to everyday life. This guarantees openness, flexibility and discourse in defining the model statement, in including and structuring values.

11. Philosophical anthropology considers the diversity of human realities in an understanding and integrating way: Sick, disabled, old people, children, criminals, neurotics, mentally ills, destitutes, outsiders, homosexuals, lesbians, prostitutes, addicts, desperates, isolateds, helpless, uneducateds, rich people, power people, gamblers, fanatics, sufferers, seekers, singles, parents, entrepreneurs, unemployed, oppressed, victims, etc. With these keywords we indicate that life crises and life course topics should also be reflected philosophically and anthropologically (see, for example: Kurzdörfer 1981, 124-128).

12. Philosophical anthropology is the "royal science". It requires its administrators (at the highest level) to complete the individuation. Expertise and fulfillment of individuation give them the highest spiritual authority in the society. Relevant andragogical experience is part of the professional competence.

We have hereby tried to make clear that the expulsion of the philosophical anthropology out of the educational science lacks any factual basis, that it is neither appropriate to place this branch of science in a reductionist manner in the back room of pedagogy resp. andragogy, nor, on the contrary, to some new fashion trends to underestimate the scientific conception of philosophical anthropology, which is an extended and constitutive concept for human education. With Plessner (1965, 26) we formulate the principle: "Without philosophy of the human there is no theory of human life experience in the humanities. Without philosophy of nature there is no philosophy of human".

Let us briefly touch the central subject areas of philosophical anthropology:

First, we can limit the human with his psychic functions. Every human has a psychodynamics, an "I" (identity formation), a will, a defense function, and a control instance. Furthermore, every human has an awareness of himself, of others, the world and in some way of the transcendence. We have determined more "psychic subsystems": The feelings, the needs, the unconscious, the dream life, the force of love and a "intelligent effect system" with the perception, the language, the thinking, the justifying, and the cognitive learning. If we define reflexivity, identity, personalization, self-determination, self-design, self-differentiation, self-limitation (Scheler 1966, 11) as "characters" (Zdarzil / Olechowski 1976, 50), so always tied back to the psychic organism and the diversity of the habitat. Is that empirical psychology? Experimental psychology? We remind you: "PSYCHE" means "SPIRIT" and "SOUL". DEATH is inherently part of life: "... as part of the infinite lifeline of the tribe, which continues through every death - in the order of life-death-life" (Kerényi 1971, 176). The finiteness implies the question of infinity (Rothacker 1970, 199). The irrational prejudice that parapsychology is not a "serious matter" persists in the social sciences, completely wrongly. Many border psychic phenomena have now been researched at least to the extent that the psychology (as science) can no longer close its eyes to it if it will be taken seriously in its basic attitude towards human being. Philosophical anthropology begins where empirical psychology stops.

Second, we can itemize and consider human activity in a variety of ways, e.g., communication (dialogue), sociality, abilities resp. skills, roles, work, forms of employment of all kinds, structuring relationships, dealing with oneself, creating culture, social resp. political engagement, ecological behavior, play, dealing with knowledge inventory, etc. The human can plan, reflect, anticipate and refuse to act. It should also be investigated, for example, why many adults refuse their "lifelong learning" (their self-education) and reject the self-reflection (self-knowledge) with all stubbornness. The "need to expand the scope for action and the ability to dispose characterizes the genus humanum in general" (Gehlen 1964, 75). The acting has on the one hand a natural side and on the other hand, of course, a psychic "inside". One of the most central questions of philosophical anthropology is the problem of the "life lie", the so-called collective oath: "Never uncover the inner psychic life; never tell the truth about it!" If one takes a thorough look behind the scenes of externalities in social life, one could well conclude that there is no difference between a total dictatorship and the "capitalist adventure society" (Schulze 1992) in the deepest psychic layers in crucial aspects of humanity and inwardness. This can and must be discovered and dealt with in a philosophical-anthropological way.

Third, the corporeality should be mentioned. Drive resp. instinct system is also necessary for human survival (Cube 1991, 122-131): Food, sexuality, curiosity, aggression, territorial behavior, desire to function. The human nature as a biological-cybernetic system still needs to be worked out to be able to determine what "respect of human nature" implies and specifically means as value. Because too much and too little of drive energy resp. drive formation has a destructive effect. In our opinion it is incredibly significant to consider the human philosophically from the point of view of the biological evolution. The fact of gender-specific differentiation is not only a topic of sexuality but has to be extended and differentiated in philosophical-anthropological perspectives. The human is always natural being. However, he can reflect and to form his nature, and to make decisions about it. In our opinion, there is not a single transcendental (metaphysical) argument to define the corporeality as something inferior. This applies not only to sexuality, which today in Christianity is still predominantly bracketed with moral doctrines under coercion and guilt. The selection in the evolution of humankind is also influenced by social behavior: "The behavior and activity of organisms also have effects on the course of the evolution" (Overhage 1965, 126). "Spirit and life are related to each other - it is a fundamental error to bring them into an original enmity, into an original state of struggle" (Scheler 1966, 87). From this point of view, human education certainly has a decisive responsibility to assume.

Fourth, we see in the biography research the decisive foundations for the development of human images for human education. Approaches to this can be found, for example, in Bühler / Ekstein (1973, 349-385), who examined life course studies under five aspects: Developmental psychological, psychoanalytical, sociological, behavioristic, and humanistic. Furthermore, the "pedagogical anthropology of life age" by Bock (1991) and the study by Pöggeler (1970, 73-110) should also be mentioned. We also refer to the various works that we have referred elsewhere in this study. A key question relates to the possible constants in the variability and diversity of possible life courses. There are topics in the human life course that the human must assign interculturally and independently of the historical-social context. Furthermore, fateful events here pose some profoundly serious philosophical questions. The human being and thus the human dignity have the highest value even under physically and materially restricted conditions. We think of the disabled, sick, unemployed, the elderly and the poor. The societies around the world are not set up to fully integrate these groups of people. The world belongs to them too, we would like to say. And finally, the interplay between past, present and future, be it as a psychological fact, be it as a generation problem, or be it as a problem of anticipating of a desired and undesired future, is philosophical-anthropological relevant and accessible to in-depth reflection.

Fifth, we find religion and belief as central characteristic of human life in all cultures. It is far from us to draft a "theological anthropology", for example in the sense of Benning (1992, 71 ff.). But the core question is anthropologically and andragogically significant: Can commonalities be recognized between religions and cultures in the overview of the last centuries (millennia)? The question of gods and God arises again and again (Wittgenstein 1994, 85). The religious belief as existential phenomenon of human being cannot be devalued and shelved with "these are just myths or dogmas". Religious experiences are not specific to religion; we find them in all forms of meditation (contemplation) and in versatile ideas about the transcendence. The passing of the biosphere of the human into the noosphere (of the spirit; Teilhard de Chardin) overcomes the anthropomorphism (Sartre; existential philosophy). Philosophy has always been concerned with that what lies "beyond the physical", certainly not out of fear of life, denial of life and flight from life.

A central problem that calls for solution paths for human education is in this context: "In the course of the Enlightenment and the industrial culture, most people have developed an emotional cavity in the place that a transcendental belief previously had occupied, where in such a changed situation, feelings flow in, that by their nature, can be expanded without limits and which easily can be merged with a rationalistic concept of utility" (Gehlen 1970, 130). According to Scheler (1966, 92) "becoming human and becoming god (are) mutually dependent ... The human only comes to that consciousness of his fellow warrior, of his co-action of god in the course of his development and his self-knowledge". We formulate this process in the context of individuation.

Sixth, the human has also to be viewed in the tension field of culture, society and environment. The different concerns of adult education on five continents (Leirman / Pöggeler 1979) show us how much education questions can vary depending on the living world conditions. Plasticity and the need for education (including talent) should not only be examined in a psychological perspective. They interact with external living conditions, including working conditions and political power structures. Socialization and the ability to learn (learning theories) must therefore also be reflected anthropologically in this historically determined context (Zdarzil / Kolechowski 1976, 22-23, 50). Gehlen formulates a warning word to the meaning of culture: "If the external safeguards and stabilizations that lie in fixed traditions are omitted and also reduced, then our behavior becomes dismantled, affect-determined, instinctual, unpredictable, unreliable" (Gehlen 1971, 59). On the one hand, that might mean: "Back to culture!", as Gehlen concludes. We can also see in it simply the need for human education. Ecological problems are to be embedded in the fundamental relation human-nature world. The most humans have widely no awareness that as part of earthly life they are not "above" the world (and thus have no total right of disposal) but are organically integrated in the biological life. The problems of environmental degradation have therefore not only to be reflected on the level of acting, but also (or rather first) on the level of fundamental relation and attitude to the natural world. We see here an important philosophical-anthropological question.

Seventh, there is a multifaceted transformation ability and some paths to transformation (cf. Murphy 1994). Psychotherapy procedures, forms of meditation, hypnosis, spiritual healing methods, extrasensory abilities, autoregulation of psychosomatic health are just a few key words. We see the human capacity for psychic-spiritual evolution as the challenge of philosophical anthropology. We do not see the "human potential in the 21st century" in parapsychic abilities or miracle events. In comparison to these facts, our concept of individuation is much closer oriented to the "profane" psychic-spiritual life: The deepest roots for the meaning and values of human being lie in the experience and the implementation of individuation. Evolutionary transformation turns out to be the real meaning of life if we understand life teleologically. Insofar, our models of the psychic organism (Illustration 3) and psychic-spiritual evolution (Illustration 4) are a philosophical-anthropological human image.

With these seven points, we have touched on some central aspects. There are still some topics that expand the research spectrum of philosophical anthropology, for example: Freedom, responsibility, procreation, determination, reincarnation, guilt, the networking of the individual with the collective unconscious, etc. These are topics that have a vital impact on the human being - yesterday, today, and tomorrow. These are the different approaches to the human today. If we take a little distance to the time, then we know very well that the human today is in an evolutionary process that has hardly just begun. The humanity has made total self-destruction possible today. But we also have a knowledge inventory that can master this difficult challenge. What do we know about the being human in a million years? Nothing.

But it is not enough to temporarily limit the generality claim ("the universal statements") to the human image to a few hundred years, for example: Even in 2500 the humans have feelings, an unconscious, dreams, a communication, cultures, forms of meditation, acting models etc. Humans will always (let us stay until the year 2500) experience meaning and value, ask to understand the riddle of the existence.

And even then, there will still be many open questions, always asked in new ways. Isn't it perhaps the case that we have enough knowledge about the human, his nature, his sociality, about the world and about "border psychic realities", at least for the next few decades, and that today it is a matter to process this knowledge philosophically-anthropologically and to make it useful to the human for daily (co-)life, for self-reflection, for personagenesis, for self-reflection as well as for the constructive handling with the basic questions of the existence:

What is the human? How should the human live? These questions are the starting point of the philosophy. Aren't these also the two core questions of human being, those preliminary answering today can achieve an enormous contribution to solving the key problems of mankind, and of the individual in his life course?

A central problem of our time is not the philosophical confession "I know that I really don't know anything", but the repression of the knowledge and thus the denial of the responsibility for this knowledge. The basic question of ethics is not whether there could be "universal values" for the whole humanity. They exist, for example: The corporeality, the psychic organism, the potentials of psychic-spiritual evolution, the living space (natural world), the diversity of cultures (as vital necessities and as creative possibilities). The crucial question is how these values of being can be respected, protected, and implemented worldwide without violating these basic values. Another open question concerns the worldwide realization of human education that is tied back to such values of being.

We think that a great deal would be achieved if philosophical anthropology succeeded in making all these aspects "discoursable", in binding the philosophical answers back to the life and in creating models for the psychic-spiritual resp. human problems in everyday life through human images (with many facets). This can activate motivations to deal with oneself and with the basic questions of the existence. If most of those humans, and especially those who have the destiny of societies worldwide in their hands, would deal with them, to a certain extent as part of personality development and individuation, the earth would be almost a paradise. Therefore, we note here the central anthropological principle of Löwisch (1982, 35-36):

"Due to his undeniable fundamental spirituality, the human is a being free to decide and open to act, to whom it is given up through his spirituality to achieve himself in his decision-making and acting, thinking and wanting in order to create his world and to prove his spirituality in all his implementations of thinking and acting". We point out that "spirit" in our sense is a transcendental-cosmic force (principle) which all humans can experience in dreams and imagination / contemplation, but nothing has to do with "intelligence" and "culture" (so-called "objective spirit"). The inwardly directed self-knowledge with methodologically clear (evaluated) procedures is the "ticket" for the discovery journey into the "inner universe" (microcosm).

We cannot find an argument to drive philosophical anthropology out of the educational sciences. Philosophical anthropology exists as term until since around the 16th century and as a science only since this century. The basic questions of human being, however, have always been a central subject of philosophy, in the Occident since the begin of the Greek civilizations. Some saw the human as the "crown of the creation", integrated into the cosmos. Others have worked out reason and spirit as essential characteristics. Again, and again, the questions revolved around morality and the conscience formation. Some have examined materialistic-biological aspects (from Democritus to Darwin and Nietzsche). Since Marx (1818-1883) we know the human image under the point of view of work, production, self-alienation, and class struggles, an becoming human in a dialectical-historical process.

Today, human images in the light of humanistic psychology, transpersonal psychology and still of behaviorism characterize the anthropological thinking, supplemented by psychoanalytic, socio-psychological, and cybernetic (system theoretical) models. The molecular-biological consideration of human behavior should not be unmentioned (Vester 1983, 1993). An expanded human image in the perspective of the transcendence and border psychology is increasingly demanded today with proven facts (cf. e.g., Capra 1986; Grof 1993; Emde 1981; Murphy 1994). And finally, C.G. Jung's depth psychology (let's think in advance of his investigations "Aion" 1978 and "Westliche Religion" 1973) explored the Christian human image in great depth. The hermeneutic in-depth analyzes by Drewermann (e.g., "Tiefenpsycholgie und Exegese" 1987) are indispensable for an expanded Christian human image in the future.

All formulate philosophical-anthropological reflections resp. conclusions for human education and the daily life, some more from the point of view of upbringing resp. educational phenomena, others more from concrete life situations and still others from border psychological or spiritual experiences, always focused on the basic questions as Kant put them at the begin of every philosophical occupation with the human: "What is the human?", "What should I do?" and "What can I hope for?". The discussion on pedagogical anthropology by König / Ramsenthaler (1980) is an evidence of the topicality of philosophical-anthropological basic questions in the educational sciences. Numerous experts in pedagogy document in that on tend agreeing: 1) Upbringing and education as need and necessity are anthropological facts; 2) The network human-environment (both as "organism") must be included in the question of human being; 3) Basically for philosophical questioning and especially for the education, the question of the determination of the human is constitutive in all anthropological reflections to becoming human (personagenesis); 4) The normative question cannot be excluded from scientific reflections and pushed into the private life of the individual; 5) The process of becoming human (and with it the human images) is to be developed "multidimensionally" ("data processing integration") and made fruitful for the educational theory; 6) The educational science is closely intertwined in all sub-areas with the basic questions of the human being, from the initial situation through the process to the goal definition.

Beck (1994, 256-267) has elaborated 13 positions on the body-soul question from the history of philosophy resp. philosophical anthropology. Does this mean that the philosophical anthropology should be abolished? We think "no". The question for the human, the psyche (the life) will remain a mystery for many centuries. We see the being on the way, that is to constantly elaborate new and expanded approaches to the basic questions of existence, as a spiritual challenge assigned to the human, which already means concrete 'life', according to the central idea: The way is as important as the goal; is already goal. Philosophical thinking is 'engine' and 'energy' for social progress in the sense of humanity, for the psychic-spiritual evolution of the human.

The question may remain open, however, how it was possible with such a huge number of philosophical-anthropological reflections on the human being, on humanity and education that Europe could ride almost the whole world into catastrophes of immeasurable proportions (first and second world wars). Anyone who seriously wants to conduct philosophical-anthropological research today cannot avoid, in a way as "detective" to uncover behind everything, first the repressions, lies and hypocrisies in the individual, in the people, in politics, in economy, generally in social sciences, and probably also on the own behalf. Knowing about the hidden realities that we are suggesting, we can only wish: The humans and the state may seriously deal with the philosophical anthropology and its "individuated" representatives (in the future). They are working on a spiritual reality that each human hold in himself; we call this the "Grail" without tying ourselves concretely to the historical tradition of this topic. The question of the meaning ultimately leads the human to himself. One thing is certain: "Meaning ... must be found" (Frankl 1993, 155). That means "hard work" on oneself. Those who do not search the "Grail" will not find it. Whatever the humans mean by the term "God", and whatever other word is used for this reality (we think that many variations are possible depending on the culture), the principle is: "God does not release the human; the human must redeem God in himself". We have practically developed how this can be achieved in our workbooks, worked up theoretically in the study book "Empirie der Individuation" (1998) and framed in this work educational-theoretically, didactically, and philosophical-anthropologically.

Hans Georg Gadamer, together with other philosophers, wrote an appeal to all parliaments and governments in the world. Among other things, it says (parts of the sentence selected and translated by us): "Today more than ever, the world needs persons who are educated in philosophical thinking ... This is the indispensable prerequisite for every true encounter between humans (peoples) and cultures ... to overcome existing contradictions and to be able to lead the humanity on the path of the good (virtue)" (SAGW 1993, 34-35).

The always open question and the never-ending human image force the human, if he is capable of self-reflection, to bethink himself always anew. We consider this to be a decisive characteristic of human being.

Perhaps, in view of the potential total annihilation of the humanity and the creation of the earth, which has become possible today, this is the only 'assurance' that the human is not Dionysian 'lost' and blinded in his hubris alongside the earth, the YOU (the other), too still wants to manipulate, control, and dominate the whole universe. Teilhard de Chardin tackles the human dilemma at the roots: "Either the life does not strive for a goal that takes up and completes its work: And then the world is absurd, self-destructive ... Or there is something (someone) in which each element gradually finds the completion in its union with the whole, what has been built up in its individuality in the salvable: Then it is worth the effort to bow to hardship and even to devote oneself to it ..." (Teilhard de Chardin 1965, 115-116).

This self-reflection has decisive consequences for the pedagogy resp. the andragogy. What kind of human image does the agogic science teach if it does not integrate the phenomenon of projection and defense mechanisms into this image? What kind of human image is it if the educational science ignores the unconscious with all its contents - the complexes, the superego, etc.? How can a human image exist in the pedagogy resp. the andragogy if the dreams with the power of the spirit are described pedagogically and andragogically as irrelevant? What kind of agogical science is it that does not focus on the love as the decisive force of the psyche and life, even eliminate it as a "scientific object"? Whom does the pedagogy and the andragogy serve if, as science and practice, they do not place the basic psychic needs and thus also the individuation above the demands of economy?

What professors, educational researchers, experts, and practitioners do not integrate into the human image, that their students - the later teachers and educators - and thus the humans in the everyday life do not take seriously. So, the child learns in school and the adults learn in adult education, that the projections, the defense mechanisms, the unconscious, the love, the dreams, the spirit in the psychic system, the psychic basic needs and the individuation can be ignored and certainly do not need education.

The logical side effect is that the pedagogy professor and education researcher, the expert and practitioner does not work through his own unconscious, does not take seriously his own dreams, and cannot interpret them, does not integrate his own projections and defense mechanisms into the "I"-guidance, neglect his own basic psychic needs and the love cares at best as private matter.

From the top of the educational hierarchy to the base, everyone becomes incapable of taking seriously the psychic life and of practicing solidarity and responsibility for the highest values of the psychic-spiritual human being.

Individuation as the appropriate concept and as a (necessary) form of the self-analysis and self-education for education experts and education practitioners of human education is certainly unknown in the sciences of human education. In this aspect, the pedagogy resp. the andragogy got stuck in the spirit of the 18th / 19th century. Compared to the psychoanalysis, that "training analysis" long maintains as a duty and a matter of course for teaching and practice, this neglect in pedagogy and andragogy is an unparalleled embarrassment. This mentioned separation of essential areas of psychic life promotes the egoism, the narcissism and above all the life lie, is even a life lie and a self-deception. So, it is not surprising that the whole people are entangled in this life lie and in this self-deception.

The solution is more than just integrating other psychic areas into the research and teaching of the educational sciences. The solution begins with a self-reflection (of the science as well as those involved in it) on the own human image and subsequently on the own philosophical anthropology. That is more than an expansion of the educational task. This is also much more than mere philosophical resp. scientific responsibility. Because environmental destruction, inhuman buildings, natural disasters, violence, fraud, psychic and social sufferings, addiction of all kinds, sects and esoteric-spiritual swamp, excesses of the pleasure and fun society, greed and envy, accidents with many thousands of dead and hundred thousand of injureds (in all life areas) are made by the humans, especially by humans who consider the love, the spirit and the individuation to be completely unimportant - or who do not even know them. One has to say: The "royal science" - that is the philosophical anthropology, hand in hand with pedagogy - of the 20th century has failed.

If this "royal science" wants to be more than just a servant of economy, leisure industry and political administration in the 21st century, if it wants to shape and promote the human being, the humanity, the spirit, and the love as the fundamental force of society, it must integrate an evolutionary philosophical-anthropological human image and realize it as an educational program.

There are innumerable voices and facts in science and practice as well as in the society in general that call for such a turnaround. Let us take a quick look there. First there are some groups of humans who may have specific expectations of pedagogy (andragogy):

1) Retirees who not / rarely take part in the active social life.
2) Humans who are mostly tied to the house because they are fragile to illness.
3) Old people in rest homes or old people's homes.
4) Sick or injured at home or in hospital, in nursing or convalescent homes.
5) Children, adolescents, and adults in social institutions (homes).
6) Convicts in prison and suspects in pre-trial detention.
7) Unemployed and part-time unemployed, which cannot manage their situation.
8) Humans who (almost) always stay at home or 'loll' for the lack of money.
9) Mentally suffering humans who for this reason are not very active in social life.
10) The consumers and professionals in the red-light district, in the porn industry.
11) Drug, alcohol, medication, game, and food addicts.
12) Shoplifters, insurance fraudsters, rip-offs.
13) Left alone children and adults who (inwardly) go to seed.
14) Single, divorced, and separated who live isolated.
15) Humans who fell victim to the economic struggle.
16) Social welfare recipients, homeless people, outcasts because of 'unfitness'.
17) Invalids, generally humans who are mentally and / or physically impaired.
18) Partial alphabets, humans with a massive educational deficit.

19) Victims of accidents and tragic events.
20) Humans who have been marginalized because of their thinking and way of life.

We estimate the total number of these groups of humans to be around two-thirds of the population. In figures (taken from the media; without guarantee) it looks like this for Germany as an example in thre year 2000:

9 (8) million suffer from depression and 10 (8) million from migraines, 3.2 million stutter, 8 million have social phobia, 5 million have chronic fears, 9 million suffer from depression, around 8 million drink too much alcohol, more than 4 million suffer from skin allergies, 7 out of 10 have spinal problems, over 0.65 million suffer from fibrillation, every tenth woman has breast cancer (47,000 new cases every year), one million lives in total poverty, one million occasionally have suicidal thoughts, every second (third) complains of insomnia, 11 million suffer from chronic pain, 3 million have headaches every day, at 7 million gnaw impotence, every day a million men go to prostitutes, 50% of adults are overweight, every German eats around 30 kg sweets per year, at 35 (45?) million torments constipation, every second child has overweight and postural deformities, every tenth child is a victim of violence in the own family and every third act of violence occurs in the marriage (partnership) and family, more than a million children live on social welfare, 6.3 million are severely disabled, almost a million people convicted, over 6 million crimes per year, around 400,000 car accidents with over 7,000 deaths and 0.5 million injureds, 1 million children with asthma, 14 million young people have hearing damages (from too much noise in the disco), every fifth child of preschool age has speech disorders (due to the lack of communication of the parents), every fifth German suffers from heartburn, more than half of all Germans suffer from back pain, 90% of the children occasionally have headaches, a third of all women in a relationship are sexually unsatisfied, every second middle-aged German is at risk of alcohol, 500,000 people use cocaine and many hundreds of thousands more Germans are addicted (nicotine, alcohol, drugs of all kinds, medication, games, consumption, chocolate, pornography, food, television, mobile phones, etc.) and again many hundreds of thousands of Germans add up in the 'categories': Homeless, accident victims, thieves, fraudsters, rip-offs, separated resp. divorced, partially illiterate, lonely, neglected, economic victims, victims of treatment (medicine, justice, administration), victims of environmental disasters, sicks of stress due to noise and pollutants (traffic) and there all those are to be mentioned (around every third person at least once in his life) who suffer from mental disorders due to their life situation, their biography, their social environment and their economic situation; etc.

These exemplary statistics predominantly reflect an inappropriately educated psychic life, mostly related with helplessness towards the "inner human". Some of the 20 groups of humans mentioned belong to the losers in the struggle for prosperity, participation, experience, and happiness; some are "away from the window" at least for a while. Some take it as if it were "fate". We find a similar mindset in lotteries: One person wins the super prize, some receive (sometimes) smaller prizes and the big rest of them get nothing. The "cool superlative" creates millions of losers and viewers of life. Does this game of inequality of opportunity in this struggle already begin at school?

The sociology professor Ulrich Beck says of our "risk society" (1986, 60-61): "Danger grows beyond the walls of the indifference". He also means that denial and non-perception of the global risks are just as great a risk as the actual risks. And: "Denied risks thrive particularly well and quickly". What will the mental health of the Germans (and other peoples) look like in 10, 20 and more years?

Professor Konrad Lorenz clearly discloses the eight deadly sins of civilized humanity (1993). We summarize (ibid, 107-109):

1. The overpopulation of earth, which forces each of us through oversupply of social contacts to shield oneself against it in a fundamentally 'inhuman' way, and which ... has an aggressive effect.
2. The devastation of the natural habitat (destroys)... also in the human himself all awe for beauty and greatness of a creation standing above him.
3. The race ... with oneself, which accelerates the development of technology to our decay, makes people blind to all true values ...
4. The disappearance of all strong feelings ... through effeminacy. Advances in technology and pharmacology encourage an increasing intolerance to anything that causes the slightest discomfort ...
5. Genetic decline ... It cannot be suspended that many infantilisms that turn large parts of today's 'rebellious' youth into social parasites may be caused genetically or epigenetically.
6. The breaking of the tradition ... the younger generation does no longer (succeed) to communicate culturally with the older generation, much less to identify. It therefore treats thus like a foreign ethnic group ...
7. The increase of indoctrinability of the humanity. The augmentation of the number of humans united in a single cultural group, together with the perfection of technical instruments for influencing the public opinion, leads to a uniformization of views that has never existed at any point in human history ... In addition, the suggestive effect of a passionately believed doctrine grows with the number of its adherents ... The de-individualizing effects are welcome to all those who want to manipulate

large crowds ...
8.   The arming of mankind with nuclear weapons …

Konrad Lorenz sees the humanity threatened. From his pamphlet (1993 resp. 1973) we take two main drivers for this development, which in our opinion run decisively against the psychic-spiritual and physical health: "One must ask oneself what is causing greater damage to the humanity today: The blinding greed for money or the grueling haste. Whichever of the two it is, it is in the interests of those in power in all political directions to promote both ... also the fear (plays) an especially important role, fear of being overtaken in the race, fear of impoverishment, fear of making wrong decisions and of no longer being able to cope with the whole stressful situation ... Fearful haste and hurried fear contribute to rob the humans of their most essential quality. One of them is reflection." (ibid., 35) And: "It must have the worst consequences if a global ideology, including the politics resulting from it, is based on a lie (the pseudo-democratic doctrine) ..." (ibid., 94).

Postmann describes central social inhibiting factors for the responsible self-education and lifestyle (1988, 170-172): "Tyrants of all kinds have always known how useful it is to offer the masses pleasure and diversion in order to appease their dissatisfaction ... censorship (is) no longer necessary as soon as the entire political discourse takes the form of amusement." ... "Disinformation means misleading information - inappropriate, irrelevant, fragmentary or superficial information - information that pretends to know something when in reality it draws one away from it." (ibid., 133)

On the freedom and responsibility of self-knowledge, Jaspers (1984, 322) says: "The evil is through freedom. What is not in the power of freedom, I do not need to answer for. What is in the power of freedom? At last, and first, I for myself, as long as I can become transparent to myself or close myself off ...". And Jung (1978, 63) writes on this: "The human nature is capable of infinite malice; only the unconscious knows no good and bad."

Our conclusion for the self-education: The facts of these eight theses are striking, profoundly serious limitations and hindrances for a free, autonomous, and creative self-education. The vicious circle is obvious: Whoever does nothing against these deadly sins is affected by them and hindered in his endeavors to self-knowledge and self-education. He promotes the obstructive frame in the future. How can the freedom be achieved and how can the evil be overcome, if not through personality development and individuation?

Let us briefly look again at the statistics presented above: This exemplary picture mainly reflects an unsuitably educated psychic life, mostly related with helplessness towards the "inner human". The twenty groups of humans mentioned above are mostly among the losers in the struggle for prosperity, participation, experience, and happiness; some are at least temporarily "away from the window". Some take it as if it were "fate". We find a similar mindset in competitions.

From the roots of the spirit of the soul (of inner-psychic life), under various aspects this is not a society with spirit, with truthfulness and love as life principles for an evolutionary human being. This reality of free social life with very many tragic victims (and perpetrators) implicitly contains expectations to the educational sciences. What "equipment" does the pedagogy (andragogy) give the above-mentioned groups of humans to constructively cope with their difficult human situation? What is it doing for prevention?

The concept of promoting talent in the world of work is largely no longer relevant today. The job market and greed for money force many people to move around in the world of work according to the possibilities. If it used earlier to say: "He who supplies something, achieves something", today one can see that very many of those who "have" (money, goods, career, reputation, participation) do not have this because they would supply something special with great dedication and inner talent, but because they acquire this "having" with tricks, aggressiveness, and power behavior. Where is the inner response to professional service with factual and social competence? The rampant lack of professional ethics points to a lack of human education and thus to a need for education.

Just as the human is psychically shaped as a personality (person), he lives with himself, with other people and with his habitat. The dealing with the own psychic organism shows itself in the dealing with the nature, the water, the air, the earth and the animal world. Just as the psychic forces are formed, thus the human shapes his own world and this is how he affects the life worlds. The enormous damages and dangers that have arisen due to the lack of inner education cannot be discussed away. Billions of francs (€) are spent annually on educational research and educational tasks. Can one ask the question whether the pedagogy (andragogy) of the 20th century needs a total revision due to educational inefficiency (deficit) in the elementary areas of human life?

And finally, the social groups outlined above could be expanded with the renaissance of totalitarian ideology. A lot of readiness to violence can be seen. Resentments towards the values of occidental culture, emotional insecurity in the people, masses of blind identifications with political and economic "leaders", regressions and assimilations in a mass consciousness, male-aggressive life forms at work and in the relationships with the woman, exclusions as model of conflict resolution, also indifference (or disorientation) in the moral issues of daily life. It is little recognized how much the thinking of the humans of all educational levels and social layers is still saturated with the spirit of the Inquisition.

The modern fascism speaks in the style of humanistic psychology, moves according to democratic customs and its lead presents itself in the finest suits and shoes. The "stage play" only runs with lies. These are also the results of human education over the past thirty years and the so highly praised ideology of prosperity. Many millions cannot participate in prosperity and never achieve the standards of modernity. What ideology and what leaders will they be leaning towards in twenty to thirty years? Does pedagogy have a future perspective and a practical answer ready? If nobody wants the love, the truthfulness, and the spirit anymore, what comes next?

The fascist and partially schizophrenic type of human is extremely widespread. If we abstract from the political aspect of the generic term "fascism", then we can recognize a human image that has main features in the way of thinking and in the basic patterns of attitudes and behavior such as:

Authoritarianism, totalitarianism, belief in myths, submission to a leader, psychic violence as warfare agent, elitist community thinking, mass manipulation and collective brainwashing, human degrading values and ideals (of the affluent culture), repression of the "inner human", denial of the spirit as psychic force, ignoring and marginalization as an instrument of ostracism, etc. Diverse life worlds are marked by it! This is where *the* destruction potential lies in the 21st century! How does pedagogy (andragogy) react to this?

If one looks at the "critical" overall picture of society, then the following statement comes to mind: *educational research, educational science and pedagogy have failed considerably in their categorical primary task. They have failed to respond to vital needs of the humans in the society.* In other words: It is long overdue to subject the lifelong popular education to a total overhaul so that in the future the humans can cope with the demands of life and at the same time those of the psyche. This can never be done without a conscious and thorough education of the entire psychic-spiritual life. If the pedagogy resp. andragogy does not do this, sects, esoteric and pseudo- religious (spiritual) movements as well as fundamentalism will proliferate. All of this is breeding ground for fascist thinking.

Such a society is not a society with spirit, with truthfulness and love as life principles for an evolutionary human being. This reality with very many tragic victims (and perpetrators) contains expectations of the educational sciences. What "equipment" does the pedagogy (andragogy) give the above-mentioned groups of humans to constructively cope with their difficult human situation? What is it doing for prevention?

It has no visions, no foresight; it only reacts to economic needs.

In the (Catholic, Christian) philosophical dictionary von Brugger (1976/1992, 430-431), the keyword responsibility is: "Responsibility is a necessary consequence of the human free will and the sanity based in it. By this, the moral person must as decisively because of his good and evil doing answer his deeds for his conscience, the moral environment and especially before the divine judge and assume the inevitable consequences of his behavior ...".

From pedagogical point of view, in Horney's "Lexikon für Pädagogik" (1970, 1287) we find aspects that clearly outline "responsibility": "... the ability and willingness to respond to a response ... with my whole person vouching for my answer. Being responsible is a basic existential orientation that has an obligatory, inevitable character.

The unconditionality of real responsibility refers to the conscience in which I become aware of what is ought and perceive its claim. The justification of the perceived claim with the strict demand for answer and responsible acting can only be given by the religion ...".

The former Vice-President Al Gore (until the end of 2000) takes a clear position on self-knowledge and the responsibility connected with it (1992, 373-375). We extract from it: "Since several years now I am intensively looking for truths about myself and about my life. And I know that many others are doing the same. More humans than ever before are asking: "Who are we? What is our goal?" ... In the end, I was simultaneously looking for a better understanding of my own life and possibilities to save the global environment ... The key is in the balance, the balance between thinking and acting, between personal worries and the commitment to the community, between the love to the natural environment and our own amazing civilization ... (My faith meaning) is rooted in the unwavering belief in God as the creator and sustainer, in a deeply personal interpretation of Christ and my relation to him ... That is the essence of the faith: Surrendering oneself of the own free will to a spiritual reality that is greater than ourselves ... we must be honest with each other and to take responsibility for our actions ... The decision is ours; the earth is at stake."

Commentary, it should be emphasized: "Christ" as the epitome of the self in the completed individuation (according to C.G. Jung, Aion) offers us in this context a bridge to the transcendental horizon of the self-knowledge and the self-education.

Our core thesis on the facts: Self-education leads out of isolation in the crowd and pushes for new forms of life where the population is balanced. Self-education promotes the respect for the creation and thus the protection of the natural habitat. Self-knowledge is a natural brake against the race of our zeitgeist. Self-education forms strong feelings and the ability to deal constructively with dislike. Self-education reduces infantilism. Self-knowledge appreciates critically the traditions and develops the cultural life progressively and evolutionarily. Self-knowledge is free from indoctrination and de-individualization. Individuation and nuclear weapons are incompatible.

Summary and Outlook:

We have founded a future-oriented concept of personality development and individuation with an educational theory, a redefinition of philosophical anthropology and tailor-made didactics for a comprehensive professionalism. Our conception is embedded in the historic tradition of philosophy, psychology, and pedagogy. To this end, we have drafted the andragogical psychology (Empirie der Individuation, 1998). Furthermore, based on this, we have created a comprehensive educational program with elementary and advanced levels for practical personality development and the individuation.

We mark the core: The human is essentially human with his psychic force systems. He has an "I". He has a will, defense, and integration mechanisms as well as a control function. The human experiences a great wealth of emotions. He has many psychic basic needs. His entire lived life since prenatal time is the inventory of his unconscious, which are the general life experiences, human images, the attitudes, and the conscience contents. The force of love can be as versatile as the intelligent functions, i.e., the thinking, the perception, the language, and the learning. The force of the spirit, (we construct this term from the achievements of the dreams, the imaginations, and contemplations) is the crucial regulatory function for the self-reflection, for conscience formation, for the transcendental anchoring of love and for the individuation process. What is alive in the human is crucial the psychodynamics, also known as the psychic energy structure.

The human includes the own (inner and external), the foreign (inner and external), the material and transcendental reality through his daily life and the way in which his psychic forces are formed. He works on these realities with thinking and inner ideas. The entire acting of the human is versatile

236

networked with all these psychic forces systems. In the presence of everyone, the own biography is the living psychic reality. The habitat, social systems, culture, religion, and the built environment created by the human are an expression of the formed psychic realities of the collective. This complicated psychic organism is versatile, malleable, changeable, and capable of development into an all-round balanced wholeness. The human can only realize his psychic-spiritual human being through the comprehensive evolutionary education of his psychic organism.

That is the fundamental object of human education for the science of andragogy and for its practice in the future, meaning primarily the enormously rich designed institutions of adult education. There is still a lot to be researched in science and practice, and to be developed in theories and practical materials. Some of what we have worked out here will certainly become new accents, be expanded, and also have to be corrected. The critical-constructive discourse on personality development and individuation is of course necessary for the further conceptual design of human education.

The freedom of the human does not consist in the fact that everyone can deny the self-education and individuation. This is just defiance and compulsion, Dionysian rebellion perhaps. The freedom shows itself in the devotion to this educational process through the responsible affirmation and the competent fulfillment of the individuation. If the humans do not complete this education, the humanity will destroy itself in the long term. Because the psychic life that is not balanced formed and not integrated into social life always "strikes" back.

Which educational institutions whatever the term "education" use, whether in connection with politics or with research or the with teaching or practice, they have no science theoretical and no factual argument to exclude any sector of the psychic organism of the "human education". Those who do this, nevertheless, deceive the human about what can make him to the human, including the love, the spirit and the process of becoming human, called "individuation". And he is in solidarity with those who say: "The psychic life is not important". Perhaps he is involved in the collective "oath" that wants to hold everyone in bondage: "Never uncover the unconscious psychic life". According to Jung (1976), the Christ archetype reflects the higher self and thus the realization of the individuation. It is not the suffering or the corresponding historical outrage (whether it was historical or not, we are not interested in here) that has become the symbol of Christianity, but rather the refusal of psychic-spiritual development resp. the individuation, and thus also the denial of encompassing psychic organism. The Christian cross symbol indeed reflects this collective vow. – The andragogy thus has a difficult position.

One might ask us whether we are not too believing in science. We have made critical comments on this in various places. The inner processes of individuation cannot be comprehensively included with the conventional mechanistic understanding of science. A new scientific paradigm is needed for the social science. The voices in the professional world are increasing.

We think it is conceivable that the science (teaching, research, professionalization) of human education, personality development and individuation will be practiced more privately than stately (at universities) in a few decades. We consider the today's conceptions (institutes with chairs, study programs, forms of qualification, knowledge collection, research, and teaching without the own individuation) to be unsuitable for the human education of individuation.

In addition, the "academic halls" are far too far removed from the life reality of the many millions of humans. Because the personality development and the individuation are for the humans. Whoever wants to have as thorough knowledge of human education as the academic standard requires, should just as thoroughly pursue his own individuation. This implies meditation, contemplation and working with dreams daily. - Fundamental changes in the entire social life of Europe are highly likely in the next century.

We also think that the psychic potential for a repetition of the "Holocaust" is increasingly explosive today. We also assume that most of the European population would shout like those then: "Crucify him!" Because our human education ultimately leads to the "living grail". This threatens every narcissistic, conceited, instinct-bound and egoistic "I", and that in all social classes, at all "educational" levels, in all professions and at all economic levels. The fascistic and partially schizophrenic human type is enormously widespread. If we abstract from the political aspect of the generic term "fascism", then we can recognize a personality profile (human image) that has basic features in the way of thinking and in the basic patterns of attitudes and behaviors such as: Authoritarianism, totalitarianism, belief in myths, subjection to a leader, psychic violence as warfare agent, elitist community thinking, mass manipulation and collective brainwashing, human degrading values and ideals of the affluent culture, repression of the "inner human", denial of the spirit as psychic force, ignoring and marginalization as an instrument of ostracism (the modern Inquisition!) etc. One replaces the political aspect of fascism with other social life worlds and finds a particularly human drama there. This is where *the* potential for destruction in the 21st century lies!

Nevertheless, we hope that there will be more and more humans who want to live the individuation, and that one day the social and economic life across Europe will be guided by the basic values of individuation. We know a hundred arguments that legitimize the psychic-spiritual evolution as a necessary process within the society in an all-round positive way. We do not know a single reason that could speak against it.

We have drafted a new concept of the human education for the 21st century - a new paradigm for the general andragogy - so that the human does not remain "stray message of the evolution" (Koestler 1990), but rather take the step from the "homo sapiens" via the "homo oeconomicus" through his psychic-spiritual development to the "living image being of the circle-cross-mandala".

From barbarism to the murder of God

Nietzsche's thoughts, summarized with a few omissions and placed in our core message on the psychic life and its education:

"The scientific man has ... got into a hurry, as if the science were a factory ... now he works as hard as ... the slave class ... Our scholars even, miraculously, cannot think of the very next question: What their work, their haste, their painful stagger is of use ... We see the scholarship already progressing terribly in the direction of barbarism ... At the end of the day, the modern man carries around an immense number of indigestible stones of knowledge ... that physical rumble rumble in him. In this rumbling, the most peculiar characteristic of the modern human is given away: The strange opposite of an interior, which no exterior corresponds, and an exterior, that no interior is equivalent ... (which is) no real education ...

Where is God? ... We killed him ... We are all his killers ... What did we do when we unchained this earth from the sun? Where is it going now? ... God is dead. God remains dead. And we killed him. How do we console ourselves, the murderers of all murderers? The holiest and most powerful thing that the earth has ever possessed, it bled to death under our knives ... With what water could we purify ourselves? ... Doings take time, even after they are done, to be seen and heard. This act is still more far away from them than the most distant stars - and yet they did it ...".

If the love, the spirit - working in dreams and meditations -, the wisdom, the growth to the living image being of the circle-cross-archetype (individuation) and the psychic-cosmic energy are a fundamental part of God, then Europe is a barbarian country with millions of 'god' killers. Regarding the scientists and practitioners of pedagogy, social education, andragogy, psychology, and philosophy: What are these humans when, in a hurry, without real basic needs they pursue science and human education like slaves, fill own and other bellies with stones? *"Everything serves the barbarism ... including science. The educated has degenerated into the greatest enemy of education."* With Nietzsche, but in our own interpretation and meaning expansion, we appeal: It is clever and wise to be vigilant if you scientist, and you, human educator does not want to be barbarians and murderers of God. Otherwise, you drag generations of young humans and whole peoples into this barbarism and murdering. Today this has consequences for thousands of years. How do you want to and how can you answer for that? Those who want to form their own human being have also to be vigilant and, above all, self-critical. Fine words and good will do not protect against folly.

For human educators and those who want human education, there is a simple test of barbarism and the murder of God: What do you do when someone comes along and speaks true: *"I received the Grail; it is mine. I was able to pull the sword of the Grail King out the earth. I will make full use of it. The destiny is sealed."*? - Who knows, maybe your answer will determine the fate of your soul for a long time, and in the sum, the fate of entire international communities. But who wants to see that? Who wants to say "yes" to love, spirit, truthfulness, wisdom, and individuation?

Quotations taken from: Nietzsche, F.: Gesammelte Werke, Vol. 1

Appendix: Classics

Some classics of the human education and their lives

As a reminder, some philosophers, psychologists, psychoanalysts and educators are presented below. We have compiled a selection of portraits and small fragments from the person's lives. All these humans, scientists and practitioners, were pioneers. They have achieved outstanding things for the humans. It is striking those men dominate this psychic-spiritual field of activity. Why should it not be possible for many women, as pioneers in science and practice, to comprehensively support the further developments of the human education?

We have also found that many pioneers have been refused by politicians and the people, rejected and in some cases even severely punished for their pioneering work. Some had to flee. Some had to pay for what they did with their live. We ask the readers and people in general a somewhat harsh question: Do the humans - the peoples - and the states - we are talking about Europe - (and thus the politicians) deserve these pioneers? Where would the peoples and states be today without these many outstanding personalities?

Isn't the human the "crown of the creation"? One must admit: Most people are closer to their evolutionary ancestors than what they could be from the plan of creation. Most people make little use of what they can live and realize from their psychic-spiritual being. It is the task of andragogues in the future to educate the humans into what they can and should become from their inner being: Living images of the "circle-cross-archetype". This requires much pioneering work, and our following list will be expanded in later future for many humans.

We present some pioneers to recall and to reflex about. The andragogy in the future builds on this history, learns from it, protects what is valuable and carries it on, renews and improves a lot, teaches in a new language and in new pictures the humans the knowledge and methods to experience and education. We do not want to forget: Many pioneers, who lived thousands of years ago, understood more about the human and his existence than the social sciences today. That is also why a look back is valuable.

As a reminder: Some philosophers and their lives

Socrates (470-399)

Socrates lived in Athens, was a sculptor by profession, but he neglected it in favor of his philosophical teaching. He did not care much about his family either. He took part as soldier in the Peloponnesian War (431-404) against Sparta, where he received several awards. His students were sons from aristocratic families. After the restore of the democracy he was accused due to dissemination of his philosophy. The reasons were: Disregard for the gods and - seduction of the youth. He had to take the poison cup. He saw himself as a "birth helper" of the ideas of his students, this was probably inspired by the profession of his mother: She was a midwife.

Plato (428-348)

Plato came from rich aristocratic family, from the mother side related with members of the tyrant regime (404-403). He was 28 years old when his teacher and friend Socrates died. He wanted to devote himself to politics to implement his philosophy into the reality of an "excellent state". He later got away from it. His opinion was: "... the misfortune of the human gender will not stop until either the gender of the right and true philosophers in the states reaches to the government or the authorities in the states become as a result of a divine destiny to real philosopher." After a few years he modified this opinion. He undertook different journeys to Italy, Sicily, Egypt, and other places more, was out twelve years and returned with forty years back to Athens, where he founded an academy that became an international meeting place. He dealt with almost everything that life has to offer.

Aristotle (384-322)

Aristotle is born in Stagira, northern Greece, as a son of a doctor: His father was court physician by the Macedonian king, the grandfather of Alexander the Great. In 367 he went to Athens to study by Plato, remained twenty years first as a student then as a teacher. Although he was an excellent scientist, it was not he but Plato's nephew who became director of the academy. Thereupon he left Athens, traveled to Asia Minor and Lesbos, and married in 344 into the rich family of one of the most powerful statesmen in Greece.

Then he followed the call to the royal court of Philip of Macedonia, this was 343, and took over the education of Alexander, Philip's son.

He stayed in Macedonia for 8 years. After Alexander became king, he returned to Athens, where he founded the Lykeion. Many years of fruitful work followed. After the death of Alexander (323) he got into political distress because of his connections to the Macedonian royal court: The Athenians revolted against the Macedonian rule and Aristotle was in danger of being sentenced to death for high treason. He fled to the island of Evia "so that the Athenians do not sin against the philosophy a second time". A year later he died in exile at the age of 62.

Epicurus (341-271)

Epicurus was born on Samos, studied with a Platonist, and traveled to Athens at the age of 18 to do his military service. It was then that he made the acquaintance of the philosophy schools that were important at the time. He studied for more years. At the age of 31 he began to teach philosophy himself. First, he teaches in Mytilene, then in Lampsakos. With some of his students he moved to Athens in 306, where he founded the "garden". There he worked in a harmonious and self-sufficient coexistence with his friends and students, which also included women and slaves.

Stoa

Stoa was one of the classical schools of philosophy in Athens. The others were Aristotle's Peripatus, Plato's Academy, and Epicurus' garden. The name has its origins in a public building in Athens, the "colorful portico" or the "Stoa poikile". Zenon (c. 332-262/1) from Kition on Cyprus was teaching, probably of mixed Greek-Oriental descent. He was the founder of the school. His scholar and friend Cleanthes, about the same age, and his successor Chryssipos laid the systematic foundations.

This first phase was called the "old Stoa" and affected the common people above all. Cleanthes himself came from humble conditions.

The "middle Stoa", on the other hand, presented itself as urban and cosmopolitan. It was represented by Panaetius from Rhodes (approx. 185-110) and Poseidonios from Apamea in Syria (135-51). Panaetius was from an old noble family. Thanks to Poseidonios close relationships with aristocratic circles in Rome, the Stoa soon found wide dissemination. The emperor Marc Aurel, the poet Seneca, and also the former slave Epictetus represented the newer Stoa; they all left extensive literature.

Plotinus (205-270)

Plotinus was born in Egypt and is considered the most important representative of the Neoplatonism. He lived in Alexandria until 242, was a pupil of Ammonios Sakkas and a soldier in the Persian campaign of Emperor Gordian. Then he settled in Rome and became head of a philosophical school. Be with about fifty years, he began at the request of his students with writing his philosophy. He stayed in Rome until the end of his life.

Augustine of Hippo (354-430)

Augustine was born in Thegaste in Numidia in what is now Algeria. The father was a landowner and city council (decurio). The mother was a committed Christian and influenced him to convert to Christianity. At the age of 17 he took a cohabitee - which was nothing unusual at the time - and two years later he became a father. In Carthage he studied rhetoric. As a student he dealt with the classical writings of literature and Cicero became of great importance for him, whose writings led him to study philosophy. He was a member of the Manichaeans, from whom he later turned away. His conversion to Christianity took place in 386. He was baptized, lived, and taught rhetoric in Carthage, Rome, and Milan. He later became bishop of Hippo Regius and died in 430 during the siege of the city by the Vandals.

Thomas Aquinas (1225-1274)

Thomas Aquinas was born in Roccasecca Castle near Naples as the youngest son of a noble family. At the age of 5 he came to the Benedictines in Monte Cassino. At the age of fourteen he went to Naples, where he studied Aristotle. In 1244 he entered the Dominican order, against the resistance of his family.

He then studied in Paris, where he met Albertus Magnus, and followed him to Cologne for four years. In 1252 he was sent to Paris to teach theology. From 1259 he taught in Italy. 1268 he was sent by the father general again to Paris to mediate in inner universitary matters of dispute. In 1272 he was called back to Naples. He died in 1274 at the age of 49 on the way to the Council of Lyon.

Master Eckhart (1260-1328)

Master Eckhart was born in Cologne. He came from a knight family that was settled in Thuringia. He studied in Cologne and Paris, became Dominican and got the highest positions in the order. He lived and taught in various places, including Erfurt, Strasbourg, and Cologne. He released the forces of faith from the rationalized theology and philosophy, which, however, earned him the criticism of the church. In 1325 an inquisition was initiated against him. In 1327 he had to submit a declaration of revocation. He did not experience the

Pope's decision; he died that same year. Later some of his statements were condemned as heretical by papal bulls.

<u>René Descartes (1596-1650)</u>

Descartes was born in La Haye, northern France, of noble origin. The father was a lawyer. The mother's side were high officials. At the age of 18 he entered a Jesuit school, studied mathematics in Poitiers, then in Paris. He served in two armies (Bavarian and Dutch armies) during the Thirty Years' War with military training in Holland. Several journeys took him all over Europe. From 1625 to 1628 he lived in Paris, then in the Netherlands, where he stayed for twenty years. His first work (1633) he did not publish because he did not want to come in the same conflicts as Galilei. He published the second work anonymously. Later his books were placed on the index of forbidden books and condemned by both Protestant and state authorities. In 1649 the philosophically interested Queen of Sweden invited him to Stockholm. The pious scholar reluctantly accepted this invitation. He died there the following year at the age of fifty-six.

<u>Gottfried W. Leibnitz (1646-1716)</u>

Leibnitz was born in Leipzig. His father was a professor of moral philosophy; he died when his son was 8 years old.

Even as a child he dealt with logic, philosophy, and theology. At the age of 15 he studied philosophy and law at the University of Leipzig and received his doctorate in 1667. He never held a scientific teaching post, but traveled a lot (Vienna, Rome, Naples, Paris, and London), to the disappointment of the princes and others courts he was minister. In 1676 he became the ducal librarian in Hanover. He had contact with scholars from all over Europe and was highly regarded. He was a member of the Royal Society, Académie des Sciences, president of the Academy of Sciences in Berlin. Later he was even offered the cardinal dignity. The last years of his life brought him a lot of hostility, for example he was accused of stealing the idea of differential calculus from Newton. Then he fell from grace. He died bitterly and lonely. No one from Georg Ludwig's court was present at his funeral.

<u>Immanuel Kant (1724-1804)</u>

Kant was born in Königsberg as the fourth of five children. His father was a master saddler. The Pietist family lived in rather poor conditions. When he was 13 years old, his mother died. He studied in Königsberg from 1740-1746, first theology, then philosophy and natural sciences. Afterwards, he was tutor at various noble estates. He received his doctorate in 1755, then he was a private lecturer, and in 1770 professor of logic and metaphysics. He never left Königsberg and the surrounding area, cultivated sociable contacts with friends and acquaintances and remained a bachelor throughout his life with a precisely regulated daily routine. He was reprimanded by King Friedrich Wilhelm II for his work (1793) "Religion within the limits of sheer reason". Like many other philosophers, he was convinced that he was doing religion a service with his religious-philosophical investigations. Unfortunately, this was not the opinion of the official representatives. He was famous beyond the borders of Germany, even during his lifetime.

Georg Friedrich W. Hegel (1770-1831)

Hegel was born in Stuttgart as the son of a civil servant. In 1788 he studied philosophy and theology in Tübingen. After graduating, he worked as a private tutor, in Bern in 1793 and in Frankfurt in 1797. Then he lived for a while on his father's inheritance. In 1802 he completed his habilitation and became a private lecturer in Jena. When Napoleon's troops occupied Jena in 1806, he fled. Firstly, he worked as an editor.

Then he became the rector of a Nuremberg grammar school. He wrote his second major work there. In 1816 he followed the call to Heidelberg and taught philosophy. He wrote an encyclopedia of the philosophical sciences. He was then called to Berlin in 1816 and became a "Prussian state philosopher". He read about various philosophical disciplines: Including art, religion, and legal philosophy. (An American critic called Hegel's works: "Masterpieces of incomprehensibility, obscured by abstraction and scarcity of style"). In 1829 he was elected as rector of the university of Berlin. In old age he was the proverbial absent-minded professor, died at the age of 61 from a chronic stomach ailment or from cholera.

Arthur Schopenhauer (1788-1860)

Schopenhauer was born in Danzig. The father was a businessman and the mother a novelist. In 1793 the family moved to Hamburg. As a child, he stayed with an uncle in Le Havre for two years. When he was 15, his father sent him on a journey across Europe. At the father's request, he began an apprenticeship as a businessman, but broke it off after his father's death (1805). The mother grew up and moved to Weimar and had a literary salon. The young Schopenhauer met Goethe, among others. He fell out with his mother and studied in Göttingen from 1809-1811. At the age of 23 he is said to have said: "Life is an unfortunate thing: I have resolved to spend it thinking about this thing." His first book was very concrete, where other philosophers have so far remained abstract, namely in relation to real life. He received his doctorate in 1813 and completed his habilitation in Berlin in 1820. He had a short relationship with Caroline Richter, who worked at the Berlin Opera. In 1833 he moved to Frankfurt. His main work went unnoticed for two decades, which made him very bitter. (Unfortunately, he attacked the university professors who could have made him known.) Fortunately, his father's inheritance made him financially independent. Only towards the end of his life did the long-awaited fame and recognition come, which softened his hardened character. He died of a heart attack at the age of 72.

Sören Kirkegaard (1813-1855)

Kirkegaard was born in Copenhagen as the youngest of seven children and grew up in financially secure circumstances in a strictly pietistic family. In 1830 he graduated from high school, then studied theology and philosophy, where he temporarily neglected the study to act out; he was considered a funny entertainer, but suffered from a widely interpreted guilt complex, whereby he said that there was a curse on his family.

After his father's death (1838) he resumed his studies in theology and passed the state examination in 1840, and in the same year he became engaged to Regine Olsen, who was ten years younger. After a few months he broke away again. In 1841 he traveled to Berlin to study Hegel's philosophy. In 1842 he returned to Copenhagen and wrote books and diaries. Through his philosophical writings, he came into the field of fire of a satirical magazine that published caricatures about him, which portrayed him as a hunchbacked "Nordic Socrates". He inherited a small fortune from his father, so he did not have to work. He dealt deeply with the official Christianity; attacked the established church vigorously, especially in newspaper articles and in his own magazine published between 1851 and 1855. He died of a stroke at the age of 42.

Karl Marx (1818-1883)

Marx was born as the son of a lawyer in Trier. His father converted from the Jewish to the Protestant faith. Already in his youth he became acquainted with the philosophy of Kant, Fichte, and the teachings of the French Enlightenment. In 1835 he studied law in Bonn, then philosophy in Berlin. He was a member of an association of time-critically committed intellectuals (circles of the Hegelian Left.) In 1841 he received his doctorate on Democritus and Epicurus in Jena. In 1842 he became editor of the "Rheinische Zeitung" in Cologne. He had to give up this position because of the Prussian press censorship. He unfolds terribly busy writing activity. In

1843 he married Jenny von Westphalen and moved to Paris. He was then expelled and had to take up residence in Brussels in 1845. Then he let himself expatriate from Prussia and was henceforth stateless. In 1848 he was also expelled from Brussels, emigrated to England, and settled in London. He constantly lived in cramped financial difficulties. His friend Engels supported him financially. He stayed in London until his death. His saying: "The philosophers have the world interpreted differently, the point, however, is to change it". Which then actually happened in many parts of the world.

Friedrich Nietzsche (1844-1900)

Nietzsche was born in Röcken into a family of pastors. His father died early. He was spoiled by the women of his family and was a rather introverted child. At the age of 18 he "lost" his faith. At 19 he read Schopenhauer.

Then he went to the recruiting school, fell ill or fell from the horse and was exempt from military service. He felt himself to be too little hardened male. (The result of the "women" education?) As a student he lived it off, studied theology (one semester) and philosophy in Bonn, then philology in Leipzig. At the age of 24 (1868) he became professor of philology in Basel, where he met Wagner, who was then living in Switzerland, and with whom he remained friends for a long time.

He broke with him in 1878. 1870/71 he made in the Franco-German War volunteer service as a military male nurse and fell ill himself. In 1872 he went back to Basel and fell in love. His book Zarathustra was not a success. Often, he put almost all his money into the publication of his works. In 1879 he had himself exempted from teaching because of his ailment and traveled a lot to cure himself: Graubünden in Switzerland, Cote d'Azur, Italy. In 1889 he suffered a stroke and fell into mental confusion, probably because of progressive paralysis. He died in Weimar in his sister's house.

Max Horkheimer (1895-1973)

Horkheimer was born in Zuffenhausen near Stuttgart into a Jewish merchant family. He left grammar school in 1911 and joined his father's company. When the First World War broke out, he was the junior manager in his father's company. At the age of 21 he began a friendship with Rose Riekher, who was eight years elder. He made up his Abitur and began to study economics, psychology, and philosophy in 1919 with a doctorate in 1923 and habilitation in 1925. He then became a private lecturer and married Rose Riekher. 1930-1933 professor of social philosophy in Frankfurt. Because of the rise of National Socialism, in 1933 he fled to Geneva, in 1934 to New

York and from there he moved in 1941 to Los Angeles. In 1949 he returned to Frankfurt and was a professor until 1959. In 1960 he moved to Switzerland and died in 1973 in Nuremberg at the age of 78.

Theodor W. Adorno (1903-1969)

Adorno was born in Frankfurt a.M. His mother was a singer, his father a merchant. The mother's sister, who was a pianist, lived with the family. His childhood was shaped by music and the two "mothers", as he called them. He was considered an incredibly talented and above-average high school student. From 1921, he studied philosophy, psychology, and musicology in Frankfurt with promotional in 1924.

He studied with the composer Alban Berg in Vienna and wanted to become a concert pianist and composer. Instead, however, he became an accomplished music theorist and returned to Frankfurt in 1926. In 1930 he completed his habilitation and became a private lecturer. With the takeover of the National Socialists, he could not continue teaching, because his father was a Jew. From 1934 to 1937 he lived in Germany and Oxford, where he studied as an "advanced student". In 1938 he traveled to the USA with his wife, where he worked on a radio project and became a member of the Institute of Social Research in New York. From 1941-1949 he lived in Los Angeles and published many writings. In 1949 he returned to Germany, and in 1952/53 he went back to Los Angeles as scientific director. In 1956 he became a professor and later director of the Institute for Social Research. Until the beginning of the sixties he missed the recognition of his colleagues, but in 1963 he became chairman of the German Society for Sociology. He died at the age of 66 while on vacation in Switzerland.

As a reminder: Some psychologists resp. psychoanalysts and their lives

Wilhelm Maximilian Wundt (1832-1920)

Wundt was born in Neckerau near Mannheim in 1832. He was a medic, physiologist, psychologist and philosopher, taught psychology, and philosophy at the universities of Heidelberg in 1864, then in Zurich in 1874 and Leipzig in 1875, where he founded the first institute for experimental psychology in 1879. He enriched psychological research with many methods and technical aids. He died at the age of 88 in Grossbothen near Leipzig.

Sigmund Freud (1856-1939)

Freud was born in Freiberg, Moravia, in 1856 as the first of seven children.

When he was six years old, the family moved to Vienna, where he attended the grammar school from 1866-1873. This was followed by a degree in medicine, while also working at the "Institut für Physiologie und Histologie" under Professor Brücke. There he met Josef Breuer, who became a friend to him and who later helped him out with financial loans. In 1881 he received his doctorate. He stayed in Brücke's laboratory until 1882 and was then an assistant doctor at the Vienna General Hospital for three years. In the winter of 1885, he stayed in Paris on the Salpetrière by Charcot. Back in Vienna he opened his own practice (1886) and married Martha Bernay. The marriage resulted in six children.

In 1887 he became a member of the Vienna Medical Society. Between 1890-1900 he mainly devoted himself to his private practice; during this time, his break with J. Breuer and a time of relative seclusion and self-analysis fell. In 1894 he suffered from cardiac symptoms, whereupon he (temporarily) stopped smoking cigars. In 1902 he became an associate professor and in the same year he founded the "Psychological Wednesday Society".

In 1907, C.G. Jung and Ludwig Binswanger visited him. In 1910 he founded the International Psychoanalytic Society with the help of his followers. In 1920 he became a full professor, three years later he fell ill with jaw cancer and had to undergo thirty operations over the years. In 1930 he received the Goethe Prize. In 1934 his books were burned in Berlin and in 1936 the entire inventory of the International Psychoanalytical Publishing House in Leipzig was confiscated by the National Socialists. In 1938 he emigrated to England, where he died in London in 1939 at the age of 83.

<u>Alfred Adler (1870-1937)</u>

Adler was born in Rudolfsheim, a suburb of Vienna, in 1870. He was the second of six children of a Jewish merchant of Hungarian descent. First, he attended a private school and then high schools in Vienna. In 1888 he began to study medicine and received his doctorate in 1895. Then he worked at the Vienna Polyclinic in the Department of Ophthalmology. In 1897 he married Raissa Epstein. Then he opened a private practice. In 1904 he converted to the Protestant faith together with his two young daughters. In 1905 and 1909 two more children were born. 1902-1911 he was a member of the Wednesday Society. In 1911 he became an Austrian citizen and in the same year he founded the Society for Individual Psychology. In 1912 he applied for a position as a private lecturer at the university, but this was rejected 3 years later. In 1916 he worked as an army doctor in neuro-psychiatric departments. In 1918 and 1919 there were publications with socialist views; but he had already given up his membership in the Social Democratic Party. In 1920 educational institutions were founded and developed. In 1924 he was appointed professor at the Pedagogical Institute in Vienna. In 1927 he attended the Wittenberg Symposium in Springfield, Ohio. In 1929 he was medical director at the Mariahilf outpatient clinic and gave additional lectures in the USA. In 1930 he became a citizen of the City of Vienna. In 1932 he taught at Long Island Medical College. In 1935 he settled in the USA. He suffered a serious illness but survived it. In 1937, on the way to a lecture tour to England, he felt cardiac pains. Contrary to the advice of the cardiologist, he traveled from Holland to Scotland. In Aberdeen, he collapsed on the street on the fourth day of his lecture tour and died on the way to the hospital.

<u>Carl Gustav Jung (1875-1961)</u>

Jung was born in Kesswil on Lake Constance, Switzerland, as the second son of a Protestant pastor. He lived in Switzerland all his life. In later years, however, he traveled extensively: He was in France, England, America, Africa and India. In 1879 the family moved to Klein-Hüningen, Basel, where he attended grammar school (1886-1895) and studied medicine. After the final exam and the recruiting school he became an assistant doctor at the "Burghölzli" in Zurich, which was headed by Professor Bleuler. He received his doctorate in 1902 and then studied for a semester with Janet in Paris. In 1903 he married Emma Rauschenbach. They had five children. In 1905 he became senior physician at the Burghölzli Psychiatric Clinic and private lecturer at the University of Zurich. In 1907 he visited Freud in Vienna. In 1909 he left the psychiatric clinic. He no longer got on well with Bleuler and wanted to devote more time to his private practice. In 1909 he became a member of the International Psychoanalytic Association but resigned in 1913 after breaking with Freud. Soon afterwards he resigned from his post as a private lecturer and until about 1919 he subjected himself to a self-analysis. During this time, his "psychological club" began. He then gave lectures in England and in 1924/25 he traveled to the USA and New Mexico and spent a few months in Kenya. In 1935 he became adjunct professor for psychology at the Polytechnic in Zurich and founded in the same year the Swiss Society for Practical Psychology. In 1937 he participated in the founding ceremony of the University of Calcutta and took the opportunity to travel through India and Ceylon. In 1943 the University of Basel awarded him the title of Professor of Medical Psychology; however, he soon resigned due to poor health. In 1944 he suffered a heart attack. In 1948 the "C.G. Jung Institute" was opened in Zurich. He received several honorary doctorates. After the war he has been variously accused to have been Nazi friendly, however due to misunderstandings. In 1955 his wife died. He himself survived her for 6 years and died in Küsnacht in 1961.

<u>John B. Watson (1878-1958)</u>

Watson was born in South Carolina in 1878. From 1894 he attended the college. From 1899-1908 he studied philosophy, then psychology at the University of Chicago, also took courses in neurology and physiology and began with animal research while still a student. A year before his doctorate, he suffered a nervous breakdown with weeks of insomnia. 1908-1919 he was a professor at Johns Hopkins University, interrupted from military service during the First World War. In 1913 the establishing of the so-called behaviorism followed. After divorcing his first wife, he married Rosalie Rayner, at the same time he separated from Johns Hopkins University, which marked the end of his research career. However, he subsequently became a successful businessman.

<u>Wilhelm Reich (1897-1957)</u>

Reich was born in Dobrzcynica, Galicia in 1897. First, he started to study law. However, influenced by Freud, with whom he was in training analysis, he switched to medicine. In 1920 he joined the International Psychoanalytic Society. He was involved in the communist movement and a member of the Communist Party. He tried to synthesize Marxism and psychoanalysis. In 1928 he became scientific director of the Socialist Society for Sexual Counseling and Sexual Research in Vienna and worked at the Vienna psychoanalytical outpatient clinic. In 1933 his book "Character Analysis" was banned in fascist Germany. In 1934 he was expelled from the Communist Party and from the International Psychoanalytic Association at the same time. So, he emigrated via Norway to the USA, where he opened a psychoanalytical practice in 1939 and developed the Orgon therapy. His book "Der Krebs", published in the USA in 1948, was withdrawn from the market by a court order and burned. It was not until much later, in the 1970s, that it could appear again. In old age he got cancer himself. The sale of the "Orgon accumulators", he had developed, was banned. He continued to evict them, after which he was sentenced to two years in prison for disobeying the court. He died of a heart attack in in the prison of Lewisburg, Pennsylvania, aged 60. His work influenced the theories of R.D. Laing, A. Lowen and F. Perls.

<u>Gordon Willard Allport (1897-1967)</u>

Allport was born in Montezuma, Indiana in 1897; he attended the public school in Cleveland, Ohio. At Harvard University he studied economics and philosophy, where he received a Bachelor of Arts in 1919.

In 1919/20 he taught English and sociology at Robert College in Istanbul. In

1922 he received his doctorate in psychology and in 1922/23 studies in Berlin and Heidelberg, in Cambridge the following year. In 1925 he married Ada L. Gould. The couple had a son. He then spent two years as an assistant professor at Harvard University, department of social ethics, later assistant professor in 1930, then an independent professor of psychology. In 1958 he received an honorary title of "Doctor of Humanities" from the Boston University. He was a member and honorary president of numerous psychological societies. He died shortly before his seventieth birthday.

Erich Fromm (1900-1980)

Fromm was born in Frankfurt a.M. in 1900. In 1922 he received his doctorate in philosophy from the University of Heidelberg. In 1926 he married Frieda Reichmann. From 1929 to 1932 he was a lecturer at the Psychoanalytic Institute in Frankfurt, then at the Institute for Social Research and at the University of Frankfurt. 1934-1939 he taught in New York at the International Institute for Social Research. In 1940/41 he was visiting professor at Columbia University. After the divorce from his first wife, he married Henny Gurland. From 1944-1946 he co-founded the William Alanson White Institute of Psychiatry and gave lectures at various universities. In 1949 he was professor at the National University of Mexico, where he became full professor of psychoanalysis from 1950. After the death of his second wife, he married Anni Freeman in 1953. He then lived in Switzerland until his death. He was a member of various associations, including the Washington Psychoanalytical Society.

Carl Ransom Rogers (1902-1987)

Rogers was born as son of a farmer in Oak Park, Illinois. The family was considered conservative Protestant. He attended the University of Wisconsin, where he first studied agronomy and then history; the graduation took place in 1924. In the same year he married Helen Elliott. From 1924-1926 he studied theology in New York. In 1928 he moved to Columbia University at the Teachers College, where he received his doctorate in 1931 (clinical and educational psychology).

Between 1928 and 1930 he worked as a clinical psychologist in the Child Study Department, the Society for the Prevention of Cruelty to Children in Rochester and from 1930-38 he was director of this children's department. In 1940 he moved to Ohio State University, where he became professor of clinical psychology in 1945. In the years 1946-1950, his theory of client-centered therapy was subject to severe criticism. But the storm subsided, and he became famous. To give his students and interested parties an insight into his therapy, he let himself film during interviews. In 1957 he had two chairs in Wisconsin: as professor of psychology and psychiatry. He received many awards and was a member of various associations. In 1987 he died. Rogers was a co-founder of humanistic psychology.

Abraham Harold Maslow (1908-1970)

Maslow was born in Brooklyn in 1908. He studied in Wisconsin and received his doctorate in philosophy in 1934. In 1928 he married Bertha Goodman; the couple had two daughters. From 1935-1937 he was at Columbia University and then until 1951 he taught as an associate professor at Brooklyn College. From 1951 he worked as a professor of psychology, later also as dean at Brandeis University. He was a member and official in many scientific societies, including president of the American Psychological Association. His studies and work brought him, along with others, together with E. Fromm and A. Adler. He was the founder and most important representative of humanistic psychology, the "third force" next to psychoanalysis, and behaviorism, but was also called the founder of the so-called "fourth force" (transpersonal psychology). He died in 1970.

Burrhus Frederick Skinner (1904-1990)

Skinner was born in New York in 1904, the son of a lawyer. He studied English literature at Hamilton College, wanted to be a writer, also wrote a few short stories, but then began to be interested in behaviorism and switched to psychology. He received his PhD in psychology from Harvard University. This was followed by the activity as a professor in Minnesota and Indiana. In 1948 he returned to Harvard, where he worked as an animal behavior researcher and developed his personality theory.

Viktor E. Frankl (1905-1997)

Frankl was born in Vienna in 1905. His father was a civil servant in the Ministry of Social Administration. The mother came from a Prague patrician family. He attended the middle school in Vienna and began to correspond with Freud; he studied medicine and philosophy and at the age of 22 gave lectures at the adult education center and at organizations of the socialist working-class youth. After completing his doctorate in medicine and philosophy, he worked at the Psychiatric University Clinic under Professor Otto Pötzl. This was followed by two years of neurological training and finally four years of work at the "Am Steinhof" psychiatric clinic. He was also a member of Adler's Association for Individual Psychology, which then excluded him. In 1937, he opened his own practice for neurology and psychiatry. During the World War he was in concentration camps for three years. His first wife died in Bergen-Belsen. His habilitation followed in 1947. At the same time, he was Professor of Neurology and Psychiatry at the University of Vienna and Professor of Logotherapy in San Diego, California. He was visiting professor at various universities, and he was awarded several honorary doctorates. He is an honorary member of the Austrian Academy of Sciences. He died in 1997.

As a reminder: Some educators and their lives

<u>Johann Amos Comenius (1592-1670)</u>

Comenius was born Jan Amos Komensky in South Moravia in 1592, of Czech descent. The father was a miller. His parents and two of his siblings died when he was a child. At the age of 16 he entered the Latin school in Prerov. Six years later (1614) he became the head of this school. This was followed by further academic studies in Herborn (Nassau) and Heidelberg. During the Thirty Years' War (beginning in 1618), as a non-Catholic, he often had to hide. His wife and children died of epidemics. In 1627 he was expelled from Bohemia. In Lissa (Leszno) he married again. He was member and later bishop of the "Bohemian Brothers". He was a respected educational writer and gained fame all over Europe. He traveled a lot: To France, England, Holland, and Sweden, where he worked at the Stockholm royal court. During this time (1642-1648) he lived in Elbing in East Prussia. Then he returned to Lissa, where his second wife died. As a bishop he traveled to Hungary and Transylvania, where he married for the third time and settled there. He then spent the last fourteen years of his life in Holland. There he died at the age of 78. His work "Orbis pictus" is the first children's learning book.

<u>Jean-Jacques Rousseau (1712-1778)</u>

Rousseau was born in Geneva as the son of a watchmaker. The ancestors on his father's side were Huguenots. The mother, who died when Jean-Jacques was born, was a pastor's daughter. At the age of 10 (1722) he was sent to a country pastor. In 1725 he began his apprenticeship as watchmaker and engraver but did not finish it. In 1728 he became a Catholic and lived with a woman 13 years older, Madame de Warens, who gave the sixteen-year-old the security he needed. It was she who stimulated his studies and sent him to Turin, where he began to study theology.

He formed himself, mostly autodidactically, literarily, philosophically, but also musically and scientifically. From 1741 he stayed in Paris, interacted with the "higher" society, and worked as a composer. He was known to Voltaire and

Montesquieu, among others.

In Paris he met Therese Levasseur, who became his partner and who gave birth to five children over the years. In 1750 he took part in a competition at the Dijon Academy. His contribution was recognized and made him famous. During a visit to Geneva, he returned to his Protestant Calvinist faith. In 1762 the educational novel "Emile" was published, along with other much-noticed writings, which earned him an arrest warrant. So began a long period of flight, first to Switzerland, then to Strasbourg and in 1766 to England, where he stayed for a year. Then he returned to France. In 1768 he married his Therese, who had before to bring their children to the foundling hospital. He spent the last ten years of his life in France. He increasingly suffered from paranoia and lived in various places, most recently at Ermenoville Castle near Paris, a property of the Marquis de Girardin. Then he died 66 years old.

Johann Heinrich Pestalozzi (1746-1827)

Pestalozzi was born in Zurich. The ancestors on his father's side came from Italy. The mother was Swiss. At the age of five he lost his father, who was only 33 years old. He left school without a qualification. Then he went into a short agricultural apprenticeship. With the help of a bank, he acquired a piece of land in Birrfeld (canton Aargau) and founded there the Neuhof an institution for poor. Then he marries Anna Schulthess. In 1774 a son was born. In 1780 the Neuhof project failed. From then on, he dealt with literary work, but also applied unsuccessfully for various positions abroad. In 1799 he began working as an educator and teacher, first in Stans (orphan father), then in Burgdorf and Münchenbuchsee (founder of the new elementary school) and at the institute in Iferten (educator of mankind). Through this institute he became known and famous. From 1812 onwards, however, there were increasing disputes with employees, and various crises led to the gradual decline of the institute, which was then dissolved in 1825. He died in Brugg at the age of 81.

Wilhelm von Humbolt (1767-1835)

Humbolt was born in Potsdam as the son of a Prussian major. The mother came from a Franco-Dutch Huguenot family. His brother, two years younger than him, was the future naturalist and world traveler Alexander von Humbolt. Wilhelm studied classical philology, history, and law in Göttingen. Educational trips took him to Paris and Switzerland.

In 1791 he married Caroline v. Dacheröden, which later inherited a considerable fortune. In 1794 he became friends with Goethe and Schiller. In

1799 he traveled through Spain. In 1802 he was the Prussian envoy in Rome. 1809-1810 he was head of the Prussian education system. He then returned to the diplomatic service in Vienna and London. In 1819 he became Minister of the Interior. He later withdrew disappointed from politics, i.e., from "his fruitless political endeavors". He then led a scholarly life as a linguist. In 1829 his wife died. He died in 1835 at the age of 68.

Friedrich Schleiermacher (1768-1834)

Schleiermacher was born in Breslau into a family of preachers. 1783-1785 he attended the boarding school near Görlitz, then he studied until 1787 at the theological college of the Brüdergemeinde in Barby near Halle. After his first theological exam, he worked as a private tutor for a count in East Prussia (1790-1793). Then he was a teacher in Berlin and completed his second theological exam. He was then assistant preacher in Landsberg and then preacher at the Charité in Berlin. In 1802 he was appointed court preacher to Pomerania for two years. From 1804-1807 he worked as a professor of theology in Halle, then moved to Berlin, where he initially lived in "the most oppressive conditions" as a privatizing scholar. In 1809 he married the widow Henriette von Willich, lived a sociable life, and got a permanent job as a preacher at the Trinity Church. Then he worked as a member of the founding committee of the University of Berlin, where he became dean of the theological faculty from 1810. From 1810-1815 he was State Councilor in the Ministry of the Interior. At all he was an active education politician, and his sermons were extremely popular. In 1813, 1820/21 and 1862 he gave lectures on pedagogy and wrote several theological treatises. At the age of 66 he died of pneumonia. Thousands of people followed the funeral procession through Berlin.

Johann F. Herbart (1776-1841)

Herbart was born in Oldenburg. His father was a judicial and senior civil servant. He remained an only child, carefully accompanied by his mother. In Oldenburg he attended high school. From 1794-1797 he studied law and philosophy in Jena. After completing his studies, he worked as a private tutor in Bern until 1800. He then lived for two years in Bremen as a private scholar and guest in a friend's house.

In 1802 he received his doctorate and soon afterwards he completed his habilitation in Göttingen. There he gave his first lectures on education and philosophy. In 1805 he received offers to the universities of Heidelberg and Landshut, which he did not accept. In 1809 he was appointed to the chair of the late Kant in Königsberg. In his house he ran a "Didactic Institute", at the university he headed the "Pedagogical Institute". He wrote books, mostly on philosophy and psychology. In 1829 he became a part-time school inspector and thus a member of the provincial school council. In 1833 he followed a call to Göttingen for the chair of philosophy. He died at the age of 65.

Friedrich Froebel (1782-1852)

Fröbel was born in Oberweissbach, Thuringia, the youngest of six children. His father was a pastor. He lost his mother in the first year of his life. So, he got a stepmother. When he was four years old, he came to live with his uncle's family, with whom he lived for four and a half years. After the confirmation, the surveyor training followed. In 1799 he studied at the University of Jena. He finished this first study in 1801 without a degree. He then worked as a surveyor, estate secretary and forest actuary in various parts of Germany. In 1805, when he was 23, he became a tutor in Frankfurt. There he taught the three sons of Caroline v. Holzhausen, a patrician from Frankfurt. He had a warm friendship with the seven-year older woman, and he found something like a mother in her. He met with Pestalozzi. 1805 and 1808-1810 he worked for him in Iferten. After his return he took up further studies; Languages, mineralogy, crystallography in Göttingen and Berlin. In 1813 he was in the Lützow Free Corps. Then he became an assistant at the Institute of Mineralogy. After the death of his brother, he took over the care of the upbringing of his children. In 1816 he founded the "educational institution" in Griesheim. In 1817 he moved to Keilhau and married Henriette Wilhelmine Hoffmeister in 1818. He wrote books. Over time, however, difficulties arose in Keilhau, including with the teachers. The educational institution was labeled as a "demagogue nest". So, he went to Switzerland in 1831. There he directed and founded various educational institutions, for example in Burgdorf, where he was director of the orphanage. In 1836 he returned to Germany and between 1837 and 1849 founded various educational institutions, including kindergartens. In 1839 his wife died. In 1850 he moved to Marienthal. In 1851 the "Froebel kindergartens" were banned in Prussia (and remained so until 1860). He was so disappointed about it that he even thought about emigrating. In America, his ideas were gaining ground. But he stayed and even remarried at the age of 69, the 36-year-old Luise Levin. He died in 1852.

Georg Kerschensteiner (1854-1932)

Kerschensteiner was born in Munich as the son of a businessman. At the age of eleven he entered the preparatory school in Freising. After three years he switched to the teacher training college. At sixteen he became a school assistant. Then he attended the Augsburg grammar school. (His brother, who was a doctor, gave the impetus for this by expressing himself critically about the "half-education of schoolmasters"). In 1877 he graduated from high school. This was followed by studies at the Technical University and later at the University of Munich. There he studied mathematics and physics. In 1880 he passed the state examination. This was followed by an assistant position at the Meteorological Central Station in Munich. From 1883 to 1895 he was an assistant and teacher for mathematics and physics at grammar schools in Nuremberg and Munich. From 1895 he was the City School Councilor of Munich and became known at home and abroad. During this time, wood and metal workshops, school kitchens and school gardens and advanced training schools with professionally oriented specialist classes etc. were set up. However, the recognition was greater abroad than at home; in addition to great approval, he also had to endure a lot of criticism. In 1910 he traveled to the USA. In 1919 he left office. In 1920 he became an honorary professor for education at the University of Munich. He was married twice and died at the age of 78.

Eduard Spranger (1882-1963)

Spranger was born in Berlin. His father was a businessman. He attended the high school and then studied in Berlin. He was a student of F. Paulsen and W. Dilthey. In 1905 he received his doctorate. In 1909 he completed his habilitation on "W. von Humbolt and his humanity idea". Afterwards he was a private lecturer for education and philosophy with teaching assignments at private lyceums in Berlin. In 1911 he was appointed to Leipzig, and in 1920 he returned to Berlin. He was friends with G. Kerschensteiner. In 1925 he was accepted into the Prussian Academy of Sciences. In 1933 he resigned. He was overly critical of the National Socialists. From then on, his books could only be published in the Academic series. 1936-1937 he worked as a visiting professor in Japan. In 1944 he was arrested. After the end of the war, he became acting rector of the university in Berlin. Due to difficulties with the occupying powers, he moved to Tübingen. In 1952 he retired. He was enormously productive in his scientific work. He also wrote about historical and cultural-political topics. He described his own student days and the resulting orientation of his science in a self- portrait (1961). He died in 1963 at the age of 81.

John Dewey (1859-1952)

Dewey was born in Burlington, Vermont, USA in 1859, the son of common people; the parents worked in retail. 1884 studies at the University of Michigan and dissertation on Kant. In 1894 he became professor and director of the seminar for philosophy, psychology, and education at the University of

Chicago. There he founded an experimental school in 1896: The Laboratory School, which became world-famous. He was also president of the American Psychological Association. In 1905 he moved to Columbia University in New York due to difficulties with the university management. There he took part in the training of teachers and published many writings. From New York, he undertook numerous travels abroad, so to Japan, China, Turkey, Mexico, and the Soviet Union. In the States he became the main representative of the "Progressive Education". He died in New York in 1952.

<u>Maria Montessori (1870-1952)</u>

Montessori was born in Chiaravalle, Italy in 1870 to an upper-class family. From 1890 she studied medicine in Rome and received her doctorate in 1896. In 1898 her son was born. She dealt with women issues at the same time she practiced her medical profession. This was followed by two years as an assistant doctor at a psychiatric clinic, where she worked as a pediatrician after the psychiatric teaching of the French doctor Edouard Seguin (1812-1880). Afterwards she was a lecturer for prospective secondary teachers and teachers for the mentally handicapped. From 1901 she studied anthropology, education, and psychology. 1904-1908 she got a teaching position at the University of Rome for Anthropology. From 1906 she was director of a day care center, "Casa dei Bambini", in a slum area of Rome. A year later a second children's home was opened and in 1908 three more were added in Rome and Milan. From 1909 on, she trained pedagogues. Meanwhile, there were Montessori schools in St. Petersburg, India, China, Japan, Australia, and the United States, where in 1913 almost a hundred Montessori institutions were. 1929 Foundation of the "Association Montessori Internationale". She had initially tried to come to arrange with the fascists who came to power in 1922, but the break with Mussolini was inevitable: The children of the Montessori schools were supposed to give "fascist" greetings. She refused. As a result, the Montessori schools were closed in 1934 and she went to Barcelona. In 1936 she settled in Holland. She still ran training courses for pedagogues, including in India. In 1949 she traveled again to India, visiting Ceylon and Pakistan. She died in Noordwijk aan Zee at the age of 82.

<u>Peter Petersen (1884-1952)</u>

Petersen was born in Grossenwiehe near Flensburg in 1884 as a child of a long-established farming family. He was the oldest of seven children. After elementary school, he went to high school in Flensburg. In 1904 he studied philosophy, history, Protestant Religious Education and Anglistics, first in Leipzig, then in Kiel, Poznan, and Copenhagen. The graduation he followed in 1908 in Jena. In 1909 he passed the senior teacher examination in Leipzig and then worked for ten years until 1920 as a lecturer at a grammar school in Hamburg. In 1912 he became secretary of the "Federation for School Reform". In 1920 he completed his habilitation in Hamburg and took over the management of the "Lichtwerk-Schule". In 1923 he became a professor for philosophy and education in Jena. There he began a school attempt in 1924, known since 1927 as "Jenaplan". Travels took him to the States, South Africa, and South America. In 1928 he was visiting professor in Hashville, USA, and in 1929 in Santiago de Chile. The Jenaplan movement received a lot of attention at home and abroad. In 1945 he became dean of the Philosophical Faculty in Jena and 1945-48 dean of the Faculty of Social Education. In addition, he worked as a professor of educational science at the University of Halle and director of the Franke Foundation. In 1946 he returned his assignment at the University of Halle on the grounds that he no longer wanted to follow the university policy that was now represented. He has been persona non grata and had to take sticks allegations and remonstrances (?). In 1948 he was dismissed as dean. He traveled around the Federal Republic of Germany, but no longer got a job at a university or college of education. In the spring of 1951, he returned to Jena, where a year later he died after a short illness at the age of 68 years died.

<u>Erich Weniger (1894-1961)</u>

Weniger was born in Steinhorst near Hanover in 1894 as the son of a pastor. The family lived in Dassel (Solling) until he was 7 years old, then in Hanover. There he attended high school. After graduating from high school in 1913, he began to study history and philosophy in Tübingen. 1914-1918 he was a war volunteer at the Western Front. In 1919 he restarted his studies and studied psychology, sociology, philosophy, and pedagogy. In 1921 he took teaching examinations, doctorate and headed the primary school for young people in Göttingen. In 1926 he completed his habilitation and became a private lecturer at the University of Göttingen.

In 1929 he was appointed to the Pedagogical Academy in Kiel as a professor for pedagogy and philosophy. In 1930 he became director of the Pedagogical Academy in Altona, which was closed in 1932. For a short time, he was director of the Pedagogical Academy in Frankfurt / Main. After the National Socialists seized power in early 1933, he was dismissed. From 1935 he dealt with military education, did active service, and was released from American war captivity in 1945. 1946-1949 he was director of new founded Pedagogical University Göttingen. He was a member of the German Education Committee for upbringing and educational system and from 1949-1961 ordinary of education at the University of Göttingen. He died at the age of 67.

<u>Wilhelm Flitner (1889-1990)</u>

Flitner was born in Berka near Weimar, the first son of a railway official. He spent part of his pre-school days in Blankenburg, where his parents belonged to the society of dignitaries. He spent his school days in Weimar. At the age of 9 he lost his mother; she died giving birth to her third children. After the visit of the grammar school, he started in 1909 in Munich with the study of literature, history and philosophy. After a semester he moved to the University of Jena, where he received his doctorate in the winter of 1912/13. He then stayed in Berlin for a year to prepare for the state examination and took the examination (1914) in Jena. At Easter of the same year, he was accepted into the Brandenburg high school seminar. When the First World War broke out, he volunteered and was released in December 1918. During the war, in 1917, he married Elisabeth Czapski, the sister of a schoolmate. She studied political science and social policy in Heidelberg.

In the spring of 1919, he joined in Jena in the high school seminar, was active in several schools in Jena and was hired as a teacher at the secondary school. In 1919 he opened the evening popular university whose leader (without pay) he became; an activity which he continued for 7 years despite inflation and hunger. Meanwhile, he had children and his wife did the doctorate at the University of Jena. In 1923 he received his habilitation. Together with Th. Litt, H. Nohl, E. Spranger, A. Fischer he founded the journal "Die Erziehung", whose first edition took place 1926. In the same year as the first Prussian Pedagogical Academies were opened in Bonn, Elbing and Kiel, he was appointed to the latter. In 1929 he followed the call to the University of Hamburg. In 1935 he gave up the editorial work for "Die Erziehung". During the Second World War his teaching was limited. From 1945 he was in the construction of Prussian teacher training involved, among other especially educational tasks (appraisers, lectures). In 1959 he retired and in 1963 he received the Hansian Goethe Prize. Since the sixties he lived in Tübingen, where he died at the age of 101.

Bibliography

Adorno, Th. W.: Erziehung zur Mündigkeit. Frankfurt 1973

Adorno, Th. W. (u.a.): Der Positivismusstreit in der deutschen Soziologie. Darmstadt 1972

Adorno, Th. W.: Theorie der Halbbildung. In: Adorno u.a. 1970

Adorno, Th. W. (u.a.): Soziologische Schriften I. Frankfurt 1970

Aebli, H.: Zwölf Grundformen des Lernens. 1983

Aebli, H.: Zwölf Grundformen des Lehrens. 1994 (8)

Albers, H.-J.: Allgemeine sozio-ökonomisch-technische Bildung. Köln/Wien 1987

Alheit, P./Tippelt, R.: Neue Forschungstendenzen in der europäischen Erwachsenenbildung. In: Zeitschrift für Pädagogik. 32. Beiheft 1994, 367-383

Alheit, P.: Biographieforschung in der Erwachsenenbildung. In: PAS 1993

Allport, G. W.: Persönlichkeit. Struktur, Entwicklung und Erfassung der menschlichen Eigenart. Stuttgart 1949

Amelang, M./Bartussek, D.: Differentielle Psychologie und Persönlichkeitsforschung. Stuttgart 1981

Apel, K. O. (u.a.): Hermeneutik und Ideologiekritik. Frankfurt 1971

Aregger, U./Isenegger, U. (Hrsg.): Curriculumprozess. Beiträge zur Curriculumkonstruktion und -implementation. EBAC-Bericht Nr.8/9. Fribourg 1972

Arnold, R.: Deutungsmuster und pädagogisches Handeln in der Erwachsenenbildung. Bad Heilbrunn 1985

Arnold, R.: Qualitätsabsicherung in der Weiterbildung. Grundlagen der Weiterbildung. 1/1994

Arnold, R./Kaltschmid J. (Hrgr.): Erwachsenensozialisation und Erwachsenenbildung. Frankfurt 1986

Baacke, D. u.a. (Hrsg.): Am Ende postmodern? Weinheim 1985

Baldwin, J.M. (ed.): Dictionary of Philosophy and Psychology. 2 Bde. Gloucester, Mass. 1960 (1925)

Balauff, Th. /Schaller, K.: Pädagogik. Eine Geschichte der Bildung und Erziehung. 3 Bde. 1969-73

Ballstaedt, S.-P.: Lerntexte und Teilnehmerunterlagen. Weinheim 1994

Baltes, P.B./Eckensberger, L.H. (Hrsg.): Entwicklungspsychologie der Lebensspanne. Stuttgart 1979

Baumgartner, M.: Verführung statt Erleuchtung. Sekten-Scientology-Esoterik. Düsseldorf 1993

Beck, K.: Das Leib-Seele-Problem und die Erziehungswissenschaft. In: Pollak/Heid. 1994, 227-267

Beck, U.: Die Risikogesellschaft. Frankfurt 1986

Beck, H. (Hrsg.): Philosophie der Erziehung. 1979

Becker, P.: Psychologie der seelischen Gesundheit. Göttingen 1982

Becker, H. Widersprüche aushalten. München 1992

Becker-Carus, C.: Grundriss der physiologischen Psychologie. Heidelberg 1981

Benner, D.: Hauptströmungen der Erziehungswissenschaft. München 1973

Benner, D.: Allgemeine Pädagogik. 1987

Benner, D. (Hrsg.): Aspekte und Probleme einer pädagogischen Handlungswissenschaft. Festschrift für Josef Derbolav zum 65. Geburtstag. Kastellaum 1977

Benner, D.: Grundstrukturen pädagogischen Denkens und Handelns. In: Enzyklopädie Erziehungswissenschaft. Stuttgart 1993

Benner, D.: Studien zur Theorie der Erziehungswissenschaft. Weinheim 1994

Benning, A.: Ethik der Erziehung. Zürich 1992

Benning, A. (Hrsg.): Erwachsenenbildung. Bilanz und Zukunftsperspektiven. Schöning. Paderborn 1986

Berger, P. L./Luckmann, T.: Die gesellschaftliche Konstruktion der Wirklichkeit. Frankfurt 1970

Biller, K.: Bildung - Integrierender Faktor in Theorie und Praxis. Weinheim 1994

Bischof, L. J.: Persönlichkeitstheorien. 2 Bde. Paderborn 1983

Blankertz, H.: Curriculumforschung - Strategien, Strukturierung, Konstruktion. Essen 1971

Blankertz, H./Theorien und Modelle der Didaktik. München 1975

Blaschek, H.: Von der Sehnsucht nach Selbstverwirklichung. In: Benning

1986, 178-197

Bloom, B. S. (Hrsg.): Taxonomie von Lernzielen im kognitiven Bereich. Weinheim. 1972

Blass, J. L.: Modelle pädagogischer Theorienbildung. 2 Bde. 1978

Bock, I.: Pädagogische Anthropologie der Lebensalter. München 1984

Bock, I.: Pädagogische Anthropologie. In: Roth 1991, 99-108

Böhm, W.: Wörterbuch der Pädagogik. Stuttgart 1988 (13)

Böhm, W. (Hrsg.): Pädagogik oder Erziehungswissenschaften. 1988

Bollnow, O. F.: Die philosophische Anthropologie und ihre methodischen Prinzipien. In: Rocek/Schatz 1972, 19-36

Bollnow, O. F.: Die anthropologische Betrachtungsweise in der Pädagogik. In: König/Ramsenthaler 1980, 36-54

Bonsch, M./Winkelmann, R. (Hrsg.): Humanität und Bildung. Hannover 1990

Born, W./Otto G. (Hrgr.): Didaktische Trends. 1978

Bourdieu, P.: Die feinen Unterschiede. Frankfurt 1994

Brezinka, W.: Werte-Erziehung in einer wertunsicheren Gesellschaft. Pädagogische Rundschau 1/1994

Brezinka, W.: Glaube, Moral und Erziehung. München 1992

Brezinka, W.: Metatheorie der Erziehung. München/Basel 1978

Brezinka, W.: Erziehungsziele. Konstanz, Wandel, Zukunft. In: Pädagogische Rundschau Nr.47, 253-260, 1993

Brinkmann, W./Renner, K. (Hrsg.): Die Pädagogik und ihre Bereiche. Paderborn 1982

Bronfenbrenner, U.: Die Ökologie der menschlichen Entwicklung. Frankfurt 1989

Brugger, W.: Philosophisches Wörterbuch. Freiburg i.Br. 1976 (1992)

Bruner, J.S.: Studien zur kognitiven Entwicklung. Stuttgart 1971

Brüwiler, H.: Methoden der ganzheitlichen Jugend- und Erwachsenenbildung. Opladen 1994

Bubner, R.: Dialektik und Wissenschaft. Frankfurt 1973

Bühler, Ch./Ekstein, R.: Anthropologische Resultate aus biologischer Forschung. In: Gadamer/Vogler 1973, 349-385

Campbell, J.: Der Held in tausend Gestalten. Frankfurt 1978

Capra, F.: Wendezeit. München 1991

Capra, F.: Das neue Denken. München 1992

Cohn, R.: Von der Psychoanalyse zur themenzentrierten Interaktion. Stuttgart 1975

Comenius, J.H.: Grosse Unterrichtslehre. Ausgabe G.A. Linder. Wien 1907

Cronbach, J.L.: Einführung in die Pädagogische Psychologie. Weinheim 1971

Cube von, F.: Verhaltensbiologie und Pädagogik. In: Roth 1991, 109-121

Derbolav, J.: Grundriss einer Gesamtpädagogik. Frankfurt 1987

Derbolav, J.: "Pädagogische Anthropologie" als Theorie der individuellen Selbstverwirklichung. In: König/Ramsenthaler 1980

Deschner, K.: Der gefälschte Glaube. München 1988

Dewe, B./Frank, G./Huge, W.: Theorien der Erwachsenenbildung. Weinheim 1988

Dewe, B./Ferchoff, W.: Die Lust am Schein - Postmodernistische Notizen über Trends, Geschmäcker und Redensarten unter Pädagogen. In: Baacke 1985

Dickopp, K. H.: Lehrbuch der systematischen Pädagogik. 1983

Dienelt, K.: Von der Metatheorie der Erziehung zur sinnorientierten Pädagogik. 1984

Dietrich, Th.: Zeit- und Grundfragen der Pädagogik. Bad Heilbrunn 1992

Dominicé, P./Finger, M.: Erwachsenenbildung in der Schweiz. Zürich 1991

Dorsch, F. u.a. (Hrgr.): Psychologisches Wörterbuch. Bern/Stuttgart 1987/1991

Doucet, F. W.: Geschichte des Geheimwissens. Freiburg 1980

Drewermann, E.: Tiefenpsychologie und Exegese. Band I: Die Wahrheit der Formen. Olten 1987 (4)

Drewermann, E.: Tiefenpsychologie und Exegese. Band II: Die Wahrheit der Werke und der Worte. Olten 1986 (2)

Drewermann, E.: Der tödliche Fortschritt. Freiburg/Basel 1991

Durant, W.: Die grossen Denker. Bergisch Gladbach 1987

Eco, U.: Apokalyptiker und Integrierte. Frankfurt 1992

Eigenmann, J./Strittmatter, A.: In: Aregger, U./Isenegger, U. 1972

Eggers, B.P./Steinbacher, F.J. (Hrgr.): Soziologie der Erwachsenenbildung. In Reihe: Pöggeler, F. (Hrgr.) Handbuch der Erwachsenenbildung. Stuttgart 1977

Ellenberger, H.F.: Die Entdeckung des Unbewussten. 2 Bde. Bern 1973

Emde, G.: Grundlagen einer transzendenzoffenen Theorie paranormaler Vorgänge. In: Resch (Hrgr) 1981, 643-702

Fink, E.: Grundphänomene des menschlichen Daseins. Freiburg 1979

Flammer, A.: Individuelle Unterschiede im Lernen. Weinheim 1975

Flechtheim, O.K.: Ist die Zukunft noch zu retten? Hamburg 1987

Flitner, A.: Schriften zur Anthropologie und Bildungslehre. Neuauflage 1984

Flitner, A.: Missratener Fortschritt. München 1977

Flitner, W.: Erwachsenenbildung. Paderborn 1982

Frankena, W. K.: Analytische Ethik. München 1972

Frankl, V. E.: Anthropologische Grundlagen. Bern/Stuttgart 1975

Frankl, V. E.: Der Mensch vor der Frage nach dem Sinn. München 1993 (9)

Freud, S.: Fragen der Gesellschaft. Ursprünge der Religion. Zürich 1974

Frey, K.: Theorie des Curriculums. Weinheim 1971

Friedrich, W./Hennig, W.: Der sozialwissenschaftliche Forschungsprozess. Berlin 1975

Frick, K. R. H.: Licht und Finsternis. Gnostisch-theosophische und freimaurerisch-okkulte Geheimgesellschaften bis an die Wende zum 20.Jh. Graz 1975

Frick, K. R. H.: Die Erleuchteten. 2 Bde. Graz 1975

Fromm, E.: Die Seele des Menschen. Stuttgart 1979

Fromm, E.: Über den Ungehorsam. Stuttgart 1982

Frommer, H.: Lernen-Wissen-Bildung. Schriften pädagogische Arbeitsstelle für Erwachsenenbildung. Neckar Verlag 1991

Fuchs, W.: Möglichkeiten der biographischen Methode. In: Niethammer 1985

Fuchs, W.: Biographische Forschung. Opladen 1984

Gadamer, H. G./Vogler, P. (Hrsg.): Neue Anthropologie. Bd.5. Psychologische Anthropologie. Stuttgart/München 1973

Gage, N. L./Berliner, D. C.: Pädagogische Psychologie. Weinheim 1986

Gagné, R. M.: Die Bedingungen des menschlichen Lernens. 1973 (3)

Galbraith, J. K.: Die Arroganz der Satten. München 1979

Gallas, H. (Hrsg.): Strukturalismus als interpretatives Verfahren. Darmstadt 1972

Gehlen, A.: Anthropologische Forschung. Reinbek 1971

Gehlen, A.: Die Seele im technischen Zeitalter. Hamburg 1957

Gehlen, A.: Moral und Hypermoral. Eine pluralistische Ethik. Frankfurt 1970

Gehlen, A.: Urmensch und Spätkultur. Frankfurt 1964

Gergen, K. J.: In: Filipp, S.A. (Hrsg.): Selbstkonzeptforschung. Stuttgart 1993

Gerner, B.: Menschennatur und Kulturmensch. In: Brinkmann/Renner 1982, 133-147

Gieseke, W. u.a.: Professionalität und Professionalisierung. Bad Heilbrunn 1988

Gieseke, W.: Didaktische Lernforschung. In: Mader 1991, 76-83

Gloger-Tippelt, G.: Beiträge einer Entwicklungspsychologie der Lebensspanne zur Erwachsenenbildung. In: PAS 1993

Gore, Al: Wege zum Gleichgewicht. Frankfurt 1992

Grimmer, F.: Pädagogik und Empathie. Pädagogische Rundschau Nr.47/3, 285-299, 1993

Grof, S.: Geburt, Tod und Transzendenz. München 1993

Groothoff, W.D.: Zur Erneuerung der Theorie der Bildung und des Bildungswesens. 1981

Gudjons u.a.: Auf meinen Spuren. Hamburg 1994

Haack, F. W.: Europas neue Religionen. Sekten-Gurus-Satanskult. Zürich 1991

Haack, F. W.: Jugendsekten. Weinheim 1991

Haag, F./Krüger, H., u.a.: Aktionsforschung. Forschungsstrategien, Forschungsfelder und Forschungspläne. München 1972

Habermas, J.: Erkenntnisinteresse. Frankfurt 1973

Habermas, J. (Hrsg.): Hermeneutik und Ideologiekritik. Frankfurt 1973

Habermas, J.: Moralbewusstsein und kommunikatives Handeln. Frankfurt 1992 (5)

Hacker, J./Olzog, G.: Deutsches Handbuch der Erwachsenenbildung. München 1985

Hamann, B.: Pädagogische Anthropologie. Bad Heilbrunn 1993

Harkin, T./Thomas, C.E.: Five minutes to midnight. Why is the nuclear threat growing faster than ever? New York 1990

Harney, K.: Moderne Erwachsenenbildung. Zeitschrift für Pädagogik 3/93

Haug, Ch.: .... Bilden oder Heilen? Erwachsenenbildung zwischen Psychotherapie und Persönlichkeitsentfaltung. Haag und Herchen 1985

Heiler, F.: Die Religionen der Menschheit. Stuttgart 1980 (1959)

Heim, R.: Die Rationalität der Psychoanalyse. Basel, Frankfurt 1993

Heitkämper, P.: Bildung als Dispositiv des Friedens. In: Zeitschrift für Pädagogik. 21. Beiheft 1986, 275-279

Hengstenberg, H.-E.: Die Frage nach verbindlichen Aussagen in der gegenwärtigen philosophischen Anthropologie. In Rocek/Schatz 1972, 65-83

Henz, H.: Lehrbuch der systematischen Pädagogik. Freiburg 1964

Hentig, H. v.: Schule als Erfahrungsraum. Stuttgart 1973

Hentig, H. v.: Eine Antwort an Theodor Wilhelm. In: Neue Sammlung 25, 1985/2, 151 ff.

Horkheimer, M.: Kritische Theorie. Frankfurt 1968

Horneffer, A.: Symbolik der Mysterienbünde. Schwarzenburg 1979

Horney, W.: Lexikon für Pädagogik. Band II. Gütersloh 1970

Hornstein, W. (u.a.): Beratung in der Erziehung. 2 Bde. Frankfurt 1977

Hufer, K. P.: Emanzipatorischer Ansatz in der Erwachsenenbildung. Grundlagen der Weiterbildung 6/93

Hügli, A./Lübcke P. (Hrsg.): Philosophie Lexikon. Reinbek 1991

Hurrelmann, K.: Sozialisation und Gesundheit. Weinheim 1994 (3)

Hurrelmann, K./Ulich, D. (Hrsg.) Sozialisationsforschung. Weinheim 1991

Ingalls, J.D.: A Trainers Guide to Andragogy. Washington D.C. 1973; Ausschnitte: "Die sieben Schritte des andragogischen Prozesses". Rohrer

SVEB Zürich 1980, Nr.4.

Ingenkamp, K.H. (Hrsg.): Handbuch der Unterrichtsforschung, Bd. I, Weinheim 1970

Isenegger, U.: Schulen und Schulsysteme. München 1977

Jank, W./Meyer, H.: Didaktische Modelle. Frankfurt 1993

Jaspers, K.: Die grossen Philosophen. München 1959

Jaspers, K.: Der philosophische Glaube angesichts der Offenbarung. München 1984

Jaspers, K.: Philosophie, Band 3 Metaphysik. Berlin 1956

Johann, T.: Erziehung und Bildung in der heidnischen und christlichen Antike. 1976

Jung, C. G.: Zur Psychologie westlicher und östlicher Religion. Olten 1973

Jung, C. G.: Aion. Beiträge zur Symbolik des Selbst. Olten 1976

Jung, C. G.: Die Archetypen und das kollektive Unbewusste. Olten 1978

Jung, C. G.: Die Struktur und Dynamik des Selbst. Olten 1978

Jungk, R. zu Ehren: Die Triebkraft der Hoffnung. Weinheim 1993

Jungk, R./Müllert, N.R.: Zukunftswerkstätten. München 1994

Kade, J.: Offene Übergänge. Zur Etablierung der Erwachsenenbildung als Erziehungswissenschaftliche Teildisziplin. In: Krüger/Rauschenbach 1994, 147-162

Kade, S.: Methoden des Fremdverstehens. Bad Heilbrunn 1983

Kainz, F.: Über die Sprachverführung des Denkens. Berlin 1972

Kaiser, A.: Sinn und Situation. Bad Heilbrunn 1985

Kaiser, R./Kaiser, A.: Begriff der Schlüsselqualifikation. In: Grundlagen der Weiterbildung 1994/4, 186-189

Kaltschmid, J.: Sozialisationstheorie, Sozialwissenschaften und Didaktik der Erwachsenenbildung. In: Arnold/Kaltschmid 1986

Kaminski, G./Bellows, S.: Feldforschung in der ökologischen Psychologie. In: Patry, J. L. (Hrsg.) 1981

Kamlah, W.: Philosophische Anthropologie. Mannheim 1973

Kamlah, W./Lorenzen, P.: Logische Propädeutik. Mannheim 1967

Kamper, D.: Pädagogische Anthropologie. In: Lenzen 1992, 311-316

Kant, I.: Grundlegung zur Metaphysik der Sitten. Stuttgart 1970

Kant, I.: Kritik der reinen Vernunft. Stuttgart 1966

Katz, D./Kahn, R. L.: The social Psychology of Organisations. New York 1966

Keller, W.: Was gestern noch als Wunder galt. München 1973

Kempkes, H. L.: Auf den Grenzen von Systemen und Alltagswelt. Frankfurt 1993

Kerényi, K.: Antike Religion. München 1971

Kerstiens, L.: Die wiederentdeckte Allgemeinbildung. In: Benning 1986, 260-280

Kessler, H.: Das offenbare Geheimnis. Freiburg i.B. 1977

Klafki, W.: Neue Studien zur Bildungstheorie und Didaktik. Weinheim/Basel 1991

Klafki, W.: Die Bedeutung der klassischen Bildungstheorien für ein zeitgemässes Konzept allgemeiner Bildung. In: Zeitschrift für Pädagogik. (32) 1986/4, 455-476

Klafki, W.: Aspekte kritisch-konstruktiver Erziehungswissenschaft. 1976

Klafki, W.: Organisation und Interaktion in pädagogischen Feldern. In: Zeitschrift für Pädagogik Nr.23, 1977, 13. Beiheft (11-38)

Klane, R.: Der irrationale Schrei des Körpers in der Wissenschaft. Oldenburg 1991

Klauer, K. J. (Hrsg.): Handbuch der pädagogischen Diagnostik. 4 Bde. Düsseldorf 1978

Klausmeier, H. J./Ripple, R. E.: Moderne Unterrichtspsychologie, Bde. 1-4, München 1978

Klein, H. (Hrsg.): Spuren in die Zukunft. München/Zürich 1993

Klemm, K. (u.a.): Bildung für das Jahr 2000. Reinbek 1985

Klimsa, P.: Neue Medien und Weiterbildung. Weinheim 1993

Kluge, N.: Einführung in die systematische Pädagogik. 1983

Klupp, A.: Planen. Managen. Trainieren. Zwanzig Bausteine erfolgreicher Erwachsenenbildung. München 1992

Knoop, K./Schwab, M.: Einführung in die Geschichte der Pädagogik.

Heidelberg. Wiesbaden 1992

Knowles, M. S.: The modern practice of adult education. New York 1970

Koestler, A.: Der Mensch - Irrläufer der Evolution. Frankfurt 1990

Kollwijk, J. v./Wieken-Mayer, M. (Hrsg.): Techniken der empirischen Sozialforschung, Band 3. München 1974

König, E./Ramsenthaler, H. (Hrsg.): Diskussion Pädagogische Anthropologie. München 1980

Koskenniemi, M.: Elemente der Unterrichtstheorie. München 1971

Kraft, V.: Die Grundlagen der Erkenntnis und der Moral. Berlin 1968

Kraft, V.: Der Wiener Kreis. Wien 1968

Krämer, S./Walter, K. D.: Effektives Lehren in der Erwachsenenbildung. Ismaning 1994

Kreyszig, E.: Statistische Methoden und ihre Anwendungen. Göttingen 1968

Krohn, S.: Der Mensch im Lichte der Grenzfragen der Philosophie. In: Resch 1972

Kron, F. W.: Grundwissen Didaktik. München 1994 (2)

Krüger, H. H.: Allgemeine Pädagogik auf dem Rückzug? In: Krüger/Rauschenbach 1994, 115-130

Krüger, H. H./Rauschenbach, Th. (Hrsg.): Erziehungswissenschaft. Die Disziplin am Beginn einer neuen Epoche. Weinheim 1994

Kruse, L./Graumann, C.-F./Lantermann, E.-D. (Hrsg.): Ökologische Psychologie. München 1990

Künzel, K.: Erwachsenenpädagoge und Erwachsenenpädagogin. In: Roth, L. (1991)

Kupffer, H.: Pädagogik der Postmoderne. Weinheim/Basel 1990

Kürzdörfer, K. (Hrsg.): Grundpositionen und Perspektiven in der Erwachsenenbildung. Bad Heilbrunn 1981

Kutschera, v. F.: Wissenschaftstheorie. München 1972

Krämer, S./Walter, K.: Effizientes Lehren in der Erwachsenenbildung.

Landmann, M.: Philosophische Anthropologie. Berlin 1969

Langeveld, M.J.: Studien zur Anthropologie des Kindes. Tübingen 1968 (3)

Lassahn, R.: Grundriss einer Allgemeinen Pädagogik. Heidelberg 1993 (3)

Lehner, M.: Didaktik und Weiterbildung. München 1989

Leirman, W./Pöggeler, F. (Hrsg.): Erwachsenenbildung in fünf Kontinenten. Stuttgart 1979

Lennhoff, E./Posnier, O.: Internationales Freimaurerlexikon. Wien/München 1932

Lenz, W.: Lehrbuch der Erwachsenenbildung. Stuttgart 1987

Lenzen, D.: Bildung und Erziehung für Europa? In: Zeitschrift für Pädagogik 32. Beiheft, 1994, 31-48

Lenzen, D./Mollenhauer, K.: Enzyklopädie Erziehungswissenschaft. Stuttgart 1992

Lenzen, D. (Hrsg.): Handbuch und Lexikon der Erziehung. Band 1. Stuttgart 1992 (2)

Lewin, K.: Feldtheorie in den Sozialwissenschaften. Bern 1963

Linden M./Hautzinger M. (Hrgr.): Psychotherapie-Manual. Berlin 1981

Lorenz, K.: Die acht Todsünden der zivilisierten Menschheit. München 1993

Löwisch, D.-J.: Einführung in die Erziehungsphilosophie. Darmstadt 1982

Luhmann, N.: Zweckbegriff und Systemrationalität. Frankfurt 1968

Mader, W. u.a.: Zehn Jahre Erwachsenenbildungswissenschaft. Klinkhardt 1991

Mager, R. F.: Lernziele und programmierter Unterricht. Weinheim 1970

Maier, K. E.: Grundriss moralischer Erziehung. Bad Heilbrunn 1986

Maslow, A. H.: Motivation und Persönlichkeit. Olten 1977

Maslow, A. H.: Psychologie des Seins. München 1973

Mattl, W.: Institutionen der Erwachsenenbildung. In: Roth, L. (1991)

Mayntz, R./Holm, K./Hübner, P.: Einführung in die Methoden der empirischen Soziologie. Opladen 1971

Meier, A./Rabe-Kleberg, U.: Weiterbildung, Lebenslauf, sozialer Wandel. Neuwied 1993

Meili-Lüthy, E.: Persönlichkeitsentwicklung als lebenslanger Prozess. Bern 1972

Metzger, Ch.: Vom Schulungsbedarf zum Schulungsplan. In: Education permanente. 2/1992, 90-93

Menck, P.: Unterrichtsanalyse und didaktische Konstruktion. 1975

Menze, C. (Hrgr.): Humanität und Erziehung. 1985

Menze, C.: Stichwort "Bildung"; in: Lenzen/Mollenhauer 1992

Merkens, H.: Wissenschaftstheorie. In: Roth 1991, 19-30

Meueler, E.: Die Türen des Käfigs. Wege zum Subjekt in der Erwachsenenbildung. Stuttgart 1993

Meyer, H. L.: Einführung in die Curriculum Methodologie. München 1972

Mollenhauer, K.: Korrekturen am Bildungsbegriff. In: Zeitschrift für Pädagogik Nr.33. Weinheim 1987

Mollenhauer, K.: Theorien zum Erziehungsprozess. München 1972

Mollenhauer, K.: Umwege. 1986

Monod, J.: Zufall und Notwendigkeit. München 1971

Mühle, G./Schell, D. H.: Kreativität und Schule. München 1970

Müller, K. R. (Hrsg.): Kurs- und Seminargestaltung. Weinheim 1994 (5)

Müller, U.: Didaktische Planung ökologischer Weiterbildung. Frankfurt 1993

Murphy, M.: Der Quantenmensch. Wessobrunn 1994

Musoloff, H.-U./Hellekamps, S.: Ist das Konzept der Wissenschaftsorientierung überholt? Pädagogische Rundschau Nr.47/6, 1993, 683-703

Nahrstedt, W./Popp, R.: Freizeitbildung: ein neues Thema für Europa. In: Zeitschrift für Pädagogik. 32. Beiheft 1994, 425-437

Nahrstedt, W.: Leben in freier Zeit. Darmstadt 1990

Nelson, C.: System der Philosophischen Ethik und Pädagogik. Göttingen 1949

Neumann, E.: Tiefenpsychologie und neue Ethik. Zürich 1949

Nezel, I.: Allgemeine Didaktik der Erwachsenenbildung. München 1992

Nezel, I.: Strukturalistische Erziehungswissenschaft. Weinheim 1976

Nickel, E.: Die Erfahrung der kosmischen Dimension. In: Resch 1973

Nonne, F.: "Postmoderne" - Ein neues Modethema für die Pädagogik. In: Baacke 1985

Nuissl, E./ Rein, A.: Die Volksschule zwischen Marktgängigkeit und öffentlichem Auftrag. In: Hessische Blätter für Volksbildung. 1993/4, 301-307

Oelkers, J.: Reformpädagogik. Weinheim/München 1992

Oerter, R. (Hrsg.): Entwicklung als lebenslanger Prozess. Hamburg 1978

Opaschowski, H. W.: Anstrengendes Vergnügen: Die Zukunft der Freizeit; in: Klein 1993, 230-248

Opaschowski, H. W.: Einführung in die Freizeitwissenschaft. Opladen 1994

Opaschowski, H. W.: Freizeitwissenschaft als neue Spektrumswissenschaft. In: Zeitschrift für Pädagogik. 32. Beiheft, 1994, 441-444

Ortner, G. E.: Bildungsökonomie und Bildungsmanagement. In: Roth, L. (1991)

Oser, F./Althof, W.: Moralische Selbstbestimmung. Stuttgart 1992

Oser, F./Althof, W./Garz, D. (Hrsg.): Moralische Zugänge zum Menschen. München 1986

Overhage, P.: Die Evolution des Lebendigen. Die Kausalität. Freiburg i.B. 1965

Pädagogische Arbeitsstelle (PAD) des DVV: Beiträge der Bezugswissenschaften zur Erwachsenenbildung. Frankfurt 1993

Parsons, T.: Sozialstruktur und Persönlichkeit. Frankfurt 1977

Patry, J. L. (Hrgr.): Feldforschung. Bern 1981

Pawlik, K.: Dimensionen des Verhaltens. Bern/Stuttgart 1971

Pawlik, K. (Hrsg.): Multivariate Persönlichkeitsforschung. Bern 1982

Pervin, L. A.: Persönlichkeitstheorien. München/Basel 1993

Petersheim, A. K.: Bildung und Kommunikation. Bern 1993

Petersson, W. H.: Didaktik als Strukturtheorie des Lehrens und Lernens. 1973

Petersson, W. H.: Lehrbuch Allgemeine Didaktik. 1983

Peursen, C.A.: Phänomenologie und analytische Philosophie. Stuttgart 1969

Pfniss, A.: Die Zukunft meistern. Graz 1988

Piaget, J.: Der Strukturalismus. Olten 1973

Picht, G.: Die deutsche Bildungskatastrophe. Freiburg 1964

Pieper, M.: Erwachsenenbildung und Lebenslauf. München 1978

Pieper, A.: Ethik und Moral. München 1985

Planck, M.: Sinn und Grenzen der exakten Wissenschaft. München 1971

Pleines, J.-E.: Das Problem in der Bildungstheorie. In: Zeitschrift für Pädagogik. 21. Beiheft 1986, 35 ff.

Plessner, H.: Die Stufen des Organischen und der Mensch. Berlin 1965

Pöggeler, F.: Erwachsenenbildung. Einführung in die Andragogik. Stuttgart 1974

Pöggeler, F.: Der Mensch in Mündigkeit und Reife. Paderborn 1970

Pöggeler, F./Wolterhoff (Hrsg.): Neue Theorien der Erwachsenenbildung. Stuttgart 1981

Pollak, G./Heid, H. (Hrsg): Von der Erziehungswissenschaft zur Pädagogik? Weinheim 1994

Pongratz, L. J.: Pädagogik in Selbstdarstellungen. 4 Bde. 1975

Popper, K. R.: Logik der Forschung. Tübingen 1969

Popper, K. R.: Das Prinzip vom Versuch und Irrtum. Ein Interview. In: Die Weltwoche Nr.38, 22.9.1994, 41-43

Portmann, A.: Aufbruch zur Lebensforschung. Zürich 1965

Portmann, A.: Um das Menschenbild. Stuttgart 1956

Postmann, N.: Wir amüsieren uns zu Tode. Frankfurt 1985 (1994)

Pribich, K.A.: Qualitätsabsicherung aus der Sicht der Aus- und Weiterbildung. Grundlagen der Weiterbildung 1/1994

Prim, R./Tilmann, H.: Grundlagen einer kritisch-rationalen Sozialwissenschaft. Heidelberg 1973

Raapke, H.D. (Hrsg.): Didaktik der Erwachsenenbildung. Stuttgart 1985

Rauschenbach, Th./Christ, B.: Abbau, Wandel oder Expansion? Zur disziplinären Entwicklung der Erziehungswissenschaft im Spiegel ihrer Stellenbesetzung. In: Krüger/Rauschenbach 1994, 69-92

Rebel, K. H.: Die Bedeutung andragogischer Fragestellungen für ein modernes Fernstudium. In: Benning 1986

Reble, A.: Geschichte der Pädagogik mit 2 Dok-Bde. Stuttgart 1981 (1951)

Reboul, O.: Indoktrination. Wenn Denken unterdrückt wird. Olten 1979

Reich Th. (Hrsg.): Didaktik als Unterrichtswissenschaft. 1976

Reich, K.: Theorien der allgemeinen Didaktik. 1977

Reifenrath, B. H.: Grundlegung einer Erwachsenenbildung. Frankfurt 1983

Resch, A. (Hrsg.): Der kosmische Mensch. München 1973

Resch, A. (Hrsg.): Welt, Mensch und Wissenschaft morgen. München 1972

Resch, A. (Hrsg.): Fortleben nach dem Tode. Innsbruck 1981

Robinsohn, S. B.: Bildungsreform als Revision des Curriculum. Berlin 1969

Rocek, R./Schatz, 0. (Hrsg.): Philosophische Anthropologie heute. München 1972

Rogers, C. R.: Entwicklung der Persönlichkeit. Stuttgart 1973

Röhrs, H. (Hrsg.): Die Erziehungswissenschaft und die Pluralität ihrer Konzepte. 1979

Rössner, L.: Kritik der Pädagogik. Aachen 1992

Rössner, L.: "Emanzipatorische Didaktik" und Entscheidungslogik. In: Zeitschrift für Pädagogik Nr.18, 1972 (599-617)

Roszak, T.: ÖKO-Psychologie. Stuttgart 1994

Roth, L.: Pädagogik. Handbuch für Studium und Praxis. München 1991

Rothacker, E.: Die Schichten der Persönlichkeit. 1952

Rothacker, E.: Philosophische Anthropologie. Bonn 1966

Ruprecht, H.: Sinnkonstitution und Leistungsprinzip. In: Ruprecht/Sitzmann 1984, XII, 81-89

Ruprecht, H./Sitzmann, G. H. (Hrsg.): Erwachsenenbildung als Wissenschaft. Bd. XII: Lebenslanges Lernen. Bd. XIII: Zur Problematik von Kriterien einer Grundlagentheorie der Erwachsenenbildung. Bd. XIV: Das Prinzip der Popularisierung als grundlagentheoretisches Problem der Erwachsenenbildung. Bd. XVI: Die Menschenwürde als Ursprung und Ziel von Erziehung und Bildung in der Grundlagentheorie der Erwachsenenbildung

Ruthven, M.: Der göttliche Supermarkt. Frankfurt 1991

Sachs, L.: Statistische Auswertungsmethoden. Berlin 1969

Sader, M.: Psychologie der Persönlichkeit. München 1980

Sagebiel, J. B.: Persönlichkeit als pädagogische Kompetenz in der beruflichen Weiterbildung. Bern 1994

Savigny von, E.: Analytische Philosophie. Freiburg/München 1970

Schäfter, O.: Die Temporalität von Erwachsenenbildung. In: ZfP 1993/3, 443-462

Scheler, M.: Die Stellung des Menschen im Kosmos. Bern 1966 (1928)

Schellhammer, E.: Menschsein in der Zukunft. Der Prozess der Individuation. Zürich 1987 (4)

Schellhammer, E.: Seelische Innenwelt im Alltag. Traum. Imagination. Psychische Energie. Zürich 1987 (4)

Schellhammer, E.: Unsere Zukunft in Ihrer Hand. Bildung für Umwelt und Frieden. Zürich 1988

Schellhammer, E.: Konzept der Individuation. Studienbuch. Zürich 2001

Scheuerl, H.: Geschichte der Erziehung. 1985

Schleichert, H.: Logischer Empirismus - Der Wiener Kreis. München 1975

Schmid, G.: Im Dschungel der neuen Religiosität. Stuttgart 1993

Schöpf, A.: in: Höffe, O. (Hrsg.): Klassiker der Philosophie. Band I. München 1985

Schöpf, A.: Philosophische Anthropologie, Sozialanthropologie und Kulturanthropologie. In: Roth 1991, 87-98

Schuchardt, E.: Innovative Forschung - Beispiel biographischer Ansatz. In: PAS 1993

Schulz, W.: Unterrichtsplanung. 1980

Schulze, G.: Die Erlebnisgesellschaft. Frankfurt 1992

Schüré, E.: Die grossen Eingeweihten. Bern/München 1979

Schütz, A./Luckmann, Th: Strukturen der Lebenswelt. Neuwied 1975 2 Bde. Frankfurt 1984

Schulze, G.: Die Erlebnisgesellschaft. Frankfurt 1992

Schweizerische Akademie der Geistes- und Sozialwissenschaften (SAGW): Bern 12/1993

Seifert, T./Waiblinger, A.: Die 50 wichtigsten Methoden. Stuttgart 1973

Seiffert, H.: Einführung in die Wissenschaftstheorie. 2 Bde. München 1972

Senzky, K.: Systemorientierung der Erwachsenenbildung. Stuttgart 1977

Sensky, K.: Selbstreflexion als Zielperspektive wissenschaftlicher Erwachsenenbildung. In: Ruprecht/Sitzmann 1986, XIV

Siebert, H.: Zur Theoriediskussion in der Erwachsenenbildung: Ideologischer Verschleiss und offene Aufgaben. In: Kürzdörfer 1981, 100-111

Siebert, H.: Erwachsenenbildung und Weiterbildung. In: Roth, L. (1991)

Siebert, H.: Aspekte einer reflexiven Didaktik. In: Mader 1991

Siebert, H.: Zukunftsaufgaben der Erwachsenenbildung angesichts der Ökokrise. In: Benning 1986

Siebert, H.: Allgemeinbildung in der Erwachsenenbildung. In: Zeitschrift für Pädagogik 21. Beiheft 1986, 137-140

Siebert, H.: Aspekte einer reflexiven Didaktik. In: Mader 1991, 19-32

Siebert, H.: Die Theorie der Erwachsenenbildung und die Praxis der Programmgestaltung. In: Hessische Blätter für Volksbildung. 1993/4, 315-235

Sitzmann, G.H.: Zu einigen Kriterien der Erwachsenenbildung. In: Ruprecht/Sitzmann 1985, XIII

Sixtl, F.: Messmethoden der Psychologie. Weinheim 1967

Skinner, B. F.: Kritik psychoanalytischer Begriffe und Theorie. In: Topitsch, E. (1970)

Speck, J. (Hrsg.): Problemgeschichte der neueren Pädagogik. 3 Bde. 1976

Speck, J.: Geschichte der Pädagogik des 20.Jahrhunderts. 2 Bde. 1978

Spitz, R.: Vom Säugling zum Kleinkind. Stuttgart 1967

Spranger, E.: Lebensformen. 1965

Spranger, E.: Philosophische Pädagogik. Heidelberg 1973

Srubar, J.: Kosmion. Die Genese der praktischen Lebenswelttheorie von Schütz. Frankfurt 1988

Steinringer, J.: Versuch einer Analyse der Beziehungskultur. Grundlagen der Weiterbildung 1/1994

Stegmüller, W.: Aufgaben und Ziele der Wissenschaftstheorie. Berlin 1973

Störig, H. J.: Kleine Weltgeschichte der Philosophie. Stuttgart 1965

SVEB (Schweizerische Vereinigung für Erwachsenenbildung): Entwicklungsplan für die 90er Jahre. Zürich 1990

SVEB: Erwachsenenbildung im künftigen Europa. Schlussbericht des Europäischen Kongresses. Zürich 1991

Tausch, R./Tausch, A. M.: Erziehungspsychologie. Göttingen 1971

Teilhard de Chardin, P.: Die Schau in die Vergangenheit. Olten 1965

Thomae, H.: Psychologische Anthropologie. In: Roth 1991, 109-121

Tietgens, H.: Zugänge zur Geschichte der Erwachsenenbildung. Bad Heilbrunn 1985

Tietgens, H.: Die Erwachsenenbildung. München 1981

Tietgens, H.: Erwachsenenbildung als Suchbewegung. Bad Heilbrunn 1986

Tietgens, H.: Professionalität für Erwachsenenbildung. In: Gieseke, W. 1988

Topitsch, E. (Hrsg.): Logik der Sozialwissenschaften. Köln 1970

Treml, A. K.: Über die Unwissenheit. Zeitschrift für Pädagogik 1994/4, 529-537

Tress, W.: Das Rätsel der seelischen Gesundheit. Göttingen 1986

Ullrich, R. (u.a.): Soziale Kompetenz. 2 Bde. München 1978/1980

Ulmann, G. (Hrgr.): Kreativitätsforschung. Köln 1973

Ueberla, K.: Faktorenanalyse. Berlin 1971

Ulich, E.: Handlungstheoretische Ansätze. In: Handbuch der Sozialisationsforschung. Weinheim 1980

US-Aussenminsterium: Global 2000. Bericht an den Präsidenten. Frankfurt 1980

Vester, F.: Unsere Welt - ein vernetztes System. München (1983) 1991

Vester, F.: Phänomen Stress. München 1993 (13)

Vester, G. H.: Soziologie der Postmoderne. München 1993

Vinnai, G.: Die Austreibung der Kritik aus der Wissenschaft. Frankfurt 1993

Wahl, D. u.a. (Hrsg.): Erwachsenenbildung konkret. Deutscher Studienverlag 1993/3

Weber, M.: Gesammelte Aufsätze zur Wissenschaftslehre. Tübingen 1968

Weber, M.: Methodologische Schriften. Studienausgabe. Frankfurt 1968

Wehnes, F. J.: Theorien der Bildung. In: Roth, L. (1991)

Weingartner, P.: Wissenschaftstheorie. Stuttgart 1971

Weiss, R.: Betriebliche Weiterbildung 1992. In: Grundlagen der Weiterbildung 1994/4

Wemmer, U./Korczak, D.: Gesundheit in Gefahr. Datenreport 93/94. Frankfurt 1993

Winkler, W.: Die Struktur der Persönlichkeit. Fachhochschulschriften Sandmann. München 1993

Winkler, M.: Wo bleibt das Allgemeine? In: Krüger/Rauschenbach 1994, 93-114

Wiersing, E.: Kontinuität oder Traditionsbruch. In: Zeitschrift für Pädagogik 21. Beiheft 1986, 19-26

Wittenbruch, W.: Schulleben - Chance oder Barriere für die Bildung des jungen Menschen. Pädagogische Rundschau 1/1994

Wittgenstein, L.: Vorlesungen und Gespräche über Ästhetik, Psychoanalyse und religiösen Glauben. Düsseldorf 1994 (1966)

Wollenweber, H.: Modernisierungsprozesse. Pädagogische Rundschau 1/1994

World Commission on environment and development: Our Common Future. Oxford 1987

Wuchterl, K.: Lehrbuch der Philosophie. Bern 1992 (4)

Wulf, Ch. (Hrsg): Einführung in die pädagogische Anthropologie. Weinheim 1994

Wurmser, L.: Flucht vor dem Gewissen. Berlin 1993 (2)

Zdarzil, H.: Pädagogische Anthropologie: empirische Theorie und philosophische Kategorialanalyse. In: König/Ramsenthaler 1980, 267-289

Zdarzil, H.: Erwachsenenbildung durch Wissenschaft. In: Benning 1986

Zdarzil, H.: Dimensionen andragogischer Theorie. In: Ruprecht/Sitzmann 1985

Zdarzil, H./Olechowski, R.: Anthropologie und Psychologie des Erwachsenen. Stuttgart 1976

Zeitschrift für Bildungsforschung und Bildungspraxis. Aarau 1988, 10.Jg.

Zeitschrift für Pädagogik: 21.Beiheft: Allgemeinbildung. Weinheim 1987

Zirfas, J.: Glück als Relais von Ethik und Anthropologie. In: Wulf 1994, 141-165

To study human education

■ The main program of human education is based on a future oriented   educational theory and on an expanded philosophical anthropology.

■ The high value of personality development and individuation is rolled up from antiquity to the present day and further developed for a modern human education. The tailor-made didactics construct the learning steps and all phases of individuation.

■ A new paradigm for pedagogy and andragogy of the 21st century is outlined: Human education through the formation of the comprehensive psychic life.

● *A study book for those who want to make expert use of the most asset of the human education.*